HELPING THE HELPERS NOT TO HARM

HELPING THE HELPERS NOT TO HARM

Iatrogenic Damage and Community Mental Health

Ruth B. Caplan
Gerald Caplan

BRUNNER-ROUTLEDGE
ALERE FLAMMAM
Taylor & Francis Group

USA	Publishing Office:	BRUNNER-ROUTLEDGE
		A member of the Taylor & Francis Group
		29 West 35th Street
		New York, NY 10001
		Tel: (212) 216-7800
		Fax: (212) 564-7854
	Distribution Center:	BRUNNER-ROUTLEDGE
		A member of the Taylor & Francis Group
		7625 Empire Drive
		Florence, KY 41042
		Tel: 1-800-634-7064
		Fax: 1-800-248-4724
UK		BRUNNER-ROUTLEDGE
		A member of the Taylor & Francis Group
		27 Church Road
		Hove
		E. Sussex, BN3 2FA
		Tel: +44 (0) 1273 207411
		Fax: +44 (0) 1273 205612

HELPING THE HELPERS NOT TO HARM: Iatrogenic Damage and Community Mental Health

1 2 3 4 5 6 7 8 9 0

Printed by Edwards Brothers, Lillington, NC, 2001.
Cover design by Ellen Seguin.

A CIP catalog record for this book is available from the British Library.
∞   The paper in this publication meets the requirements of the ANSI Standard Z39.48-1984 (Permanence of Paper).

Library of Congress Cataloging-in-Publication Data
Caplan, Ruth B.
  Helping the helpers not to harm : iatrogenic damage and community mental health / Ruth B. Caplan & Gerald Caplan
      p. cm.
  Includes bibliographical references and index.
  ISBN 1-58391-095-6
  1. Community mental health services. 2. Psychiatric errors. 3. Iatrogenic diseases. I. Caplan, Gerald. II. Title.

RA790.5.C346 2001
362.2′2—dc21   2001037975

This book is dedicated to the memory of
Paul J. Siebenberg (1919–1999)

It is also dedicated, with our gratitude, to our son/grandson,
Jonathan J. Moskovich,
who deciphered and typed countless drafts of this manuscript
during his army leaves. Without his generous help and experience
with computers, this book would not have been completed.

CONTENTS

FOREWORD

When I first met Professor Gerald Caplan and his daughter, Dr. Ruth Caplan, they presented me with their book *Helping the Helpers to Help* (Caplan & Caplan, 1972). Upon reading it, I realized how very relevant its contents are for so many important facets of our rabbinic duties. As Rabbis, we have to deal with family matters and face family crises. Even more so, those of us who serve as judges in the Rabbinic Courts, will find that book of inestimable value. Frequently, when we reach a decision in matters of marriage and divorce, we must deal with the subject of the custody of children. On such occasions, it is always my innermost feeling that, in making these decisions, the matter must be approached as if we were deciding on matters of life or death. The responsibility is very hard to bear, and a mistake may sometimes be fatal for the future of the children and their parents. Indeed, we have much to learn from the Caplans' new approach to the subject of *Shalom Bayit* [peace in the home].

Bringing peace to a family, and ensuring the proper education of children are both very important Jewish values. Every morning we recite in our daily prayers "Those are the things whose fruits one enjoys in this world, while the principal remains for him in the world to come. . . . Acts of kindness and making peace between a man and his fellow" (which is interpreted by the Rabbis to refer particularly to a husband and wife). The welfare of children is one of the major factors in keeping a couple in crisis together and is frequently the crucial issue in times of separation and, certainly, during the process of a divorce.

That earlier book by the Caplans was indeed a major contribution in helping all of us involved in the process of family relations, both in our efforts to restore peace to families, or, if this proves impossible, in helping family members caught in the web of emotional stress and guiding them towards constructive solutions. Hence, I was very happy to read their new book *Helping the Helpers Not to Harm*.

This new book is certainly an important contribution. It describes the potential harm which can be caused by those with a desire to help, but who, due to insufficient training or experience or both, actually sometimes trigger a chain reaction which causes major damage to both husband and wife, and even more so to the children.

My revered father and teacher, the Nazir of Jerusalem, Rabbi David Cohen of blessed memory, used to bless the sick when he visited them by quoting a verse from Psalms: "May He send His word and heal them, and may He save them from being harmed" (Psalms 107:20), which he then proceeded to explain: "I bless you and pray for your complete recovery, but even more importantly, I pray that G-d should save you from whatever harm the doctors may cause you in the course of their efforts to treat and heal you." Time and again over the years, I have seen, when visiting the sick, how important this blessing is. The same is especially true respecting the emotional trauma experienced by families in crisis.

The Caplans are right in saying

> Divorce procedures provide fertile ground for iatrogenic damage, because they require the opening of the hitherto private domains of a family's circumstances and relationships to public scrutiny by a range of legal and child welfare professionals, any one of whom may interpret and direct the situation into a potentially pathogenic direction. Since, in many cases of divorce, parents are engaged in intense conflicts, each of them seeks to persuade the professionals to identify with them in condemning the other parent and to help them wrest the children from the other. Divorce cases are particularly conducive to triggering loss of professional objectivity on the part of the professionals, with unconscious or preconscious biases invading their professional functioning. (Caplan & Caplan, 1999)

The harm caused by professionals may not only stem from sympathy, but is often also caused by insufficient training. To quote the Caplans' present publication: "It has been recognized that well intentioned professionals may harm clients because of a lack of knowledge, skill, empathy, or objectivity."

We, as Rabbis and Rabbinic Judges, must always bear this in mind when, unfortunately frequently, we face a situation where each party brings into court its "expert" who sides with him or her, or when a couple separates and the parents go to live in different cities, and the welfare agency in the father's city offers an opinion in his favor, while the agency in the mother's city offers an opinion in hers. The recommendations of such conflicting experts always puts the court in a real quandary. I have had situations like this happen in my court, and I prayed that G-d would give me "an understanding heart," like King Solomon's, to reach a just and fair decision.

I feel I should add that according to Jewish *Hallacha* [religious law], the only consideration that should guide a Rabbinic Court when making a decision on child care and custody is the "welfare of the child," not the "rights" and "privileges" of the parents.

It is my sincere hope that the Caplans' new book will help us when we are forced to determine what is in the child's best interests. I also hope that it will help the welfare agencies relate wisely to the parties involved in a divorce and guide them in the right direction.

I would like to end my brief remarks by quoting from a prayer we recite in the synagogue every *Sabbath* morning: "May G-d help and guide all who deal faithfully with the needs of the public. May G-d give them their reward. May He remove them from all sickness, heal their bodies, and forgive their sins. May He send blessings and success to all their activities. Along with all Israel, their brethren, let us say, 'Amen.'"

Rabbi Shear-Yashuv Cohen
Chief Rabbi of Haifa
President, Haifa District Rabbinic Courts

ACKNOWLEDGMENT—FOR OUR CRITICS

Unlike any of our earlier writings, the drafts of this book were shown, both by us and by the publisher, to a series of critics and reviewers. Consequently, in its later stages, this volume evolved as a kind of dialogue, responding both directly and implicitly to questions, reservations, and requests for clarification from these colleagues, the identities of most of whom are unknown to us. We would like to express our sincerest thanks to these people for the time and care they spent raising issues that have added considerably to our own understanding and analysis of the themes involved. They have thus contributed significantly to the development and balance of this book, for which we are most grateful.

The subject of this volume, elucidating and reducing damaging professional practices, requires us to weigh and consider criticism, though it may distress and disturb us. If we are to minimize harming our clients, and if we are to expand our knowledge of the forces involved in this complex field, we must not ignore the voices of dissent. Therefore, we do not only preach this message in what is to follow, but we have long found it advantageous to practice it as well.

Introduction

Iatrogenic harm is a term that originated in medical practice to denote the damage induced in a patient as a by-product of a therapeutic intervention, such as undesirable side effects of medication or secondary infections caused by invasive procedures. We are extending the word here to refer to the harm that is caused to a patient or client by any caregiver, whether physician, teacher, psychiatrist, school guidance counselor, social worker, or judge, in the course of a professional intervention such as that which has the declared intention of curing or preventing psychosocial disorders.

In reviewing cases that have been referred to our clinic in Jerusalem after passing through local religious and secular courts, the adoption service, the welfare-child protection office, and other agencies, we have been struck by the irony that community services ostensibly dedicated to preventing psychiatric and social disorders are prone to generating them. Such damage to individuals and families can be so severe as to dwarf the client's original problem, and may lead to more psychological suffering and social maladjustment than could have been expected to emerge from the predicament that first brought the client to the notice of caregivers.

Colleagues in a number of countries have privately agreed that harm caused by the caregiving system is a serious and widespread problem, but one on which they have been reluctant to speak out for fear of spoiling relations with fellow professionals and of being blacklisted by key agencies. As the head of a British social agency told us, "After I raised questions about the harmful handling of a case by another agency, I was treated as a pariah." Efforts to combat these abuses have been hindered by an absence of criteria for delineating the problem and for identifying patterns of factors involved that would allow us to devise programs to prevent and counteract the suffering of vulnerable individuals.

We had never planned to study iatrogenic damage, nor were we particularly aware that the phenomenon existed on any scale that made it noteworthy. The subject obtruded itself gradually on our attention during 15 years of efforts to organize a community service in Jerusalem to reduce the incidence of mental disorders in the population of children of divorcing parents. In this primary prevention mission, we were basing ourselves on a conceptual framework that we have developed over the last 50 years, and that we have explicated in a series of publications.[1]

Our interest in children of divorce led us to study a variety of harmful patterns of professional interventions in their lives by community caregivers in various fields. Gradually, the phenomenon of iatrogenic damage emerged as a subject of research in its own right whose noxious effects on mental and social well-being, we found, were not confined to children of divorcing parents. These effects could be seen to pose a potential hazard in any situation where professionals and lay people of good will intervene, often with the best of intentions, in the lives of others, ostensibly in order to help them. Therefore, while this introductory chapter will focus on the conceptual and historical background of our interest in professional malfunctioning which was rooted in our efforts to study and establish a primary preventive community psychiatric program for the children of divorcing parents, this book as a whole will not dwell exclusively on the effects of damaging behavior on this particular subpopulation. Instead, it will also draw on the experience of individuals from other high-risk categories whose weaknesses and needs rendered them vulnerable to mismanagement by caregivers.

Before we discuss the issues associated with iatrogenic damage, it may be useful to briefly describe the theoretical framework on which our work is based, which also colors our assumptions, analyses, and definitions of professional malfunctioning, and to describe the setting in Jerusalem in which we have been working.

☐ Primary Prevention

At the core of our activities lies the concept of *primary prevention*, a concept borrowed from public health (G. Caplan, 1964a). This refers to

---

[1]All our writings listed in the bibliography deal with the topics of this book. Successive articles record the development of our thinking, and are not merely reformulations of the same ideas. See, particularly, Caplan, R. B. (1982).

organizing programs for reducing the *incidence*—or the *rate of new cases*—of a disorder in a particular population. In our community mental health work, this means attempting to reduce the incidence of psychosocial disorders that we have reason to believe occur in identifiable subpopulations in reaction to particular stress or misfortunes. We base ourselves on studies that we and colleagues have conducted which have identified certain circumstances of loss, actual or threatened, or sudden life changes, as precipitating a rate of psychosocial disorder in an exposed group that is higher than the rate of mental breakdown found in a similar population that has not been exposed to such stressors. Put most simply, the focus of our work involves identifying particular subpopulations that are vulnerable because they have experienced certain potentially damaging events, and then working out ways to help and support those people so that they do not develop pathology.

This goal, beneficent in theory, involves inherent dangers in practice. In the course of our work, we have been forced to confront the unwelcome fact that when one moves from traditional therapeutic intervention in situations of present illness to intervening in the lives of people who are currently healthy with the purpose of preventing future pathology, we confront ethical and procedural problems for whose ramifications we may not be sufficiently prepared. Proactive intervention is a basic feature of programs of primary prevention, whether in public health campaigns of mass inoculation or of adding antibacterial substances to the public water supply, for example, or engaging in the community mental health equivalents. We thereby intervene, often uninvited, in the lives of healthy people because, based on the evidence at hand, we have decided that they have been exposed to circumstances that pose a statistical risk of their incurring future disorder. Usually, however, the individuals concerned are not aware of this danger. They may feel, in fact, that they are coping adequately in their own way and time, and they may object to our reaching out to change their lives by trespassing on their privacy and autonomy and by intervening in their relationships. Here we see one possible factor among many that may predispose to iatrogenic damage and which, in consequence, should make us very cautious about how and under what circumstances we move from a preventive program that is oriented towards an entire at-risk population, to a qualitatively different type of intervention in the lives of particular individuals.

A primary preventive program for a population involves an educational approach—the dissemination of information whose contents are based on research findings about the expected hazard, and on possible ways of avoiding or lessening the intensity of ensuing stressors. It may also involve attempts to change public policy so that those institutions that may be mobilized to act in circumstances associated with the particular hazard do so in ways that reduce, rather than exacerbate harmful forces. Preventive style intervention in the lives of named individuals, however, should be confined to those people who manifest symptoms of strain that show that they are having difficulties in coping. Those who are free of symptoms of strain, on the other hand, should not suffer direct professional intrusion in their lives just because they belong to an identifiable population known to be at statistical risk. We will return to this subject in later chapters in relation to concrete examples, since the confusion of some caregivers about when and how to move from primary preventive intervention in a population to an individual case orientation can cause iatrogenic damage.

Let us continue, then, with the theoretical models on which we have based our Jerusalem program for the children of divorce.

☐ Psychosocial Support

People in communities are rarely exposed to adverse circumstances entirely on their own. They are usually helped in times of stress by interaction with other individuals and groups, as well as by the values and problem-solving traditions of their culture. We refer to these forces as *psychosocial support systems*. They act as a buffer between the individual and the full impact of the short-term crisis situations.

Empirical researches have consistently found that individuals exposed to high levels of stress who, at the same time, receive adequate psychosocial support are usually able to master the stressful situation without any reduction in their level of mental health. Similar individuals exposed to similar levels of that stress, but without psychosocial support, subsequently have about two or three times the rate of mental disorder of the general population (Brown, Bhrolchain, & Harris, 1975; G. Caplan, 1981a, 1989; Cobb, 1976; DeAraujo et al., 1973; Kalter, 1977; Kalter & Rembar, 1981; McDermott, 1970; Nichols, Cassel, & Kaplan, 1972; Rutter, 1985; Wadsworth, 1979; Wadsworth & Maclean, 1987; Wadsworth, Peckham, & Taylor, 1985; Wadsworth et al., 1990; Wallerstein & Kelly, 1980; Weiss, 1975). These support systems that have been found to lower the risk to mental health are characterized by providing a solicitous group that helps stressed individuals to lower their emotional upset marked by anger, anxiety, depression, shame, and the like. Supporters instill hope, and they help sufferers deal with the cognitive burdens of the stressful situation by guiding them to collect essential information so as to overcome possible confusion and to work out effective ways of solving the problems raised by the adversity. They also help with the concrete tasks involved in coping with the predicament, and they may provide extra material and financial resources and services, so that an organized life can continue despite the upsetting and preoccupying circumstances of the stress (Antonovsky, 1974; G. Caplan, 1989; Cassel, 1974; Garmezy et al., 1978; Halpern, 1978; Tayal, 1972; Wallerstein & Kelly, 1980).

Most studies have found that raised levels of anxiety and other negative emotions are associated with a lowered capacity for effective problem solving. The essential core of the kind of support that protects against mental disorder is help in making up for this cognitive deterioration. That help may be supplied by providing guidance and by sharing the tasks of overcoming the difficulties involved in the situation, or else by encouraging the individual to resign himself or herself to the realities of nonfulfillment of previously satisfied needs and of finding alternative sources of satisfaction (Beck, 1970; Blaufarb & Levine, 1972; G. Caplan, 1982, 1989; Crawshaw, 1963; Hansell, 1976; Hiroto, 1974; Janis, 1951; Seligman, 1975, 1976; Shader & Shwartz, 1966; Tayal, 1972; Tyhurst, 1951, 1957). The harmful effect of short or long-term exposure to stressful circumstances results from the negative pressures of the adversity interacting with the individual's existing capacity to cope with difficult circumstances. These, in turn, are linked with his or her inborn personality characteristics and with what that individual has learned from previous experience. The main factor in determining whether the nature of the outcome will be healthy or pathological will be the type and level of the buffering offered by the psychosocial support system operating at that time.

These ideas have led to the development of our conceptual model of primary preventive psychiatry: To monitor the reactions of a population exposed to types of adversity that have been shown to be pathogenic; and to ensure that people are receiving effective psychosocial support that is helping to reduce the level of their negative emotional tension, that offers guidance about the hazardous situation and how to master it, that provides helpers who intervene personally to deal with the current difficulties, and that also assists by providing money and concrete goods and services to foster a positive outcome.

A number of studies of "vulnerable but invincible high-risk children" —highly resilient children who spontaneously master high levels of stress—show that these youngsters elicit from helpful adults nurturing attention that replaces the psychosocial and socioeconomic supplies of which they are deprived by the absence or malfunctioning of their parents (Werner, 1989, 1997). These temperamentally gifted young people actively reach out and make the contacts which allow them to create the supportive environment that enables them to overcome their adversity no matter how pathogenic this may be for most children. We may copy the way these resilient children operate in order to achieve similar results for ordinary children involved in such stressful situations. In other words, our primary preventive psychiatry mission calls on us to study the psychosocial and the socioeconomic hazards involved in a stressful life situation that empirical research has shown to be associated with high rates of mental disorder in a particular population. Then it calls for us to introduce measures that increase the likelihood that more children will be enabled to overcome these difficulties in ways similar to those used by the invincible children.

From both stress researches and the studies of vulnerable but invincible high risk children, we have learned that we need to guide community leaders, strategically positioned care givers, parents, and other family members to reduce the impact of the stressors, and to provide emotional support and cognitive guidance to the children and to their parents or guardians. Such support and guidance will enable them to evade or overcome the burdens, or to find ways of putting up with the pain and discomfort of the irreducible elements of the adversity and to focus on more rewarding aspects of their life.

☐ Crisis Theory

While we believe that most mental disorders occur as a result of the operation of factors of adversity over a prolonged period, the course of pathological development is not smooth but occurs in a series of steps, each of which is preceded by a short period of upset to which we have given the term *crisis*. These are temporary periods of cognitive and emotional upset precipitated by sudden changes in life circumstances when threats or challenges to essential psychological supplies confront the individual with novel problems that he or she is not able to solve quickly (G. Caplan, 1963, 1970; Hansell, 1976; Lindemann, 1944; Parkes, 1970; Rutter, 1985). It appears that these crisis periods are way stations when the trajectory of the mental health of individuals may change and lead them in the direction of improved mental health or of mental disorder.

We have studied the short-term developments that characterize such crisis periods, which are not only periods of change, but also turn out to be periods when individuals, because of their temporary disequilibria, become more open to being swayed by outside influence and more amenable to being modified by it than they are during a stable state. During the crisis, individuals may change their level of mental health significantly. They may be influenced by those around them to try novel ways of managing which then become incorporated into their ongoing coping repertoire, or they may use ineffective ways of problem solving, or may evade the presenting problems, thereby failing to deal adequately with the current crisis. They may also integrate these weakening tactics into their ongoing pattern of coping.

From this, it follows that the intervention by support and guidance that is at the core of primary prevention must be organized to operate during the period of crisis which will occur as the hazardous factors impinge on the members of the population at risk. We have found that, by harnessing such crises, we can achieve profound psychological changes that would have required far greater professional time and effort to bring about during a more stable state.

☐ Epidemiological Model

While crises enable us to use scarce and expensive professional manpower and time more efficiently to gain maximum therapeutic effect in the interests of wide coverage of the needs of a population by intervening during these short episodes when an individual's mental state is unusually malleable, we also employ a public health epidemiological model rather than an exclusively individual patient oriented approach. Investigating or treating individual psychopathology in depth requires highly skilled professionals who are expensive to train and employ and of whom there will never be enough to satisfy the needs of a total population of sufferers. Therefore, it is more efficient for these specialists to study their necessarily limited number of intensive treatment cases in order to discover common leverage points and generally recurring issues that apply across a whole population of cases irrespective of individual personalities and varying details of each person's history and relationships. This knowledge can then be used to instruct less skilled and less specialized professionals in how to modify the life situation of the target population.

For example, instead of uncovering and resolving the burden of the past for each distressed family member, a protracted and agonizing procedure requiring a high degree of skill, it is possible to modify some of the damage caused by that past through helping individuals to deal successfully with a present life predicament. Thus unresolved conflicts and failures which may have contributed to the client developing maladaptive patterns of coping and which may be reawakened by any subsequent trauma, like the process of divorce, can be counteracted by supporting individuals embroiled in a current crisis and encouraging them to overcome the present situation. Supporting and promoting success in the present forms a corrective emotional experience that enables individuals to assert mastery over other facets of their lives as well, thereby counteracting debilitating aspects of the past. This supportive and educational function does not require the time or level of professional sophistication needed to engage in the reconstructive therapy of each individual, and it will enable a larger population to be helped by more readily available resources. But as we will see presently, this epidemiological model that mobilizes caregivers less specialized in mental health issues and techniques unwittingly increases the risk of iatrogenic damage, even as it increases the availability of help for those in need.

☐ Elements of a Preventive Program: Preventive Methods and Techniques

Over the past years, much of our effort has been spent in developing a number of preventive methods and techniques which are based on the above conceptual models and have been refined and evaluated in our clinical programs with stressed individuals and their families. Such methods as preventive crisis intervention, anticipatory guidance, convening supportive groups for stressed individuals and their families, and the like, designed as they are to reduce specific stressors or to increase psychosocial support for individuals and their families, all have common logistical characteristics. They are all designed to make maximum economical use of skilled mental health manpower, which will always be in short supply. Consequently, all these methods are time limited, and wherever possible they focus on the clients' conscious or preconscious processes, not on their unconscious ones, using methods of counseling rather than uncovering psychotherapy. They focus on improving the clients' ability to cope based on an examination of the current realities of the stressful situation, and on how to improve the adjustment to present circumstances, rather than on attempting to delve into the intricacies of improving personality structure. These methods also involve, as much as possible, transferring the tasks of helping to other relevant parts of the caregiving network, both professional and nonprofessional, rather than keeping them within the traditional confines of psychiatric or psychological practice.

☐ Logistic Aspects of Organization of Preventive Programs

What differentiates an organized primary preventive program from activities that merely involve the use of preventive methods is that the former is characterized by specifically planned efforts to reduce the statistical probabilities of disorder. Crucial in this process is that of making policy choices that maximize our active contribution to lowering the incidence of cases of disorder in the total bounded population for which we have accepted responsibility and accountability. This usually means that we must collect data about how caregiving agents and agencies work, and about the social values and practices in the population. Based on this new knowledge, we then choose where and how to intervene in order to improve, whenever possible, those forces that affect the population-wide statistics of disorder. To do this, we must understand the network of forces that affect individual sufferers and their families. For instance, we must pay particular attention to institutional and social facets of such caregiving systems as divorce courts, and the roles and attitudes of judges, as well as other community-wide issues that may affect the attitudes and practices of health workers, educators, religious denominations, and the like in relation to family breakup. All of these may affect how individual children and their families perceive the issues of parental divorce, and all of these may significantly increase or decrease their difficulties of coping with, and mastering the burdens of the situation.

As we collect information about these broader environmental influences, we must select among them those which are likely to be amenable to change, so that we may concentrate our efforts on those that yield the best chances of improving the statistical picture. This approach has made us realize that, to intervene effectively in this extremely complicated field, we must dramatically change our own traditional role. We cannot just sit back and refer our cases to other caregivers. We must actively collaborate with our fellow workers in exploring and grappling with the problems. Once we have jointly arrived at a solution, our colleagues can finish the job and will then be prepared to deal effectively with a similar problem on their own in the future. As in the process of consultee-centered mental health consultation, a method of preventive psychiatry that we pioneered at Harvard Medical School Laboratory of Community Psychiatry 40 years ago and whose terms we will describe later in this book, we penetrate the work field of our consultees, and immerse ourselves in the realities of their situation as a basis for helping them acquire major new mental health sensitivities and skills.

Taking part in a serious primary prevention program, however, makes very much bigger demands on our time than offering occasional, on-demand mental health consultation to a caregiving colleague on a possibly one-session-a-week basis. For instance, in the 1980s when we established our first primary prevention programs on the wards of the Hadassah teaching hospitals in Jerusalem, we seconded Dr. Hadassah

LeBow, a senior child psychoanalyst on the staff of our Department of Child Psychiatry, to work on a 70 percent basis in the very busy Department of Pediatric Surgery (G. Caplan, 1993; LeBow et al., 1983). Over a four-year period, she worked as a preventive psychiatrist on the multidisciplinary pediatric surgery team in a role analogous to those of such other nonsurgical members. Each professional, such as nutritionists, specialists in infectious diseases, or occupational therapists, makes his or her own specialist contribution, as well as enhancing colleagues' understanding of each one's activities on ward rounds in order to involve other workers in sharing their tasks. As the head of our department, Gerald Caplan had less time available than did Dr. LeBow, but he spent 20 percent of his work week doing a similar job on the team of the adult oncology department, focusing on developing a program to help children deal with the insecurities of living with a parent suffering from cancer.

This intensive collaboration in the work of colleagues in other fields alerted us to the problems involved in, and the possibilities opened by systematically integrating our own preventive mental health approach into the core activities of other professional groups. Our understanding of not only the advantages, but also the organizational and practical pitfalls involved now became more sophisticated than it had been when we were acting as intermittent mental health consultants who were outsiders moving in and out of key community agencies for a few designated hours a month.

When our team retired from the Hadassah hospitals, we changed our focus in order to concentrate our preventive efforts on the major risk factor of parental divorce. Our Hadassah experience had enriched our expertise in the community organization aspects of how to obtain the approval of leading caregivers in other health fields, so that we might enter their workspace and operate as preventive child psychiatric members of their team. We have now begun to clarify some of the practical issues involved in the process of obtaining and maintaining this approval, and this is also providing us with a window onto iatrogenically damaging behavior.

☐ Iatrogenic Damage as the Reversal of Psychosocial Supportive Mechanisms During Crises

Our findings on iatrogenic damage reveal that part of the harm generated is due to the reversal by malfunctioning professionals of the mechanisms of beneficial support and guidance. Damaging behavior typically exacerbates anxiety, anger, shame, despair, and guilt; it brings about the deprivation and depletion of material and social resources; it deliberately increases obfuscation and consequent cognitive confusion; and it induces additional crises that render clients particularly vulnerable to on-going psychological deterioration because of the disproportionate impact of stressors and the negative feedback produced by damaging caregivers during the disequilibrium of the crisis state.

☐ Focus on High-risk Populations

Our theoretical model borrows another fundamental concept from public health practice that guides us in ways of handling the large numbers of individuals in a population who may require our intervention. We focus on subpopulations at high risk of disorder because they are exposed to particularly harmful adverse circumstances, or because they have inadequate resources, or else because they are not receiving adequate psychosocial support. We are particularly interested in subpopulations who in the absence of specific preventive intervention are likely to become disordered and yet, if we intervene appropriately, can be helped to master the stressful situation. The practical model resembles triage programs used by armies to determine the timetable of priorities in treating battlefield casualties. In order to reduce loss of life, most armies develop the policy of providing immediate treatment for the moderately wounded for whom prompt medical and surgical intervention will make the difference between whether or not they will survive. These are separated from the less seriously wounded, who can recover on their own or with delayed care, and the most critically wounded, who will probably die irrespective of what is done for them (Glass, 1947).

☐ The Jerusalem Program for Children of Divorced Parents

Fifteen years ago in Jerusalem, we chose a sample high-risk situation for children and then began developing a model program of primary prevention to deal with it, a program that we could describe in sufficient detail so that other workers in other places might replicate it. Our goal was to reduce the incidence of mental disorder and social maladjustment in the general population of children exposed to the particular hazard of divorce to a level that would be expected in the absence of that hazard. We chose parental divorce for our sample adversity because it is sufficiently common to constitute a major social problem. For example, in Israel there is currently about one divorce for every four marriages. It also entails a high risk of disorder— 30–40% percent of children of divorced parents become psychologically or socially disturbed. Finally, we chose it because it is possible to locate the entire population of children at risk, since all their parents are obliged to ratify their divorce in a particular court of law. This divorce court, which for Jews in Israel is the regional Rabbinic Court, not only dissolves the marriage but, in many cases, also controls the postdivorce arrangements for the future care of the children, offering us the opportunity to intervene preventively in the life situation of the entire population of children involved in this adversity if we can succeed in building the necessary collaboration with the judges.

In 1984, therefore, we established a governmentally authorized, nonprofit public agency that operates in accordance with a registered constitution and with approved guidelines, subject to annual financial audit and ongoing controls by a board of governors made up of recognized community leaders. A full account of the vicissitudes of establishing and maintaining sanction for a community-based project within so unfamiliar a cultural and organizational setting as the centuries-old Rabbinic Court system, the lessons we learned, and the programs that grew out of them are the subject for a separate forthcoming book. However, a brief summary of our activities may help to explain the way we became aware of the impact of iatrogenic damage.

☐ Initial Explorations

In a preliminary study, we had found that the approximately 500,000 Jewish inhabitants of Jerusalem and its surrounding region are served by six Rabbinic Courts, each consisting of a panel of three Rabbinic judges, all housed in a building in the center of the city. The Rabbinic courts have exclusive power to grant bills of divorce, but other related aspects of family law, such as marital separation, custody of children, contacts of children with noncustodial parents, child maintenance payments, and division of family property, may be adjudicated either in that religious court or in the recently created secular Family Court system. Parents are free to choose the court system in which they sue, but once a file is opened, it cannot be transferred to the other jurisdiction. A total of about 1,400–1,650 divorce-related files are opened annually in Jerusalem courts, and about 500–600 of these couples are granted a divorce each year in the Rabbinic Courts. Organizing a service for that number of cases seemed feasible.

☐ Establishing a Clinical Framework

We decided to carry out our study in a clinical framework, first because we, as clinicians, are accustomed to conducting research while simultaneously providing a diagnostic and therapeutic service for patients who thereby feel that we are giving them something of value in return for their giving us the opportunity to collect our data. Second, we needed to offer a concrete service to the divorce courts in order to be admitted into their domain, and a specialized clinic would provide them with high-level expert evidence about the mental health factors in their difficult cases. We also, incidentally, thereby created a setting to which other types of cases could be referred, cases involving not only divorce but also adoption and other aspects of family-based disturbance and disintegration as well as criminal cases involving suspicions of sexual abuse.

Having established the framework for our clinic, we initiated contacts with the Chief Rabbis and the Director of Rabbinic Courts of the Ministry of Religious Affairs, and offered our services as community mental health specialists to help the courts deal with complicated cases.

During the next decade and a half, we were appointed Specialist Consultants in Mental Health to the Directorate of Rabbinic Courts of Israel and to the Rabbinic Courts of Jerusalem, and we appeared as expert witnesses in many cases. We received referrals from panels of Rabbinic judges for psychiatric evaluations in issues of custody in pre- and postdivorce suits, and we consulted regularly with the courts' social worker who deals in marriage and divorce counseling. Unfortunately, we were never given the hoped-for access to a total, or even a random sampling of cases because these courts are governed by centuries-old rules of stringent confidentiality that are designed not only to protect the privacy of clients from the prying eyes of neighbors in traditional small, ingrown communities, but also to shield judges from outsiders who might influence their decisions. Access to Rabbinic courtrooms is consequently restricted. Access to files by outsiders is against the law, and consultation with judges without the presence of the parties to a case is largely forbidden. Each panel of judges is fully autonomous and is linked to the Directorate of Rabbinic Courts of the Ministry of Religious Affairs and the Chief Rabbinate by administrative ties only, so no directives or authorization from these bodies could grant us access to a representative sample of cases. We were therefore left with a skewed sample of extreme cases on which to base our findings. This has hindered our attempts to gain an accurate picture of the needs of the total divorcing population, but has probably increased our chances of exposure to instances of iatrogenic damage.

☐ A Research Paradox

This research paradox may be understood as follows: In Israel, Great Britain, and, we suspect, other Western countries as well, only about 10% of divorcing couples come to court in a state of acute, open conflict that requires active and often protracted intervention by judges to bring about agreements necessary for the future welfare of the children. About 90% of divorcing couples, on the other hand, only appeal to the courts to formally ratify agreements arrived at by the parties themselves. These couples are not openly contesting the divorce, and they have arrived at apparently mutually tolerated agreements about division of property, child custody, visitation schedules, and the like. The courts feel no need to delve into these cases and the issues behind the configuration of the agreements in part because they are already grossly over-burdened by the contentious 10% of cases. However, those uncontested cases that pass through the system without triggering judicial concerns—partly because they appear so peaceable and uncontested, and partly because the system is so overwhelmed by the instances of open conflict that judges are reluctant to stir apparently untroubled waters—may be presenting a deceptively innocuous appearance. What are presented as mutually acceptable agreements, for example, may not have been arrived at by free and equal choice, but may be the result of manipulation and bullying by a powerful party who has overridden the will of a weaker spouse. This could lead to simmering antagonisms and ambivalence that could flare after the divorce and impinge on the well-being of the children. This suspicion may be suggested by the numbers. If we remember that 30–40% of children of divorcing parents develop subsequent pathology, such a high proportion is unlikely to emerge only from the approximately 10% of openly conflicted cases that stimulate judicial concern and intervention. Somewhere among the 90%, therefore, unobserved pathological forces must be festering.

Moreover, when the courts refer troubled and troubling cases to us, they are choosing, out of only the 10% that concern them, those instances that they find particularly perplexing and that they cannot handle according to their own tools and experience. Thus, we are not only seeing a skewed sample from the point-of-view of the total divorcing parental population, but we are seeing a skewed sample of a skewed sample—only that fraction of the 10% that individual judges or panels of Rabbinic judges feel is beyond their own idiosyncratic capacities to manage.

To skew our sample further, another factor may be operating. In Israel, when a judge feels that a case is beyond his or her understanding, he or she has to persuade both parties to agree to call in a particular expert. One or other of the litigants may refuse to accept the designated expert, claiming to believe that this specialist is likely to produce an evaluation prejudicial to his or her interests. The dissenting party may then demand that another expert of his or her own choice be appointed. Thus, the choice of an outside expert to help defuse and resolve the impasse can itself become a source of yet more conflict. Israeli law allows judges to overrule such objections, but by and large they are loath to do so because they want the expert's opinion to be accepted by both parties. With disagreement from the outset, the end intention of reducing conflict may begin with two strikes against it. Thus, when we wish to see a representative case sample, the clients' preconceptions and possible misconceptions about us, fuelled perhaps by the stories of lawyers and caregivers against whose clients or cases we may have given unfavorable opinions in the past, play a further role in limiting our access.

From this, it follows that, if we wish to provide a service designed to lower the rate of pathology among the total population of children of divorcing parents, we will be severely limited in identifying the needs and creating hopefully effective service options. This is especially so if we base our findings only on the contentious cases that are referred to us according to criteria that reflect the individual needs of individual judges, each of whom may have differing capacities to tolerate and handle different types of obstreperous or disturbed litigants.

From the point of view of our present study of iatrogenic damage, however, this acute skewing of the research sample is positive, since it highlights those instances of troubled and troubling clients that evoke the most frequent interventions by caregiving authorities and, hence, offers the largest pool in which professional malfunctioning may arise. Since for our present study we are not searching for data on the prevalence of iatrogenic damage, but rather on the conditions that may encourage it and the characteristics of its manifestations, these complex, ambiguous, emotionally burdensome cases offer a convenient medium for examining professional bias, misapprehension, and mismanagement, a medium that enables us to see most clearly the etiology of the damaging processes.

☐ Harmful Factors

To return to our description of our Jerusalem project. The most important preventive feature of our clinic is that it provides us with a vehicle for collaborating with the courts, both Rabbinic and secular, and more recently, with the newly established, secular Family Courts. Many of our clients have been referred by the judges who ask us to investigate the relative competence of parents in unusually contentious cases in order to assign custody, and to help the bench decide how best to arrange contact between the children and the noncustodial parent.

Although the sample of cases referred to us is not so representative of the general population of divorcing parents and their children as we had hoped it would be, it has still been possible, based on our studies of these cases, to list specific harmful factors that may overburden the coping resources of children who do not receive sufficient psychosocial support. Such stressors must be identified and reduced in intensity and duration throughout a population as part of a program of primary prevention. These stressors can also act as trip wires, energizing caregivers who, as we will presently see, may then engage in stereotyped and damaging behavior that can make bad situations far worse.

Among these stressors are the following:

- Parental quarreling, particularly after one of the parents has decided to divorce. Such quarreling becomes especially stressful when it continues after the dissolution of the marriage.
- Conflict of interest between parents and children, since most children oppose divorce, while parents see no alternative to escaping a union that makes their own lives intolerable. This makes many children feel like passive victims of adults, whom they may come to regard as caring less for the children than for themselves and who are, therefore, seen through the children's eyes as behaving selfishly.
- Partisanship of children in which they take sides, because they have been recruited and incited by one parent against the other, or because the children on their own may have grown to hate one of the parents because of memories of violence or because of the parent's threatening or belittling personality.
- Communications issues in which parents hide the preparations for divorce from the children, leading the latter to feel passive victims. After the divorce, parents may burden the children further by using them as channels to pass hostile messages.
- Deprivation of parenting, because one parent has left the home and the other is so fatigued and depressed by the burdens of coping that he or she is no longer functioning at full capacity. This may leave the children feeling insecure and abandoned by both parents.
- Complete abandonment by a parent, which may be accompanied by the loss of concrete resources like income and the disruption of

the network of the parents' contacts which adults normally invoke to ease a child's progress through social, educational, and vocational hurdles—contacts such as "old boys networks."

- This latter deprivation may be exacerbated by residential mobility when not only are the child's contacts with school and friends disrupted, but the parents' supportive network may also be left behind, leading to greater burdens on parenting capacity and requiring the building of new channels to social influence and security.
- Stigma. Even in cultures that formally accept divorce, many children feel intense, irrational shame about the breakup of their family, so that they deliberately isolate themselves from otherwise available sources of support.
- Sex. Children may overhear accusations of sexual irregularities that stimulate intensified curiosity about the sex lives of parents. After divorce, the children may intervene in their parents' attempts to date and remarry. Sometimes, the child may try to replace the absent spouse and, especially in adolescence, may take on the role of arbiter of the sexual behavior of a parent. This may lead to the child being deprived of parental guidance in handling the complications of his or her own sexual development.

A central focus of our preventive program has been the organizing of systematic efforts to reduce the intensity and duration of these specific stressors. This has been done, in the main, by alerting family members to the harmful significance of such issues, and by enlisting their collaborators in attempts to modify them. For example, one major pathogen selected out of our list, occurs after the divorce when children rebel against being passive victims of their parents' endless quarreling. As the recipients and transmitters of hostile messages between parents, they may begin not only to take sides, but also to contribute to and manipulate the drama. They may do so by the nature of their reporting, both true and false, about each parent to the other, and particularly by their accounts of how they may have been treated, or mistreated by each parent. This is another factor that can energize caregivers and can lead to their acting on a misinterpretation of the child's actual situation, thereby generating iatrogenic damage.

In cases like these, our efforts to reduce continuing stress and prevent possible future pathology involves influencing the parents to stop using their children as message carriers and as informers to be interrogated after each visit between households. We also alert both parties to the possibility that children may distort information either in order to become active in increasing antagonism between their parents, perhaps in order to ensure a maximum of attention and solicitude focused on themselves, or in order to ingratiate themselves with one parent by providing ammunition that the latter seems to crave. Alternatively, children may be trying to make peace as part of an attempt to control the forces that are upsetting their lives.

While diagnosing and intervening in such situations may reduce the stress on specific children and their parents, such preventive processes require the expenditure of significant staff time, so that, necessarily, only a limited number of individuals can ever benefit in this way. In order to intervene on a populationwide scale, therefore, we must create a system of priorities by defining certain categories of cases as of higher risk than others, and by focusing our efforts selectively on those particularly vulnerable subpopulations. In doing this, we are adopting one method of a public health approach—choosing to put our emphasis on a defined subpopulation with which we can deal effectively given our limited resources, rather than dissipating our effectiveness by trying to stretch inadequate resources to cover the entire population.

☐ Defining Target Intervention Groups

In order to obtain the maximum benefit from what will always be inadequate manpower resources, we advocate focusing on high-risk subpopulations or *target groups*. A target group has enough common characteristics so that it can be readily identified and labeled, and so that specific programs can be developed by means of which that subpopulation need not be dealt with exclusively by mental health specialists. Either its members can be guided to help themselves, or suitably primed nonmental health specialists can be enabled to handle them adequately. In order to identify such target groups, we need detailed studies of regularly occurring phenomena in the interplay of traumatic and helpful forces in a particular harmful situation. For instance, among the heterogeneous populations of cases of children of divorced parents referred to us in our exploratory studies in Jerusalem, we identified three such target groups with enough common features that we were able to plan for them to receive specific programs of intervention.

☐ Target Group I: Children of Ineffective but Healthy Parents

The first of these is composed of the children of parents who are mentally healthy and generally reasonably effective, but who lack the knowledge needed to deal adequately with the stresses faced by children of divorce. Consequently, they cannot offer enough support in ways that will help shield the children against psychiatric disturbance or social maladjustment during childhood or later life. However, if we provide such parents with the knowledge of what is likely to be involved for their children and how other parents have helped their children to cope with divorce, most will then be able to adjust their own behavior so as to reduce the impact of some of the stresses of family breakup, and will pay increased attention to the needs and fears of the children, and give them greater psychosocial backup.

We have developed simple, short, printed guides that offer ways for parents to help their children cope adequately. The administrative staff of the divorce courts hands these out to every parent opening a file for a divorce-related issue. Each guide also contains a number of covert messages that enunciate basic principles concerning the responsibility of parents to cater to the special needs of their children after divorce, to be sensitive to the turmoil of the children, and to provide the children with essential emotional support and cognitive guidance. It also emphasizes that the expectable upsets and discomforts of all concerned are signs of healthy adaptive effort and not of illness; and it implies that with nonprofessional guidance of family and friends and more experienced divorced parents, most couples will be able to set aside their mutual antagonisms in the service of collaborating with each other for the benefit of their children.[2]

It is an axiom frequently misunderstood by caregivers that primary prevention is not traditional clinical practice carried out on a mass scale, but differs in its nature and methods in order to use scarce professional time as economically as possible. Consequently, the guides are designed not to recruit cases or to increase dependency on caregivers by raising anxiety and by suggesting that a dire outcome is an expectable consequence of divorce unless there is professional intervention; but rather we try to enhance the parents' autonomy and self-confidence.

☐ Target Group II: Children of Disturbed Parents

The second intervention target population is that of children at least one of whose parents is exploiting them, either by covertly manipulating

---

[2]The full text of these guides is included in our 1993 article "Organization of Preventive Psychiatry Programs," *Community Mental Health Journal, 29*(4), 367–385.

them in order to solve unconscious problems of their own, or by using them as auxiliaries to attack the other parent without sensitivity to the needs of the children. Many of these parents are suffering from personality disorders and are often impervious to mediation or rational persuasion either because of their narcissistic or paranoid tendencies, or because they are driven by a hatred for their spouse which is so intense that they are prepared to use, and even sacrifice, their children as weapons in an interminable battle even after the marriage has been dissolved. In one such battle, for example, a parent with a paranoid disorder was engaged in turning the child against the former spouse in an attempt to gain custody. In the course of protracted legal battles during which the child began to show symptoms of major psychological maladjustment, the disordered parent said to the other, "If you ever get her back, all you'll get is a lump of flesh!"

In our clinical practice, we have found these situations hard to handle by education or by psychotherapeutic verbal techniques; and often mediation that seeks to stop such fighting for the sake of the love parents bear their children also fails. In such cases, primary preventive measures lie in the hands of the divorce court judges, who should be alerted by mental health specialists to the likelihood of psychological damage to the children unless the judges use their power to ensure that the disordered parent is not permitted to dictate future patterns of child care. This is an example where we must beware of romanticizing the rights of all parents to have contact with their children, and of the universality of the dictum that a child should maintain contact with both parents after divorce. Where there is reason to believe, after a careful study and objective judgment, that a parent is likely to make use of his or her "rights for contact" in such a way as to harm the child, the duty of the courts is to take steps to prevent this happening.

In order to carry out our primary prevention mission in the case of this second target population, we are currently organizing study groups for Rabbinic judges, secular Family Court judges, and mental health specialists to provide us with the opportunity to learn from each other how to deal with these problems. Later in this book, we will describe this program in some detail, not only as it relates to issues of divorce, but also as a possible tool for inhibiting or aborting iatrogenic damage.

☐ Target Group III: Children of Iatrogenically Damaged Families

Our third target group is that of children of families that are the victims of harmful intervention by malfunctioning professional caregivers, a group that may coexist with the other categories. Divorce procedures provide fertile ground for iatrogenic damage because they require the opening of the hitherto private domains of a family's circumstances and relationships to public scrutiny by a range of legal and child welfare professionals, any one of whom may interpret and direct the situation into a potentially pathogenic direction. Most cases of divorcing parents are characterized by intense conflicts between the parties, each of whom seeks to persuade caregivers to identify with them in condemning the other parent and in helping them to wrest the children from the other. Thus, divorce cases are particularly conducive to generating charges and claims by clients that trigger loss of professional objectivity, allowing unconscious or preconscious biases to invade professional functioning. It was the discovery of this target group that first alerted us to the dangers of iatrogenic damage, and stimulated our interest in exploring this as a part of our program to seek to reduce crippling stressors.

☐ Iatrogenic Damage as a Widespread Problem with Shared Features

We soon realized, however, that victims of iatrogenic damage were not confined to divorcing families. We found that many forms of adversity that we had briefly researched increased the danger of their sufferers becoming the targets of professional malfunctioning. These could include, for example, children of cancer patients, or children of parents killed in road accidents. Other cases appeared as we, in our role as mental health specialists, were consulted by a variety of community agencies that serve needy populations in such fields as adoption and child abuse. We soon realized that, among such clients, damaging professional interventions are often significant pathogens. A commonality of characteristics began to emerge in all such examples. Such shared features included an apparent abrogation of a balanced point-of-view by caregivers and a Kafkaesque, nightmare quality that was particularly arresting when seen not as an isolated, aberrant situation but as yet another example within an increasingly recognizable category. A distinguishing feature that we found marking all examples was the reaction it evoked in most observers of the situation in which clients were placed as a result of damaging professional interventions— that the case was "impossible" and "absurd." As we shall see, such cases are impossible only in the sense that conjuring tricks are impossible. Like conjuring tricks, they present a false superficial appearance that distracts the observer from what is actually happening. Once one views the case from the right angle, it is understandable, both in causation and in its drive towards an "absurd" end.

As we began to collect and study these cases, we came to recognize the warning signs of immanent professional malfunctioning, and wondered whether it might be possible, therefore, to forestall the psychic damage that often scars victims of iatrogenic harm. As specialists in community mental health, we saw that iatrogenic damage constitutes a significant pathogen threatening the psychosocial well-being of many vulnerable members of the community, not only in cases of divorce, but also in many other situations in which people come to the attention of caregivers. Consequently, we felt that a determined effort must be made to understand its etiology and to reduce its incidence.

☐ A Possible Consequence of Any Intervention

Our concern became even greater when we realized that the possibility of causing iatrogenic damage is an inevitable consequence of any type of intervention by would-be helpers in the lives of people who are initially weak and dependant, or who are rendered more so by the misplaced efforts of caregivers. The sobering evidence seems to show that any kind of intervention, whether professional or lay, that is intended to be benign, may inadvertently lead to damage unless attention is paid to forestalling or aborting this unwanted outcome. We can now understand the hesitation of conservatives, who wish to limit the "meddling" of public bodies in private lives, and who oppose conceptualizing and labeling categories of human problems as possibly needing third party intervention. Their ideas contain a pessimistic logic that is well worth considering. For example, in Great Britain at the present time, most of the judicial procedures involving divorce are conducted by ratifying forms filled in by couples without any personal interaction at all between the divorcing parents and the bench. Only the openly conflicted 10% of cases actually come into contact with judges. As community mental health specialists, we may feel that it might be well to modify this bureaucratization of the divorce process in order to inject more direct contact between the 90% of uncontested cases and the judges and, thus, to identify hidden sources of problems that are apparently generating pathology in a proportion of the children despite the innocuous outer appearance of temporary arrangements that their parents may have cobbled together. However, unless we are simultaneously trying to lower the ensuing risk of iatrogenic damage, we may also be raising new chances of harming these children. Thus, for those of us committed to a community and preventive mental health approach, issues associated with iatrogenic damage have a grave and urgent importance. As we look for ways to intercede to reduce the prevalence of psychosocial pathology in the population, we must simultaneously find ways to control the prevalence of system-generated harm throughout the full range of the helping fields we are mobilizing to our cause.

☐ Stressing Negative Issues

This study began with no preexisting theories, professional or political, about the origins, mechanisms, or possible results of iatrogenic damage. All our findings have been derived from long-term exposure to actual clinical material, and we expect that the ideas that have emerged will be further developed and modified by continuing study.

It should be noted that, by the very nature of the subject examined, this book accentuates the negative. It dwells on distressing case material and it highlights unhelpful professional behavior. In describing these phenomena, we had to contend with a serious technical problem—how to use such material to illustrate instances of malfunctioning without readers concluding that we are thereby implying a condemnation of entire professional groups. Some of those who read the preliminary drafts of this book felt that it lacked balance and was possibly unfair to certain categories of community caregivers. There was no intention, however, to single out particular professionals as perpetrators of iatrogenic damage, nor to imply that certain instances of damaging behavior represented the general practice of particular caregiving fields. It so happens, however, that as we were dealing predominantly (though not exclusively) with divorce and custody battles, we saw a disproportionate numbers of instances that involved welfare and child protection social workers. This is not to say that other fields are immune from carrying out damaging behavior, or that we see welfare workers as unusually harming. It is necessary to state from the outset that we believe emphatically and sincerely that most caregivers in these and other community service fields are doing a vital, difficult, and sometimes thankless job, and that most of them are deeply committed to the present and future well-being, both physical and mental, of their clients. In most cases, they carry out their publicly mandated role with compassion and professionalism. This book, however, dwells on the darker side—on cases whose prevalence in the general population we do not know, but which occur at a sufficiently significant rate that every single professional to whom we have spoken on this subject has immediately agreed, "I have seen cases like that."

Despite the unfortunate possibility that there will be those among the population of caregiving professionals who will feel offended by what is to follow, if they give the matter some consideration, they too may come to see that whether such cases constitute an occasional aberration or a more frequently occurring phenomenon, responsible professionals should accustom themselves to the unwelcome idea that the best intentions, and even the best training, do not comprise invincible bulwarks against harming clients. If we as community caregivers are to carry out our duty to the public, we must arrive at methods for identifying and then aborting damaging behavior as early as possible, and not allow defensive denials and an allegiance to any particular professional group to obscure an unpalatable reality. In Chapter 12, we attempt to consider and answer criticisms of our study by professionals who saw this material before publication, and some of whom found it threatening or biased. We felt that the issues they raised required a respectful and thoughtful consideration on our part that hopefully has served to clarify our arguments for a larger audience and has also helped us to think more deeply about questions that we might otherwise have glossed over.

☐ Catchment Areas

While our work relating to preventing pathology in children of divorce drew cases from the catchment area of Jerusalem, the instances of iatrogenic damage that we have seen have come randomly from all over the country, since, apparently, it became known that we were prepared to brave the consequences of trying to intervene in such cases. Therefore, no impression about the geographic distribution of such cases in Israel can be derived from this book, nor can any consequent conclusions be drawn about the general quality of professional functioning or supervision in any particular locality.

☐ Organization of this Book

The next chapter will contain an overview of some major sources of iatrogenically damaging behavior. This abstract presentation will be filled out and added to in Chapters 3–7 through detailed analysis of typical, though disguised, cases. These cases were chosen to illustrate certain commonly occurring issues of causation and process in iatrogenic damage. They are all distressing. They form a continuum according to the severity and deliberateness of the steps taken by caregivers to perpetrate a damaging course of action, until they move from the category of individual "honest mistakes" into another, more worrisome category, where damaging behavior becomes reinforced by the concurrence of a wider professional climate in their caregiving system. With these examples in mind, Chapter 8 will discuss why programs to control harmful professional behavior do not always fulfill our expectations. In Chapter 9, we will suggest some practical ways of combating the issues involved, and Chapter 10 will consider the possible role of mental health consultation theory and techniques in modifying attitudes in unwelcoming agencies that may host iatrogenically damaging situations. In Chapter 11, we will consider how judges may be sensitized to some of the issues involved. In Chapter 12, as we have already mentioned, we will consider questions raised by the criticism of early readers. Chapter 13 will discuss helping the victims of iatrogenic damage and will offer some final observations based on our own experience as clinicians.

Let us stress again that we will be dealing throughout with upsetting material that may offend those who feel that their profession or its theories have been unfairly characterized. But we have derived our findings from clinical experiences, and we are describing facets of reality that must be acknowledged and dealt with frankly, unwelcome as they are to all of us, if we are to improve our services to the community.

2

CHAPTER

An Overview of Some Causative Factors

Within long-established caregiving fields, it has been recognized that well-intentioned professionals may harm clients because of a lack of knowledge, skill, empathy, or objectivity (G. & R. B. Caplan, 1999). The statistical possibility of malfunctioning taking place has been recognized and integrated into the planning of medical, educational, legal, and other human services, and avenues have been provided by custom and statute for clients to protest and seek redress. Professional guilds and service providers have evolved, or have had imposed on them by governing and funding agencies, ways of monitoring and documenting staff and peer performance in order to ensure ethical and quality control over the practice of colleagues and to forestall both damage to clients and also possibly baseless complaints against professionals for negligence, incompetence, or insensitivity to clients' needs. Despite such efforts, iatrogenic harm continues to occur, because precautions against it fail or can be evaded, and because certain areas of potential danger have not been delineated or acknowledged with enough urgency. Supervision of staff performance and avenues of redress for clients may not operate effectively in such cases, because the need for them has not been sufficiently anticipated, or because they have been deliberately blocked by damaging caregivers.

☐ Awareness of Iatrogenic Harm in Medical Practice

In regulating medical practice, for example, the inescapable fact that iatrogenic harm can take place has had to be faced openly and frankly. "Stay away from doctors, they will only make you ill" is a piece of folk wisdom that has long reflected a general awareness of the dangers of iatrogenic damage. Over the ages, it has forced the medical profession to try to prevent the harming of patients and to do so visibly enough to reassure the public.

A growing number of recent books and articles have discussed the scientific and legal aspects of the identification and prevention of iatrogenic damage. These have included analyses not only of possible causes for malfunctioning in carrying out the physical aspects of medicine, but also of potentially harmful shortcomings in the intangible, psychological dimensions of the doctor–patient relationship. As Richard P. Kluft pointed out in his article, "The Physician as Perpetrator of Abuse" (1993), there is an imbalance of power inherent in the doctor–patient relationship that may facilitate damaging behavior since the patient in his or her needy and crisis-prone situation is in a regressive, dependant state. The abuse of a malfunctioning physician can then assume the characteristics of child abuse or incest, producing deep psychosocial harm to augment any physical damage. We may add that this imbalance of power exists and has significant ramifications wherever any caregiver deals with troubled clients.

Identifying and preventing the perpetration of iatrogenic harm has become a priority of regulatory and licensing bodies like the British General Medical Council. In the aftermath of some recent, highly publicized malpractice cases that have shaken public and governmental confidence and have resulted in a number of colleagues being struck off the rolls, the British General Medical Council has produced two booklets that were sent to all its licensees, *Good Medical Practice* and *Maintaining Good Medical Practice*. These publications set out guidelines to be used as norms to judge physicians whose right to remain licensed is in question. These guidelines are of particular interest to us because they deal in large measure with aspects of professional behavior that have a psychological component, and, while composed for doctors, they could apply equally to most other caregiving professionals. Each booklet, for example, begins with the following declaration.

> Patients must be able to trust doctors with their lives and wellbeing. To justify that trust, we as a profession have a duty to maintain a good

standard of practice and care and to show respect for human life. In particular, as a doctor you must:

Make the care of your patient your first concern;
Treat every patient politely and considerately;
Respect patients' dignity and privacy;
Listen to patients and respect their views;
Give patients information in a way that they can understand;
Respect the right of patients to be fully involved in decisions about their care;
Keep your professional knowledge and skills up to date;
Recognize the limits of your professional competence;
Be honest and trustworthy;
Respect and protect confidential information;
Make sure that your personal beliefs do not prejudice your patients' care;
Act quickly to protect patients from risk if you have good reason to believe that you or a colleague may not be fit to practice;
Avoid abusing your position as a doctor; and
Work with colleagues in the ways that best serve patients' interests.

In all these matters, you must never discriminate unfairly against your patients or colleagues. And you must always be prepared to justify your actions to them. (*Good Medical Practice*, 1998)

This concern with the need to consciously guard against the possibility of doing not only physical harm but also psychological damage by insensitive and unethical behavior has been recognized in medicine at least since the time of Hippocrates, more than 2,000 years ago. Hippocrates understood not only that there is an interrelationship of body and mind, but also that there is a danger of doing harm inherent in the discrepancy between the powerful caregiver and the dependent sufferer. He bound his disciples, therefore, by an oath that is still taken by physicians today to avoid causing not only physical damage but also harm by committing ethical offenses.

The standards for good patient care advocated since the days of Hippocrates down to our own time represent a professional ideal that unfortunately may not always reflect practice. Iatrogenic harm, both physical and psychological, continues to occur in a significant number of cases despite official directives and warnings. Well-worded directives may not affect the practice of physicians who may not read, or who may fail to absorb the message of the British General Medical Council's booklets, and more seriously, regulatory powers may not be used with sufficient and timely force, thus allowing those who breach the guidelines to continue their practices with sometimes tragic consequences. For our present purposes, we take medicine as a model not because it has succeeded in eliminating iatrogenic damage—very far from it—but because it has recognized the problem openly, and is actively and publicly defining the issues involved.

☐ Iatrogenic Damage and Other Professions

While medicine has had millennia to evolve norms of professional conduct, other caregiving fields, especially those associated with psychological counseling and with social and welfare services, have found iatrogenic harm harder for practitioners to acknowledge, define, monitor, and control. In contemporary Western societies, a growing list of ills once considered the private concern of the individuals involved are now often dealt with on a formal, community level by regulatory laws and by specialized, often publicly funded, human services. The community has been sensitized to the human and economic cost of deprivation, and the evidence of physical and mental health specialists has impressed on the public the social cost to their communities of long-term damage associated with such stressors as family violence, divorce, disputed custody of minors, neglect and abuse of children, inattention to learning disabilities, rape, chronic intergenerational poverty, and a host of other problems once regarded as the exclusive business of those directly involved.

In order to deal with these issues, new professions, subprofessions, and paraprofessions were, and are continuing to be, created within the health, welfare, law enforcement, mental health, education, and counseling fields. Not all of these have clearly delineated identities and areas of assured, formalized expertise. Some are endowed with statutory powers that obligate their intervention in the private lives of families. This has led to improvements in the lot of many vulnerable people, but it has also opened the door to iatrogenic damage. Most of these professions have had a far shorter history than medicine in which to evolve a unified identity and generally binding criteria for what constitute correct functioning, and they may lack the corporate unity and self-confidence that enables physicians to acknowledge, at least in theory, the need for self-imposed vigilance and to accept surveillance by colleagues in order to forestall undesirable results. Medical students are taught the imperative of self-consciously guarding against oversights and bias. Other caregiving professions, whose job carries less open risk of causing the maiming or death of a client, are apparently less inclined, or less aware of the need, to drill into their students the possibility that their interventions, however well-intentioned, may in fact cause harm.

☐ Lack of Precise Criteria for Establishing Professional Roles, Especially in Recently Created Professions

Because of recent social trends, a demand has been created for new role functions to be entrusted to mental health, welfare, and law enforcement professionals and paraprofessionals. For example, new professional missions have been forged from the need of judges to get advice about the custody of children in divorce cases. That advice comes from experts on parenting capacity in a variety of professions, each of which may see the family from a partial viewpoint that is molded by its particular background. One source of iatrogenic damage is the ad hoc nature of the appearance of these fields in response to the community's immediate needs and the lack of standardized criteria for establishing relative degrees of expertise and assessing competence. For example, some years ago, a foreign colleague told us that he was disillusioned by the caliber of many of those involved in the "custody evaluation industry." These evaluators might be psychologists, psychiatrists, or social workers with varying levels of academic qualifications in their respective field, appointed by courts to assess the divorcing parents in custody disputes. Our colleague felt that many of these professionals were not qualified to make the important decisions involved. Once their evidence had been presented in court, its validity became difficult for judges not trained in mental health matters to weigh, and it became very difficult for a parent to challenge. Such evaluators, our colleague said, tended to be appointed because of their relationship with lawyers for whose clients they had written "nice reports," while their actual competence and experience were "secondary." This colleague felt that established standardized criteria were needed to mark true expertise. While several organizations in his country apparently grant credentials in this area, this colleague suspected that such certification was not always based on examination of qualifications, but rather on the payment of a fee.

Certain categories of experts in the mental health and child protection field are subgroups of traditional career categories, and the precise delineation of their qualifications and areas of legitimate activity are still in flux. Among the pioneers in a given field or subspecialty may be those who have achieved their position despite inadequate training. Some may have had the aptitude and motivation to build up their own competence to a high level, but others may have occupied key positions by virtue of having arrived first, survived long, and guarded well against the encroachment of better-qualified newcomers. Such veterans may oppose or evade raising the standards and delimiting the legitimate area of competence of their fields more precisely because they feel threatened by these moves.

This phenomenon persists in part because the community caregiving system generally calls for more people to occupy job slots than there are talented candidates to fill them. Staff positions may be endowed with statutory obligations and prerogatives that presuppose incumbents of quality. Yet many of those who are actually available and prepared to do the sometimes unpalatable work that is involved in front line fields may not reflect the image anticipated by the people who set up that part of the system. The system, therefore, has to muddle through with less than ideal staffing, demanding that often low-level personnel deal with the most complicated jobs. Meanwhile high-level professionals tend to become administrators, supervisors, and educators whose sense of community realities may be filtered through the observations and reports of less qualified subordinates. Other professionals, like judges, suffer from input overload that makes their need for advisors more pressing, and in consequence, they are sometimes forced to place undue reliance on whatever "experts" present themselves. The latter may include those with more nominal than actual competence, thereby increasing the risk that their advice will damage clients.

☐ Ambiguity in Determining Damaging Behavior in Nontechnological Fields

Because of the nontechnical, nonphysical nature of their interventions, it may be legitimately difficult for certain categories of community caregivers to realize that their own interventions have caused damage. In the medical field, at least in theory, the suspicion that a course of treatment has caused harm can be supported by the onset of unanticipated physical deterioration. In cases of distress that involve no physical damage, the question of what harm has been caused and by whom becomes more slippery. Consequently, successful malpractice suits to allot damages in tort cases involving psychotherapy have been rare. In their article on "Psychiatric Malpractice" Joel I. Klein and Steven I. Glover explain that, "tort law has always been slow to provide remedies for purely emotional injuries . . . since courts reasoned that emotional injuries are too evanescent, metaphysical and variable" (Klein & Glover, 1983), and it is difficult to show that the damage has been caused by the misconduct of a caregiver. As R. E. Kendell, President of the British Royal College of Psychiatrists, wrote in an editorial for the *Psychiatric Bulletin*:

So far, none of the great scandals has involved psychiatry, but this is probably simply because the nature of psychiatric practice does not lend itself to early detection of incompetence. We do not put patients' lives at immediate risk in the way that surgeons and anesthetists necessarily do, nor do we participate in routine procedures like breast and cervical screening which lend themselves to simple forms of audit. Luckily too, the public has the wisdom to realize that dissatisfied patients, of whom we have many, do not always have sound reasons for their dissatisfaction. (Kendell, 1998)

Furthermore, what we, because of our own biases, may perceive as system-generated harm may not be identified as such by those who define acceptable means and attainable goals in terms other than ours because they have different professional values, point of view, and timeframes for measuring results. For example, the primary cause of manifest damage may be plausibly disputed. It may be claimed that the client suffered harm as a result of those earlier forces which the supposedly malfunctioning caregivers had identified as necessitating their original intervention, and that this damage would have been even greater had no action been taken at all. We may argue, on the other hand, that the original, undeniably damaging factors were needlessly exacerbated by the quality of the professional intervention.

David P. H. Jones argued, in an article on "Professional and Clinical Challenges to Protection of Children" (1996), that in sexual abuse cases, for example,

In any consideration of iatrogenic harm, it can be difficult to distinguish what is truly iatrogenic from the natural harm and disruption of the abuse itself. In the case of intrafamiliar sexual abuse, discovery itself is disruptive and traumatic, and in a very real sense the family can never be the same again.

Jones goes on to caution,

When the professionals in a sexual abuse system respond to abuse, frequently casual observers such as the news media, as well as child psychologists and psychiatrists who are not directly involved with cases, leap to the conclusion that simply because the crisis of discovery is followed by disruption and distress among family members, that these features in themselves must have been caused or created by the professional response. They forget that when a stable system, which may have existed for some time in a relatively predictable state, is suddenly disrupted by discovery, that change is likely to be radical, because the whole of the previous status has depended upon the relative subjugation and silence of one or more family members. While that person is contained and persuaded to remain silent, the remainder of the system manages to exist in apparent contentment and stability, as though one or more members of the family are sacrificed for the sake of the greater good. (1991)

The ambiguities inherent in psychologically weighted issues make for a murkiness through which we must struggle if we wish to identify the process associated with iatrogenic damage. For, despite all caveats, professionals do on occasions malfunction in clearly discernable ways, and they do so for often identifiable reasons.

☐ Unselected, Minimally Trained Personnel Recruited For Primary Prevention

The theory and practice of community mental health and primary prevention unwittingly increase the risk of iatrogenic harm when they are based on a model in which a wide range of caregivers add to their own traditional professional service missions that of interesting themselves and intervening in the crises of their clients in order to prevent potential psychological disorder in a statistically significant proportion of a group deemed to be at risk. By mobilizing these caregivers and giving them a double agenda to do not only their own work, but also part of ours, we energize a heterogeneous and largely unknown population of professionals over whose selection, training, and supervision we clearly have little or no control. Among them are the empathic, wise, and humane, who are well suited to assuming a role in protecting and promoting mental health. There are many others, however, who lack the tact, warmth, insight, and judgment to handle individuals in crisis, especially if members of their profession now feel they have a license to inquire into the privacy of a client's feelings and family circumstances, to give unsolicited advice, and to inform on clients to the authorities or take punitive measures because of mistaken or misunderstood cues. Therefore, we may be asking those least qualified to make the most critical judgments, to become the gatekeepers for clients to reach supportive care, and also possibly to initiate punitive consequences against clients for their suspected weaknesses and misperceived faults.

The fact that many people are not suited by background or temperament to be active in the field of mental health does not necessarily discourage them from working in it. Training workshops or a course or two that give a smattering of knowledge in this area can promote an unwarranted sense of competence in those with an exaggerated notion of their own talents, and this can be fatally matched by the mistaken trust in their judgment and expertise by laymen and professionals in other fields. This paucity of preparation can undermine the judgment and effectiveness of caregivers whom one might assume to be necessarily sophisticated in mental health areas, such caregivers as many child protection workers and specialized investigators charged with questioning children who are the supposed victims of sexual abuse. Yet on examination, the scantiness of the training in normal, abnormal, and child psychology, and in the techniques of assessing family relationships of many who are in positions to make radical decisions about the fate of children and parents is unsettling.

☐ Shallow Understanding of Mental Health Principles

Even if they have had some preparation, such professionals may lack a depth of understanding of the principles that govern the mental health aspects of their work. This may lead them to turn complex theories and general guidelines into rigidly enforced rules and simplistic, superficial formulae that make no allowances for individual characteristics and needs of clients. This rigidity may be caused by lack of experience, so that professionals cannot judge when it is appropriate to make exceptions to general guidelines. To stereotype and apply a ready made formula taken from an authoritative source may also be a defensive reaction when confronting the complexity of real human situations, thereby resolving the professional's own confusion and discomfort. However, it may also stem from the distortion of theories within the process of their transmission from teacher to student and from one colleague to another. As in the children's game of "broken telephone," a message gets progressively more garbled as it passes from one person to the next. Even when it is enunciated with clarity and precision, a theory tends to emerge out in the field of practice in a mutated form that may give it an imperative tone that was never intended, and that may even negate the spirit of the original concept. Some dutiful caregivers then enforce these apparent dogmas in defiance of common sense on any case that they stereotype as fitting an immutable category.

Such, for example, is the way some welfare officers and judges, in a number of mismanaged cases that have been referred to us, have dealt with the refusal of some children from divorced families to associate with a noncustodial parent. The caregivers have apparently accepted uncritically the concept that this refusal constitutes an inevitable danger to the child's mental health. If the child cannot be forced— often by physical propulsion and what is euphemistically termed "treatment" or "psychotherapy"—which can have more in common with indoctrination and brain-washing than with real therapy—into a room with the rejected parent, then the child must be separated from the preferred parent, even if necessary, by institutionalization until he or she accepts contact with the other. Some children, however, have good reasons to avoid a parent who appears benign and inoffensive to adults, but whose violence and abuse they may have witnessed or whose personality they may find threatening, belittling, or manipulative. Even if the antipathy has been influenced by brainwashing or intimidation by the preferred parent, as caregivers often suspect, it is not long before the child internalizes this view, and it becomes very difficult to reverse the situation. This reversal can seldom be accomplished by force, since the child will correctly see this as the long arm of the rejected and victimizing parent who will not thereby endear himself or herself to the child.

☐ Population at Risk

There is, however, an even more fallacious basis for this pressure, and that is a failure to instill in caregivers an understanding of the meaning of a "population at risk," in whose lives caregivers are encouraged to intervene in order to prevent a threatened pathology. It may be true that a statistically significant number of children who reject a parent may suffer in the future from some form of consequent psychosocial disturbance that one would ideally aim to prevent. However that danger is theoretical; it refers to the chance that such cases will occur at an increased rate in a total population. It does not prophesy that *this* child *will* become ill. If, in order to prevent this possible future damage, we subject the child to present, certain damage by inflicting trauma through forcing him or her into stressful situations and by isolating him or her from a parent whom the child loves and with whom he or she feels safe, we have grotesquely caricatured the concept of primary prevention.

☐ Primary Prevention vs. Privacy and Autonomy

We are beginning to realize that the methods and techniques that we are developing in the field of primary prevention may cause harm rather than the good we hope to achieve. Our well-meant actions must be carefully controlled and limited by sensitivity to the rights of people for privacy and autonomy in deciding about intimate aspects of their own lives. It may be that we pioneers in community mental health are sufficiently experienced and interpersonally sensitive to be able to recognize the early signs of potential harm when we cross the boundaries of privacy, but it remains for the future to determine how, if at all, it is possible to recruit the large numbers of line workers who will intercede with that same level of sensitivity and skill in the intimate lives of a whole population.

For instance, many people who are grappling with current situations of adversity will be weakened, rather than strengthened by well-meaning intervention that is aimed at supporting them. If asked, such people are likely to say that they want to be left alone to struggle with their difficulties at their own pace, rather than being forced by the pressure of others to deal with the issues according to some universal timetable. Clinicians experienced in dealing with posttraumatic reactions have learned to allow victims to deny and evade particularly burdensome issues until such time as they show signs of being able to handle them. Less skilled workers will increase the posttraumatic pathology by prematurely attacking defenses and forcing confrontation with upsetting realities. The problem for those who will explore the practical implementation of our primary preventive program over the coming decades is how to develop techniques to guard against harming a population by well-meaning intervention that overpowers defenses linked with privacy and autonomy, and that fail to respect idiosyncratic timetables and methods of coping.

We are reminded of an example that was brought to our attention by a group of adolescent volunteer youth leaders who came to ask for our advice. They worked in an underprivileged neighborhood in which a number of school children had just been killed or wounded in a terrorist incident. The authorities had immediately sent teams of mental health workers to engage in crisis intervention in each classroom in the local school where the incident had occurred. The volunteers told us that these mental health personnel were resented by the children and their parents, who saw their intervention not as the help it was intended to be, but as an invasion of officious outsiders who, they felt, were heartlessly probing their fresh wounds. The local people felt that the professionals were trying to turn them, in the midst of their justifiable grief, into psychiatric cases and were forcing treatment on them. The volunteers respected the reluctance of the children to speak about their feelings and the traumatic events that they had just witnessed, understanding that this was in line with their culture that frowned on introspection and encouraged a stoic control of emotions. The volunteers were less concerned about a stereotyped professional intervention that offended against the local culture, than they were about a particular child who, unlike the rest who wept quietly and clung to each other, laughed loudly, and made silly gestures and flippant remarks about the incident. This child had been punished for rough play just before the attack occurred and had been sent off the playground into the building. She had thus watched from the safety of an upper window as the classmates, whom she had just been pushing around, were shot. The other survivors were now calling this child vulgar and callous because of her indecorous outbursts. The volunteers were worried that as the child was being extruded from the group, she was being made psychologically vulnerable both by her increasing isolation and by what must have been complicated feelings about her chance survival because of naughtiness. Thus, the professionals, in their rush to engage in crisis intervention and to be proactive in a tragedy that had presumably upset them as it had shocked the whole country, had not only unwittingly antagonized and insulted those whom they had set out to help, but in their flurry of stereotyped and premature activity, they had missed identifying at least one child in acute danger of becoming another casualty. As we will see presently, one aspect of damaging behavior by professionals is to be so wedded to a preconceived focus that targets what they are certain is a source of vulnerability, that they overlook unanticipated, but possibly more authentic and immediate dangers.

☐ The Bounded Population and Iatrogenic Damage

One of the cornerstones of the community-based model of prevention is that of the bounded population for which particular agencies are given service obligations. One source of damage comes from the fact that this traps both clients and caregivers in an obligatory relationship that one side or the other may find unsatisfactory. If an already distressed client in the midst of the disequilibrium of a crisis finds himself or herself being dealt with by an insensitive, ignorant, overbearing, or prejudiced professional, it becomes difficult to escape to a more congenial caregiver. If one's domicile places one inside the jurisdiction of a particular school, or welfare office, or medical practice, it may require energy not readily available to those already burdened by a crisis to change to another service provider. According to the first letter of one's name, one automatically belongs to a particular panel of judges in Rabbinic divorce courts, even if they are found not to be objective, sympathetic, or culturally congruent by their clients. If vulnerable people actually manage to switch to another branch of an agency, or to another professional in the same institution, the file that contains the assessment that the client finds unsatisfactory, or that contains his or her reputation for obstreperousness may accompany him or her, so the change may not alleviate the problem.

The other side of the coin of a populationwide approach is that once community agencies must accept responsibility for an entire bounded population and may no longer choose "suitable" cases, they will have to deal with "unsuitable" ones—those whom they do not know how to handle, or those whom they find obnoxious or threatening. Like their clients, these professionals cannot easily escape if they want to continue to be employed. Ideally, in-service training, supervision, and mental health consultation should help professionals deal with situations that are beyond their current capacities. However, what works on paper may not work in the field. Supervisors for example may not be purveyors of psychological knowledge and sagacity, though expert in their primary area of responsibility, their own profession, and they may well share the prejudices and limitations of their subordinates.

☐ Vulnerable Clients

This can be particularly damaging for certain categories of cases. For, while any client may incur iatrogenic damage, some are especially vulnerable. Those most obviously at risk belong to populations regarded by particular caregivers as being of low status and inherently problematic. In Israel, that can mean members of large ultraorthodox families, members of North African or Middle Eastern communities, especially if they hold menial jobs, recent immigrants from Ethiopia and provinces of the former Soviet Union, and those who hold what are considered extreme political views. Other clients may be victimized if they are not compliant and have a history of protesting against the way they have been treated in the past. This is then entered in their record to discredit and stigmatize them in future encounters with the system.

☐ Loss of Professional Objectivity

One source of iatrogenic damage that has long interested us, and whose prevalence is increased by the mobilization into the front ranks of preventive mental health of professionals from different disciplines, is the normally competent caregiver who unwittingly and repeatedly mismanages particular categories of cases. Within an heterogeneous caseload, they may encounter occasional instances that trigger a loss of professional objectivity and consequent lapses in judgment and performance. Such lapses can also occur systematically, when caregivers compulsively hunt out cases that link onto unresolved themes or conflicts in their own lives, manipulating clients so as to reenact the caregiver's own unconscious inner drama. Such professionals typically identify in a case issues that are not necessarily based on observable facts, and they distort the evidence to fit the mold of their own making. They may work compulsively, for example, to "rescue" children whom they erroneously perceive to be at risk, stereotyping the family as degenerate, uncaring, and perverted, and rejecting all evidence that contradicts their conclusions. The hallmarks of this category of damaging professionals are their almost religious zeal and self-righteousness, the repetitiveness with which they discover and pursue similar cases, the tenacity with which they cling to a distorted image of the clients, and their resistance to acknowledging any indications that run counter to their own apocalyptic predictions about the client's fate should the professional's own directives for management not be followed. It is as though these caregivers are being driven by forces outside the case that have little to do with concrete reality.

Among the most damaging of such professionals are those who have been drawn to fields where they are most likely to meet the category of cases that stimulates them to engage in damaging behavior. Working in such an area endows them with a formal mission that may mask the irrational quality of their functioning and legitimizes their victimization of certain types of clients. For, if child protection workers, for example, identify and prosecute many cases of abuse and remove supposedly victimized children from their families, they will be regarded as fulfilling their public mandate in exemplary fashion. Some observers may point out, however, that, while a proportion of their cases indeed requires extreme forms of intervention, others may be largely fabricated and mismanaged and do not, in fact, warrant the draconian measures that are meted out to them.

☐ Collective Lack of Professional Objectivity

The situation may be aggravated further if a number of caregivers with a similar irrational and compulsive drive to hunt down the cases that excite them come together in the same institution. They may gain control of its policy making and of hiring staff, thereby causing considerable damage to clients. This may make it virtually impossible for those who are harmed to gain redress because of the solid front that validates the irrational interpretation of a case. We will return to this sensitive and important issue when we discuss clinical examples.

☐ Theme Interference and Why It Endangers Clients

We have been concerned with this type of loss of objectivity, a phenomena we have called *theme interference*, since our days at Harvard Laboratory of Community Psychiatry in the Harvard University Medical School when we were conceptualizing and refining our techniques of consultee-centered mental health consultation in order to counteract certain types of lapses in professional functioning (G. Caplan, 1970; R. B. Caplan & G. Caplan, 1972). In trying to help caregivers such as public health nurses, clergymen, and teachers overcome current problems in their daily work, we became aware that these difficulties were not infrequently associated with a loss of professional objectivity when some problem or theme from the private life of the caregivers invaded their professional work, generating a "theme interference."

Theme interference is an irrational, unconscious maneuver engaged in by the caregiver in order to solve an unresolved problem in his or her mind or life. The caregiver projects onto a current work situation his or her own unconscious or preconscious issue that is triggered by an evocative cue in the characteristics of a client or in a feature of a client's case. Theme interference is a psychic defense, whereby, to use psychoanalytic terminology, a displacement is effected so that the caregiver confronts and struggles with his or her own problem "out there," where it is relatively unthreatening because it is supposedly taking place at a safe distance in someone else's life and not, obviously, within the life of the caregiver.

This process endangers the client for two reasons: First, the reality of the client and the configuration of the unconscious theme in the caregiver are not totally congruent. In order for the theme to fit the client, the caregiver cannot permit himself or herself to perceive the client and his or her surround clearly, because the idiosyncrasies of the latter and possible discrepancies between his or her situation and the caregiver's own unconscious problem would spoil the match. Consequently, the caregiver typically stereotypes and demonizes the client and figures in the client's life. The caregiver's capacity to gather undistorted information about the realities of the case is therefore inhibited and blinkered because, if he or she permitted himself or herself to scrutinize the facts too closely, the mismatch would be revealed and the unconscious displacement would be disrupted.

The second danger to the client comes from the fact that the theme is a complex of thoughts and feelings that are linked in the unconscious mind of the caregiver with a past problem that he or she has found insoluble. For this reason, when the theme is activated, the caregiver feels helpless and hopeless to deal effectively with the issues, and acts accordingly. When the theme is displaced onto the client's case, namely when the caregiver perceives the relevant stereotyped pattern that is identical with his or her unconscious memory of what occurred to him or her in the past, he or she uses this as an opportunity to get relief from the pressure caused by the repressed memory of the old difficulties that continues to burden the caregiver, because it represents a past failure to solve an important life problem (Caplan & Caplan, 1972).

It must be remembered that repression may not be a permanent solution to unresolved issues. Ghosts of past failures and unresolved conflicts may chronically threaten to bubble up to the surface of consciousness and may require a constant, significant, and sometimes draining input of psychic energy to keep them out of the individual's awareness. The caregiver gets some relief from the pressure of this struggle against unwelcome memories breaking through to the surface of consciousness by the fact of displacing the problem onto the client, because he or she can now feel that the erupting worries are due to concern with the difficulties experienced by the client and not with any threatening personal issues. The memory of what took place in the caregiver's past can then continue to be unconscious, while the associated negative feelings can now be allowed into conscious awareness and can be ascribed to a praiseworthy professional concern with the predicament of the client.

Typically, the caregiver perceives the client as inevitably heading towards disaster. The caregiver may struggle to avert that doom, but does so in a way that unconsciously ensures a bad outcome in real life to match the caregiver's fear of failure in his or her own dilemma. This entire maneuver must be suppressed from consciousness in order to form an effective defense mechanism. If the caregiver is made aware of what he or she is doing, this particular case would be unlinked from the theme. But usually, the caregiver will find another, similar case to be clicked into the same pattern and to take the place of the previous discarded case in "solving" the caregiver's problem.

☐ Consultee-Centered Case Consultation

At Harvard Medical School, our Laboratory of Community Mental Health developed techniques for remedying this situation in which a theme interference blocked effective professional functioning. In this technique, a consultant trained in a specific and definite method called *consultee-centered case consultation* dealt with the caregiver's work problem within the defense structure erected by the consultee's unconscious. Paradoxically, the technique hinged on not making the theme conscious by forcing consultees to become aware of how they had been defending themselves against a rejected or frightening issue by the subconscious defense of displacing it onto the story of the client and unsuccessfully grappling with it "out there." The consultant had to identify the theme from the consultee's account of the case, but was never to probe into the privacy of the latter's conscious or unconscious life, nor was the consultant to bring the theme itself to the consultee's conscious attention. Instead, the consultant looked at the case alongside the consultee, and brought the latter to realize that its outcome might not be inevitably disastrous after all. This not only enabled the caregiver to see the case as potentially soluble, it could also lead to a reflexive, unconscious effect, since if this client in this situation was not lost, perhaps the caregiver or someone close to him or her was not without hope either.

☐ Theme Interference and Iatrogenic Damage

Nowadays, we realize that these theme interferences were examples of minor episodes of iatrogenic damage in which the consultees were covertly exploiting clients to relieve their own inner psychological tension. A characteristic feature of this process, as we have said, was that the caregivers often perceived the clients as fixed stereotypes which were related to the part they were supposed to be playing in the drama that reenacted the caregiver's own theme. One sign of the success of our theme interference reduction techniques was that the consultees became able to perceive and deal with the clients as real, complex human beings and not as dehumanized stereotypes.

After observing many clinical examples, we have come to suspect that the particular attributes of unconsciously motivated mismanagement caused by a theme interference are characteristic markers for many instances of iatrogenic damage, whether caused by unconscious or conscious forces. *Typically, the damaging professional, consciously or unconsciously, creates a false picture of the client's situation in order to achieve an ending that is, for whatever reason, predetermined and rendered inevitable by the professional from the very outset of contact between client and caregiver. This, then, leads to premature cognitive closure since it obviates any felt need in the caregiver to pursue and analyze the client's actual circumstances, because to look at reality might threaten the achievement of a prefigured, inappropriate end towards which the damaging caregiver consciously or unconsciously drives the hapless client.*

☐ The Limits of Mental Health Consultation

The mental health consultation techniques that we developed to deal with theme interference cannot readily abort the type of damaging behavior that may well be the result of inappropriate treatment by an individual caregiver but may also be system-linked and embedded in the cozy collegiality of a hospitable institutional setting. In our experience working as mental health consultants among school teachers, public health nurses, Episcopalian parish clergy and bishops, and other professional groups, intrusion of unconscious material into the caregiver's work was regarded by superiors and coworkers as an uncharacteristic and unwelcome lapse in the caregiver's accustomed level of effectiveness. A worker who was usually competent was seen as having inexplicable difficulties in a case, which thereby disturbed the mission of the caregiver's agency. The caregiver himself or herself would also be upset by this apparently mysterious inability to manage a case at his or her usual level of functioning. Thus, mental health consultation depends on workers or supervisors asking for help from a specialist consultant because they realize that a problem exists and they are disturbed by it. Our recent practice has taken place in a wider and more varied context where many cases of iatrogenic damage have been fuelled by unconscious bias and stereotyping in which neither the individual caregiver, nor the supervisor, nor the higher echelons of their agency have been able or prepared to acknowledge that they have any problem at all. Thus theme interference can be not merely the handicap of an individual worker, but can become legitimized within the social fabric of the organization from which fortified position it becomes very difficult to dislodge. As we will see presently when we analyze cases, disciplined workers whose actions are supported by and are consistent with the apparently explicit policy of their superiors can produce "absurd" and "irrational" damaging processes.

Up till now, we have described possible sources of iatrogenic damage that may seem logical and familiar to many colleagues. We will now turn to some that may seem less obvious, more controversial, and perhaps more abstract, and whose implications for practice in the field may be less readily grasped. The reader's patience is needed at this point, therefore, while we list some of the possibly less familiar issues, all of which will be illustrated in forthcoming chapters in detailed examples that show how they may manifest themselves in distorting the treatment of clients.

☐ Caregivers as Agents of Social Control

Professionals dealing punitively with clients who might be more appropriately treated by supportive means may cause iatrogenic damage. The punitive drive behind the work of caregivers driven by theme interference can be intensified by the fact that their role may be a hybrid one. Outwardly, certain community agencies appear to be therapeutic, but the other side of their mission is to act as branches of law enforcement and social control. The publicly mandated goal of these protective agencies is to prosecute offenders who, for example, are deemed a threat to child welfare, and to do so if necessary at the cost of the survival of the family. A senior Israeli social worker lamented the fact that the local child protection system has impressed on the public that it is *the* address for reporting all suspicions concerning the wellbeing of children. Laymen and caregivers now accept that its workers are the correct recipients of any information about family problems, thereby ensuring that the field is monopolized by agents of social control, not by those exclusively dedicated to social support. This hybrid role may explain an Orwellian distortion of terminology that we keep encountering, in which "therapy" and "treatment" may actually designate imposition of social norms. The goal of this "treatment" may not be to restore the client's wellbeing, but to force compliance with the values espoused by the caregiver and his or her agency, which may actually lower a client's sense of wellbeing. Clients who turn to such agencies for help may find that they have walked into a virtually inescapable situation, where vulnerability and the evidence of their need for guidance may be used as evidence to take punitive measures against them.

People may also be damaged by caregiving professionals who are bound by laws that force disclosure of suspicions of abuse to the legal authorities. Clients may then find that confidentiality is unexpectedly suspended, and that because some aspect of their case triggers somebody's alarm—rationally or irrationally—they suddenly become criminally suspect, subjected to frightening, humiliating, interminable investigations, and even temporary imprisonment.

☐ A Double Agenda and the Danger of Iatrogenic Damage

Mental health professionals recruit caregivers in other fields to give early warning of ominous symptoms among individuals in crisis whom the latter encounter in the course of their own work. In the same way, workers in other community agencies may also encourage other professionals and paraprofessionals to follow a double agenda while performing their own primary role. For example, an acclaimed preschool enrichment program that teaches immigrant and disadvantaged mothers to stimulate their children's learning capacity is staffed by "counselors"—often mothers who have themselves graduated from the program—who conduct home visits. An admiring newspaper account of this program included the following:

> In the subculture where immigrants do not allow welfare or community workers into their homes, the only person who can get into the house and see what's happening is a counselor, who is not seen as a threat. When counselors come to the homes, they both ensure the parents' commitment to the program, but at the same time also see what's happening in the child's environment and can report on bad conditions or suspicions of maltreatment. (Rotem, 1998)

The issue that concerns us here is not the exposure of genuine abuse, which is a goal to which we all subscribe, but rather the encouragement of denunciations based on superficial observations and the "suspicions" of informants whose unthreatening appearance is in some measure a deception as far as the clients are concerned. This use of a double agenda, coupled with a legal demand for reporting by caregivers of every suspicion on pain of facing prosecution themselves, may drive even normally careful professionals to sound alarms before giving themselves time to check their facts. It may also lower the threshold beyond which those in need of guidance and treatment in the traditional sense of the words may be subjected to legal proceedings with all the attendant stress and expense that such a status entails. Cases that are trivial or illusory are in danger of being lumped together with others that are gross violations of decency and safety. Within the ensuing prosecutory atmosphere, the possibility of a client being treated or reeducated in the old-fashioned meaning of those words is reduced. Instead of teaching parenting skills to an inadequately prepared, impulsive mother who lashes out at a hyperactive, intractable child, for example, the prosecutors' solution may be to deprive her of parental rights.

☐ Legal Powers of Certain Community Caregivers

A potential magnet for damaging workers in hybrid institutions is legislation that gives unusual powers to those whose jobs bring them into contact with clients who may be at special risk. In countries like Israel, Great Britain, and the United States, child protection workers, for example, are allowed to leapfrog the usual civil safeguards to mobilize courts and police in order to snatch children out of what the professional deems to be harm's way with little or no delay. The good intentions of those who propose these measures can lead to abuse, not only because the evidence for emergency action may be misjudged, and because many children are traumatized by this process, but because the wrong type of people may be drawn to fields that grant such control over the lives of others. We might have hoped that the courts or the supervisory structures of each professional group might forestall the abuse of powers that have been lavishly granted in the field of child protection, for example. In fact, however, for a variety of reasons to be discussed presently, this may not happen.

☐ The Hidden Agenda

The probability that the caregiving system will damage clients can be increased even further if the motivating drive in such professionals is not only an unconscious irrational theme but also a consciously held, hidden agenda that contributes to intensifying the impact of that theme by focusing it on an outwardly legitimate goal like the prevention of psychosocial pathology in members of vulnerable subpopulations, which is used as a screen to disguise the real motivation behind an intervention. The covert agenda cannot be openly acknowledged, because it often runs against the prevailing ideological currents in a society where the appearance of caring, and where adhering to democratic practices and fair legal processes are generally held to be paramount. One of the marks of such cases of iatrogenic damage is that complaints by dissatisfied clients are stifled because an open and fair review of grievances might expose this hidden agenda that is often antidemocratic and self-serving.

The stated goal of child protection and adoption services, for example, is the welfare of the child. Advocating this is rather like invoking the wishes of the dead, an unimpeachable piety that tends to project the views of the one invoking the slogan rather than any ascertainable wish of the voiceless principal. Its invocation may camouflage other, less socially acceptable wishes in the service of which the real welfare of the client becomes secondary and may even be sacrificed entirely. In many cases of iatrogenic harm that we have studied, except for the rhetoric, the welfare of the child and that of the family figured low on the actual priorities of the damaging caregivers. More significant were issues of protecting the existence and prerogatives of the system and fending off censure and political pressure, satisfying a vocal interest group like would-be adoptive parents, or ideologically motivated positions involving religious vs. secular interests, for example, the profeminist leanings of the professionals, or even nationalistic motives that favor the raising of a child in one country rather than in another.

The hidden agenda might be driven by administrative or idealistic motives. An example of the former might be an agency's efforts to maintain and augment its funding level by recruiting clients. If, for example, appropriation of funds is pegged to the number of beds occupied in a residential institution for deprived or abused children, and this, in turn, determines staffing levels so that if the number of inmates drops job slots would be eliminated, an agency might be tempted to fill beds artificially by institutionalizing children who might otherwise be safely left in the community, and by extending the stay of those already in residence. In a similar vein, more staff could be maintained by prescribing tests and treatment that would not otherwise be indicated. This would serve a second purpose of maintaining contact with, and surveillance over clients for extended periods in order to move them eventually into another facet of the agency's operations when the opportunity offered. Similarly, in an article on wrongful adoption suits in the United States (Vobedja, 1998), in which adoptive families attempt to divest themselves of severely disturbed adoptees about whose early history and vulnerabilities they had not been told by the authorities, it was suggested that one motive for placing unsuitable children was new governmental funding that gave incentives for agencies to arrange for older children to be adopted.

☐ Social Engineering

A hidden agenda may also be driven by ideology. Among the more ubiquitous items in a hidden agenda is a cult of social engineering that seeks to create a "new man" by modifying the social milieu, in pursuit of which the interests of the individual may be sacrificed. Social engineering is common in revolutionary and emerging societies that try to dispel what are seen as primitive and retrograde aspects of traditional culture and to integrate immigrants and others who are outsiders because of class or caste by imposing conformity to a way of life that fits the idealized self-image of that society. Historically, implementing such Utopian visions has implied that caregivers and policy makers hold to an implicit hierarchy of racial, physical, and cultural norms. Those in authority tacitly regard themselves as exemplars and arbiters of the higher standards, though objectively they may not be of the elite of their own defining but may only aspire to be regarded as such and attempt to prove their identification with the ideal by treating more harshly members of certain other groups who may be tacitly seen as inferior, undesirable, incorrigible, and ultimately expendable. In such ideologies, preserving the family unit is not necessarily seen as essential because families by their nature are culturally conservative, carrying the past into the future.

In Israel, as in other emerging and ideologically based societies, there is a tradition in certain political circles and professional groups of deliberately loosening the ties between generations in order to create a modern, "liberated," homogeneously westernized mentality. Agencies that are the heirs of this tradition have a low threshold for removing children from families and derogating parenting capacity in those deemed to be the analogue of the Biblical generation condemned to 40 years' of wandering in the desert. Suspicion about the welfare of the children of such subgroups is more readily and harshly acted upon, and evidence to support removing children from families, if lacking, is more readily manufactured.

☐ Stereotyped Case Files

When there is an hidden agenda, official case files tend to manipulate evidence to point towards a solution arrived at by the caregivers in advance. Those cases that involve social engineering, for example, tend to contain particular stereotyped imagery and language. The biological parents of children whom the caregivers wish to remove are inevitably described as dirty, brutal, primitive, immoral, carnal, and "mildly retarded." Their world is depicted as abounding in head lice, cockroaches, and excessive appetites for sex, drink, and drugs, though in certain cases that we have dealt with, examination of the actual people and their homes did not bear out this picture. The environment to which the court is asked to transfer the child, on the other hand, is idealized and equally stereotyped as clean, punctual, orderly, technologically modern, and, above all, spiritual—not in a religious sense, but in an intellectual one. That world is marked by organized after-school activities, help with homework, music lessons, computers, and mental health counseling.

☐ Complex and Grey Areas

In all these possible sources of iatrogenic damage, clients are unconsciously, mistakenly, or even deliberately misidentified and shunted into stigmatized categories by caregivers. This imposes on clients, who may already be in need of support, an additional burden of trying to correct the misidentification of their problem and of having to fight the system that may be subjecting them to stress while removing their psychosocial supplies, thereby increasing their vulnerability to mental disorder.

In our Jerusalem program, we took on the responsibility to create a population-oriented program of primary prevention, which means, according to our value system, that we cannot pick and choose where we can work most comfortably. Instead, we must go where the major threats to the well-being of the target population are to be found. Since we have determined that one of these threats is iatrogenic damage, we must consider the elements involved in its etiology and perpetuation.

The first issue to be faced is the behavior of the individual harming professional. Here, we are on relatively familiar ground, since we often recognize characteristic aspects of a theme interference with whose anatomy and manifestations we have grown familiar over years of practice. However, the second element may be less familiar, namely the institutional cocooning of the individual damaging caregiver. This involves the protection and support for what we regard as irrationality, which stems from the fact that it is in line with the prevailing ethos of that system. This consequently reinforces what is, to us, a clearly pathogenic manner of case management, and the concomitant rejection of all questioning by outsiders. That, in turn, ensures that, while such agencies' salience (that is, their strategic importance in affecting the mental health of the community) is high, their feasibility (their openness to accepting help) is very low indeed.

In considering this situation, we have to face two facts. First, the defensiveness of some leading, highly salient agencies is influenced by their operating with embittered and deprived clients who are prone to complain about whatever treatment they receive. Thus these agencies develop a protective posture and are apt to attack any critic in line with the sentiment expressed by one embattled agency head, "Those who don't act, don't make mistakes." Second, in Israel, a country of immigration and consequent cultural heterogeneity, there are two main, discrepant value systems in the field of human services: That which focuses on the rights and needs of the individual and his or her family, holding that the healthy collective is the product of healthy individuals, and that which emphasizes strengthening the collective, holding that its well-being promotes the health and welfare of each of its members. The adherents of the latter view demand conformity with generally accepted norms and tend to discount the discomfort of individuals, especially those who deviate from its values.

We follow the former tradition, whereas certain key Israeli agencies, especially in the child welfare field, identify with the second philosophy. Therefore what we designate as damaging, they may tend to discount as the inevitable sacrifices on the path to establishing a better end.

In the next chapters, we will analyze clinical examples in order to begin illustrating and amplifying the points raised so far.

Some Typical Features of Iatrogenically Damaging Behavior

In order to clarify and expand our understanding of how iatrogenic damage occurs, we will now turn to some typical cases. While these disguised examples are derived from our clinical experience, which happens to be based in Israel, the phenomena described have resonated with colleagues from other countries who have confirmed that the same type of lapses in professional functioning occur in the United States, Britain, Canada, Australia, and doubtless in other places as well. Different cultures and laws may produce variations, but there appear to be generic characteristics that mark and warn of the malfunctioning of caregivers wherever they practice.

We begin with two examples that came to us neither from the courts, nor from our primary preventive caseload of children of divorcing parents. Instead, they were private referrals of cases of damage or potential damage generated by the educational system, and they involved hitherto normal children from stable families. In our first example, professional malfunctioning appeared to arise mainly from cognitive and administrative shortcomings. In the second case, more complex and less obvious elements seem to have led to distortions in professional behavior. By reviewing these cases, we will begin to flesh out the abstract issues we have been discussing so far.

☐ A Well-Intentioned Plan

Thirteen-year-old Alice was beginning her second year of junior high school. Attractive and intelligent, she had always been a social and academic success and was well liked by teachers. During her first year in the new school, her parents were surprised, therefore, to see an uncharacteristic drop in certain of her grades in subjects in which she had previously excelled. Alice explained that the low marks were coming from classes taught by a particular teacher who demanded a regurgitation of memorized details. Alice found these classes boring and concentration difficult. When she studied for frequent tests, she found that the material she had laboriously memorized fled at the sight of the questions. Her panic was increased by her realization that the teacher disliked her and even expected her to fail. In episodes whose occurrence was corroborated by Alice's friends, the teacher had humiliated the girl in class by announcing her latest bad marks and by comments like "I bet Alice will not be able to answer any of these questions." When Alice's parents offered to intervene, the girl said that she was "no longer a baby," and that she wanted to deal with her own problems. Since Alice was indeed mature for her age and poised in the presence of adults, and since her classmates were supportive, she was allowed to struggle on her own.

When summer arrived, and the unsympathetic teacher was left behind, Alice was optimistic despite the few expected low grades, and she was confident that she would improve her marks the following year. In the fall, however, Alice began to develop increasingly worsening symptoms of school avoidance, coupled with uncharacteristic expressions of low self-esteem that nobody could explain. After some weeks, with reluctance and deep shame, Alice revealed that because she had done badly in certain courses the year before, the guidance counselor had placed her in a remedial class to raise her grade average. In order to fit this class into Alice's schedule, the girl had been taken out of a favorite elective—a foreign language at which she had been doing well, and in which her closest friends were also enrolled. When Alice had protested, she had been told that electives had to be sacrificed to improve her average in core subjects. Alice pointed out to the remedial teacher that the class to which she had been assigned covered material that may have fitted the needs of its other participants, but in fact did not even cover the subject in which Alice was supposedly weak. So the whole exercise was, Alice said, futile as far as her grades were concerned. Alice reported that the teacher had agreed with this view but had said that she had no authority to free the girl from an attendance that had been decreed by the teacher's superiors. Alice told her parents bitterly, "the teachers keep saying: 'We are here to help you, dear,' but they aren't helping me at all. And the worst thing is that when I get good grades, they are going to take the credit, when actually it will be due to my own efforts, but they won't believe it. And anyway, I'm not good at any school subjects, so it's a waste of time to go to school at all." Alice's mother, shocked and incredulous that the school had taken these steps without notifying or consulting her, arranged to meet with the guidance counselor and the head of the remedial program.

At the meeting, Alice's mother discovered that these pleasant, clearly well-meaning staff members knew remarkably little, if anything, about her daughter. They had automatically moved Alice into the remedial program, they said, because computerized records showed that she had more than two grades below a C. They had not found it necessary to discuss their intentions in advance with the child or with her parents. They were unaware of any friction with the previous year's teacher that might have contributed to last year's poor showing, nor had they noted that the low grades had all come from classes taught by one person. They were unaware of Alice's high intelligence or her record of high marks in primary school in these very subjects. And, indeed, they were unaware of Alice's present misery and consequent avoidance of not only the remedial classes but also, by now, of the school itself. They had dismissed Alice's protests, they admitted, since they felt they were negligible and transitory. "All the children object to going to these classes because they see them as a social stigma," the head of remedial teaching said, "but they come to accept it." When Alice's mother insisted that the classes were doing the child more harm that good, and that however good the teachers' intentions might be, they would have great difficulty helping someone who rejected their help, the staff members agreed to release Alice from the remedial class "on the responsibility of her family," and to assess the situation anew at the end of the term. By then, however, Alice's rejection of the school had become so entrenched as to require treatment and transfer to another framework.

In this apparently simple case, we can see a number of not uncommon issues that can turn conscientious, well-meaning professionals unwittingly into damaging caregivers.

☐ Professional Enthusiasm for an Idealistic Plan

First, we see professionals enthusiastically committed to their own well-intentioned idealistic plan, whose benefit they regarded as axiomatic and so intuitively obvious that they did not feel that it might require explanation on their part to convince the intended clients of its value or to elicit their cooperation. As professionals, they apparently assumed that their superior knowledge would confer unchallenged authority in implementing what amounted to a program of primary preventive intervention. That is, they identified a high-risk subgroup, designated as children who received two or more grades of C or lower in core subjects, and set out to bolster the performance of those students. In doing so, they were not only intending to raise these children's chances of admittance to elite high schools, (coincidentally, thereby raising the academic reputation of their own establishment), but they were also intending to free parents from the widespread local burden of hiring tutors to improve a child's grades. The school had seen no need to inform parents of their child's selection for inclusion in this program because the staff had regarded it as self-evidently beneficial. They were shocked and uncomprehending when faced by the "eccentricity" of Alice's parents who were rejecting their help. The objections of the children themselves had been dismissed as inconsequential and temporary, although one might have thought that the fear of incurring social stigma, though possibly "irrational," should have been discussed seriously with young adolescents.

☐ Failure to Gather Data

A major contributory factor in causing harm which we meet repeatedly in most, if not all, iatrogenic damage cases, is the failure of professionals to realize the decisive importance of gathering data, both in the early stages of enrolling clients, and also on an ongoing basis in order to monitor any unexpected pitfalls that might hinder the intended benefits of their intervention. While the school had assumed a way of identifying a high-risk group, this involved a stereotyped categorization, for the staff had failed to examine the history of each tagged student and his or her possibly varying, and complex reasons for poor performance—reasons that might have called into question the appropriateness and effectiveness of developing a standard program of intervention for all outwardly similar cases. This failure to gather data at best had led to waste, since those whose low grades might have been due to transitory conditions, and who might have been well able to manage on their own, were lumped together with those whose general intellectual capacities might have been lower, and who might have required specialized individual help that could not be offered in a group setting.

☐ Ignoring Logistical Problems

In the course of the meeting with the guidance counselor and the head of remedial teaching, Alice's mother discovered that their plan had proved too ambitious for complete implementation. It demanded a virtual duplication of the school's regular program, so that children took regular subjects in tandem with parallel remedial classes in the same area. In practice, it turned out that there were not enough staff available to teach all those who had been enrolled. Consequently, Alice had found herself in remedial classes that did not suit her supposed profile, because a relevant teacher was on maternity leave, and no substitute had yet been found.

One aspect of damaging professional behavior is the attempt to place clients in less than suitable frameworks because they have been tagged as requiring help, but the available options to serve them are limited and even unsuitable. In Alice's case, the frustration of an already unwilling client was increased by the professionals' insistence, for their own bureaucratic reasons, that she remain in a patently unsuitable setting.

☐ Snowballing Damage

The failure of the staff to gather feedback data as the program progressed, or to listen to the complaints of students, meant that damage was not only not corrected, but it even snowballed. The professionals assessed their results according to their own limited criteria—whether or not grades rose. They ignored, however, the emotional consequences of their intervention, which in Alice's case developed into a major loss of self-esteem and motivation and a growing tendency to run away from the teachers who, she felt, belittled her. This narrowing of focus and selective inattention to a client's overall well-being, so that obvious damage is ignored, is a warning signal of professional malfunctioning that we will encounter in other examples.

☐ When is an Intervention Helpful, and When is it Damaging?

As we consider Alice's case, another crucial issue emerges that we will recognize in subsequent examples, namely the professionals' failure to grasp the cardinal concept that any preventive intervention is not what intuitively feels suitable, but, rather, it must be governed by certain consciously enunciated principles. The aim of the intervention should be to provide guidance and to widen the clients' view of available options of how to deal with his or her predicament in such a way as to increase that client's autonomy and ego strength. Unless the intervention is molded to accomplish these ends, it risks becoming destructive, by sapping the client's sense of autonomy and by rendering him or her more dependant. It may then reduce not only self-respect, but also the client's confidence in the rationality and good intentions of the helping system. In light of this, any preventive style intervention must be deliberately plotted and calibrated to build the client up, and not to tear him or her down. In order to ensure the former outcome, the effect of the intervention and the inevitable ripples that are thereby set in motion must be monitored throughout its course in order for the professional to be sure that the means are leading to a mentally healthy, rather than a destructive outcome.

☐ Causes of Malfunctioning in this Case

The malfunctioning of professionals in this example can be ascribed to readily identifiable, nonesoteric cognitive and administrative short-comings. The staff's naive enthusiasm for their own ideas was coupled with an apparent low capacity for realistic planning and implementation of a scheme that involved more complex variables than they seemed to be aware of. This was matched by a lack of psychological sophistication that led to their stereotyping and misjudging the complexity of their students' personalities and needs, and thereby, in turn, to their overlooking the emotional damage that they were causing. There was no evidence in this case, however, of any hidden, unconscious themes that might have determined the behavior of the professionals. They accepted information about Alice's history without resistance; and despite their enthusiasm for their intervention program, they were not so unduly invested in it as to oppose Alice's mother's insistence on her daughter being moved out of the remedial class, nor did they deny the validity of her suggestion that, in future, parents be included in decisions about their children's participation in the program.

In the next case, we will examine a more complex constellation of social and emotional issues that can distort professional functioning, creating a potentially more worrisome situation than that which upset Alice.

☐ A Child's Game

Four-year-old Dan, the youngest but one in a large family of Moroccan origin, was enrolled in the neighborhood prekindergarten. A student teacher playing with the little boy observed him taking a female doll, pulling up its skirt, and shouting, "No, don't!" When the student showed considerable interest in this, Dan gleefully repeated the sequence. He did so again with more hilarity when the student called the kindergarten teacher over to observe the proceedings, and he was even more triumphantly boisterous when the latter called her assistant over to watch yet another performance. A hastily convened staff conference established that Dan's father had recently suffered an injury in a car accident so significant that he was now unemployed and was "prone to episodes of violence," and that an older sister had "attempted suicide." The mother was called in and interrogated. She was told that the child protection services would have to be informed that there was a suspicion of sexual abuse.

Puzzled by her child's unaccountable behavior and frightened by the threat of being denounced to the authorities, the mother went to her family doctor who phoned the teacher and assured her that he knew the family's circumstances thoroughly and that there was no cause for alarm. To the doctor's surprise, however, the teacher refused to be swayed by his information.

The family was referred to us. It turned out that while the father had indeed been injured, he was not violent, but only prone to loudly cursing the severe back pains and vertigo that were his legacy of the accident; and, while he was currently unemployed, he was successfully retraining for a less physically demanding job. The "suicidal" sister had never been significantly depressed, though she had been much saddened by the death of a friend in a military incident a year earlier. While stressed by the father's incapacity, the family was well supported by friends and relatives. Dan himself was mischievous and cheerful, showing no signs of trauma or anything out of the ordinary, except that he seemed not to be very articulate. He was bored when the subject of his game came up, but was in no way anxious or evasive. Whatever the inspiration for the game might have been, he was certainly not the victim, nor, as far we could tell, were any of his sisters.

When the mother told the kindergarten teacher that we had concluded that there was no cause for concern, she was struck by the teacher's reaction. "I said to her," the mother told us, 'you sound disappointed. Why aren't you relieved?'" The teacher said that of course she was not disappointed, but she insisted that she could not let the case drop. She would have to report it to the social workers.

Realizing that if they were reported to the authorities they could be trapped in a web of accusations that might involve legal fees that they could not afford, the family began to panic. Then the neighbor's daughter remembered that while babysitting for Dan some weeks earlier, she had caught him out of bed, peeping around the living room at the farcical TV program she was watching in which a woman, consorting with someone else's husband, had pulled her skirt over her face and shouted, "No, don't!" when her lover's wife unexpectedly opened the door. When the teacher was told of this, the situation seemed to cool down. But a few days later, she became suspicious of something else Dan said, and she again announced that she was going to inform the child protection service. It was then deemed expedient by the family and their advisors for Dan to develop an "infection" that would keep him at home until the term ended and he could be transferred to another kindergarten.

From this example, in which quick action by people aware of the dangers of iatrogenic damage prevented long-term consequences, we can begin to identify more characteristic warning signs in professional behavior.

☐ An Accusatory Stance

Given what we know about the prevalence and pathological sequellae of child sexual abuse, and given the severe penalties that now exist in Israel for nondisclosure to the authorities of suspicions concerning it, the kindergarten teacher was fully justified in noting and questioning Dan's game, in asking his mother whether she could explain it, and in discretely watching for any evidence in Dan's demeanor and circumstances that might corroborate the possibility that something was indeed amiss. The teacher's malfunctioning lay in her jumping to a conclusion from insufficient evidence, her subsequent absolute refusal to test and correct her perceptions, and her emotional investment in maintaining that sexual abuse had happened as evidence threw increasing doubt on the probability of any impropriety having taken place.

From the first, the teacher's stance had been accusatory, punitive, and self-righteous. Though sometimes clothed in solicitude, the attitude of the professional in most such iatrogenic damage cases is aggressive and threatening to the client, who finds himself or herself on the defensive. The emphasis is not on understanding a puzzling occurrence or on helping the client support a burden, but on establishing guilt or deficiencies. The professional is filled with crusading zeal to right a moral wrong, a zeal that cannot be deflected by denials, excuses, or facts.

☐ Compulsive Belief in Dire Threat

Usually, the professional clings tenaciously to a conviction that there is a dire threat to someone in the case, although the objective evidence may fail to sustain this belief. The professional typically refuses to accept suggestions that he or she is on the wrong track or to consider evidence that may throw doubt on his or her anticipation of catastrophe. The compulsive energy with which the professional tries to make the charges stick, and his or her refusal or inability to see how much harm he or she is doing to the clients should always be a cause for concern. In many such cases, the real circumstances, like our little client's hilarity when he played his game, are ignored. This lack of congruence between the professional's suspicions and the objective evidence confuses the clients, who are generally slow to realize what is happening and to mobilize defenses against the attacks leveled against them. Typically, such clients are incredulous as they tell us what charges they are confronting because the accusations strike them as so absurd.

☐ The Pinball Effect

In the early days of our developing mental health consultation techniques at the Harvard Laboratory of Community Psychiatry to deal with theme interference, we worked out a technique that we called "dissipating the stereotype," which consisted of consultants getting consultees to identify with their own realistic view of the client. When this was accomplished, the consultees were suddenly able to deal with the case with their usual effectiveness, since our maneuver had "unlinked" the consultees from their covert exploitation of this particular client as an unconscious symbol to relieve their own inner tension. We eventually gave up this technique when we discovered that although it rescued *this* client from being exploited in *this* way, it often left the underlying mechanism in the mind of the consultees unchanged, with the result that, usually and quickly, they found some other client or some other situation to exploit. We called this the "pinball machine phenomenon," because it reminded us of the game where one fires off a ball only to have it replaced by another that pops into place to be fired off in its turn. In this case, the pinball effect came into play when the teacher was obliged to accept that the child's statements did not indicate abuse. She then found grounds for renewed suspicion in some other equally innocent remark that he made.

☐ The Multi-problem Image

In many cases, the misfortunes of the clients—here, the father's accident and loss of work and the daughter's sadness at the death of a friend—are exaggerated and woven into a pattern of linked evidence to adduce further weaknesses and ills, thereby using people's vulnerabilities and bad luck that are often random and coincidental to prove a pattern of degeneracy. We have noticed how official files of families trapped in cases of iatrogenic damage list, not always accurately by the way, misfortunes and deprivations in a family's history that are often irrelevant to the current question, like allegations of marital disharmony in the grandparents of a child taken away for adoption. These descriptions take the tone of ill-concealed accusations, creating a possibly spurious picture of a multiproblem family. This makes further charges of depravity, neglect, or cruelty seem plausible and even expectable.

The teacher's expectation that the family would have problems may also have been stimulated by its North African ethnicity. Certain groups appear to be suspected more easily than others of being abusive or negligent, and interventions in their lives are more readily carried out. Caregivers of many nationalities have stereotypes about local subpopulations, perceiving them as more likely to exhibit and engender social and other forms of pathology. Immigrants to Israel from North African and the Middle East, as well as the ultraorthodox from various European backgrounds have tended to be both poor and underemployed, which place them in a high at-risk category, and all of these subpopulations have traditionally valued large families. Some of those caregivers of secular, European decent who have long occupied policy making positions have tended to see such large families as "third world" and necessarily neglectful, since, they reason, two parents cannot provide adequate care for so many children. Those who stigmatize large families, however, have apparently failed to notice that they are organized differently from small ones. Families in these communities traditionally maintain a clan structure in which children are cared for not only by parents, but by grandparents, aunts, and uncles, and others. Furthermore, unlike small families, those parents who expect to produce many offspring arrange from the birth of their oldest children to train them not only to share household chores, but also to care for younger siblings. Thus, not only is the burden on parents reduced, but younger members of well-managed large families may be stimulated and cared for adequately, even in relatively low socioeconomic conditions. In an attempt to assimilate and modernize immigrants, however, there was a tendency to denigrate and disrupt the traditional authority structure of these families, which tendency, in fact, contributed to the development of social pathology and deviance. Thus, the stereotyping of certain groups has an element of a self-fulfilling prophecy, as interventions disrupt traditional mechanisms of control.

Both Eastern and European ultraorthodox families have further raised the concern of welfare authorities because, while neither group accepts abuse, the borderline between what is and is not permitted in the way of corporal punishment and patriarchal authority may not be regarded as normative according to current dominant Western values. An ultraorthodox client, for example, told us that her estranged husband hit their children not in the interest of education, but in anger. She regarded the former as acceptable, but the latter as abusive. Caregivers may not be prepared to countenance this distinction, and many of us might agree. Within each of these groups, poverty and some measure of intergenerational conflict about the authority of seniors, opposition to the dominant Western attitudes to sexual roles and mores, as well as the legacy of persecution and possible torture in countries of origin have incubated cases of family violence.

The ultraorthodox community has only recently publicly acknowledged problems in this area (Shahar, 1999). Hitherto, there has been a tendency to deny the problem internally and to hide inescapably obvious cases from secular authorities in order to shield the community from shame and to fend off the interference of "foreign" courts and alien ways. Within the group, cases of family violence and sexual abuse are often taken for adjudication to rabbis known for their grasp of family issues. In various instances, we have learned how particular rabbis who were experts in mediating family conflicts have handled such issues imaginatively and effectively. Their solutions have taken into account issues not generally considered by the secular caregiving system—for example, the fact that family instability and open scandal can lower the value of children in arranged marriages. Therefore, problems must be handled discreetly and outer appearances of respectability and family unity have to be maintained in order to shield children from social stigma and suffering during their adult years as well as from abuse during minority. This can require Solomonic judgements that the community often does not choose to entrust to secular authorities. We were told of a case which was brought before a rabbi respected for his knowledge of religious family law in which a widowed mother with a history of violent rages had hit her 16-year-old daughter so hard that she had opened a deep gash in the girl's head. The Rabbi summoned the girl and asked her whether she wanted to be moved into foster care or into a boarding school. The girl, who was the eldest daughter in the family, said that she preferred to stay at home despite the danger because she felt responsible for her younger siblings. Since she was destined to marry at eighteen, as is the custom in such communities, and since her value with the matchmakers would drop if she was fostered or put into an institution, she wanted to try to stay with her mother for two more years until she married, and then she intended to take her siblings with her into a new home. The Rabbi arranged to support her in her choice. He called in the mother and ordered her to accept psychiatric care and medication on pain of Divine displeasure. With the help of neighbors and relatives, the situation was kept under observation and control and the family was kept together until the girl was old enough to set up a home of her own.

Clearly, instances such as this can be viewed as conflicting with the publicly mandated legal obligation of caregivers, possibly exacerbating their suspicions and their determination to preempt cases by treating rumors against members of these communities with marked attention. The problem of iatrogenic damage arises when assumptions based on ethnic stereotyping replace thorough, open-minded assessment of the actual data, and when the expectation of high prevalence turns into a certainty that because suspicions are aroused in a case that fits some criteria of a particular risk category, the case necessarily demands maximum intervention.

☐ Demonic Crimes

It was no coincidence that, in the instance of Dan's game, the suspicions of the teacher revolved around sexual abuse. At particular risk, we have found, are those cases that can be linked to issues considered demonic—charges so emotionally loaded for a particular historic period or culture that the mere suspicion of their occurring, however scanty the evidence, can so shock public and judicial feeling that they distort critical judgment. Nowadays, perhaps as a reaction against past indifference and skepticism, a demonic crime is child abuse, especially if it is sexual—a crime that rightly outrages public opinion, but only if such an act has actually taken place and if the evidence for conviction is plausible.

In our experience, some of the most mismanaged cases have been stirred up by poorly supported suspicions and a consequent failure to realize the need to assess ambiguous evidence critically. In one of our cases, for example, a father was jailed for performing an indecent act on his two-year old daughter. The day-care center director claimed that she had long suspected that "something was going on," while the not very prepossessing-looking father played with the child in his car before the institution opened. Some weeks earlier, the parents had questioned the director about remarks made by the child, which seemed to suggest that she had witnessed some sexual episode. The woman had vehemently denied that any such thing had occurred on her premises. Later, there was a story that the girl had been sexually interfered with by some older boys in the center, one of whom was said to be the son of the director's close friend. When the director denounced the father for abuse, the authorities, including trial judges, refused to consider the possibility that an indecent act could have been performed by one child on another. Three years later, as the result of a number of unambiguous cases referred for police investigation, it was realized that assaults involving some form of sex play or exploitation by schoolchildren of classmates were indeed taking place, even among children as young as kindergarten age. At the time of the father's trial, however, prevailing stereotypes about "wicked" parents and "innocent" children apparently prevented the authorities from looking at evidence that contradicted these stereotypes.

We once allowed our own judgment to be swayed by such demonic charges in an adoption case in which a social worker described to us a mother's behavior when visiting her 18-month-old son in a shelter for abused children. According to the social worker, while changing the toddler's diapers the mother was observed to suck his penis. When challenged, she was reported to have said, "Why shouldn't I? I do this to all my little princes." We had all felt that the mother was being unjustly treated, until we heard this story. Horrified, we agreed that this placed a different complexion on the case. Then we came to our senses, and asked, "Does this fit the person we know?" We asked the mother about the charge. She too was horrified. "I would never do anything so disgusting, even with my husband," she said. "What I actually did was kiss the baby's little, soft tummy."

☐ Failure to Examine Evidence

It must be stressed again that a major, if not *the* major and recurring factor in creating iatrogenic damage is a failure on the part of professionals to examine evidence. This failure is a final common path phenomenon.

It may be due to unconscious forces in the individual that inhibit his or her ability to look at reality; to individual or social prejudice about demonic, unthinkable, or "impossible" situations which give the illusion that the situation is "obvious" and needs no further investigation; to lack of professional experience so that the need to search for evidence is not fully realized; or to a hidden agenda that deliberately ignores inconvenient evidence because it might conflict with the outcome that the damaging caregiver is determined to bring about. Whatever its reason, the failure of a professional to survey the realities of a client's situation is a major sign of potentially damaging behavior.

☐ "Demonic" Issues Erase Thresholds

One by-product of the treatment of what we may designate as "demonic" issues, is that everyone becomes oversensitive. The threshold between the normal and the culpable grows ambiguous, so that spontaneous, harmless behavior raises suspicion and endangers individuals because it superficially resembles forbidden activities. We once witnessed a sensible, experienced marriage counselor calling in the child protection service when in the course of a mediation session between divorcing parents, she learned that the father permitted his three-year-old daughter to walk in and out of the bathroom when he was on the toilet. The counselor was a religious woman for whom a requirement to observe personal modesty was axiomatic. We could not convince her that in local secular culture, where youth groups and army units track through wilderness landscapes devoid of sheltering bushes and far from modern sanitation, a certain casualness and communality may develop round processes that are generally kept private in urban settings, and this can cross over into daily life. Thus, the father's behavior in the presence of a toddler was, if not normative, at least not necessarily sinister. Just as in the McCarthy era in the United States when it was dangerous to hint at any "leftist" sentiments, today a continuum may be perceived linking abuse to a disciplinary slap, or fondling a child, or photographing a child naked in the bath, or allowing a child to climb into one's bed. This thereby lowers the threshold over which authorities can be mobilized and threaten prosecution. Such linkage not only harms innocents who suddenly find themselves suspects, it also damages those who, aware of this value system and fearful of being denounced, are inhibited in expressing affection or in disciplining children. We are reminded here of an anecdote told us by the grandmother of an unusually intelligent and mischievous preschooler whose parents found him difficult to manage. His grandmother, being direct and old-fashioned, advised the parents to give the child a smack on his bottom when he grew particularly obstreperous. The parents referred this politically incorrect advice to the parenting group to which they belonged. The grandmother told us that the entire session then turned, not to finding strategies to manage the child, but to earnestly inquiring whether or not the grandmother had abused her own children during their minority.

While these observations may strike a reader as a superficial glance at a complex subject, in fact, they point to a significant category of causal factors in the genesis of many iatrogenic cases—the shifting of border posts, whereby the markers between what is seen as permitted or forbidden are eroded or moved for reasons of expediency. This may refer to judgments about the activities of clients; but it may also mean a blurring of necessary boundaries between the personal and professional lives of caregivers; distinctions between what are perceived as ethical or unethical professional practices; or the designating of the legitimate claimants to professional expertise and executive authority in arriving at and enforcing case dispositions. Throughout this study, implicitly and explicitly, the issue of blurred boundaries will recur and should be noted. Such boundary shiftings were described in newspaper articles about the result of zero-tolerance policies for violence in U.S. schools. For example, two 8-year-olds who pointed a paper gun during games of cops and robbers or cowboys and Indians, while making traditionally fierce noises, were arrested and tried for making "terrorist threats" (Haughney, 2001). School officials throughout America are reportedly "turning children over to the criminal justice system for punishment of what was once seen as childhood play." An offocial of the school board in the district where the two 8-year-olds were arrested explained, "They were children playing achild's game. Unfortunately for everyone, the wrong words ('I'm going to kill you all') were used." What we see in such examples is a tendency on the part of professionals to let fear govern their actions. Unless they enforce politics with a literalness that defies common sense by carrying logic to an illogical conclusion, they apparently fear that they will be held culpable for any future outbreak of lethal violence. In various iatrogenic damage cases we have studied, fear is a major factor distoring profesional behavior. It may have irrational roots, but it can also be based on an all to realistic perception of the public's intolerance for mistakes coupled with the tendency of society to find scapegoats whenever tragedy strikes. This can thereby inhibit even the best trained and balanced caregivers when they face a boundary between the acceptable and the forbidden that has been moved in response to suddenly changing societal concerns.

☐ Resolution by Escape from the System

We now return to the consequences of Dan's game. It is further characteristic of iatrogenic damage cases that the caregiving system may be so intractable that the plight of the little boy's family could be resolved only by the escape of the clients from that particular framework. In such cases, the system tends to be self-validating, so that, as we will see in other instances, normal channels of recourse for injured clients are blocked. Once clients are enmeshed in an iatrogenic damage situation it becomes virtually impossible to escape within the terms of the system.

☐ The Hidden Agenda

As in many iatrogenic damage cases, the apparent illogic of the caregiver's behavior could be explained not merely by some psychological oversensitivity on his or her part, but by a consciously held hidden agenda. A politically influential member of their community, to whom Dan's family had turned for help, discovered that two years earlier, the Welfare Department had blamed the teacher for not reporting some suspicious circumstances associated with another child who subsequently had been found to have been abused. Since then, the teacher had been trying to reestablish her credit with the social workers by identifying a case to make up for her past mistake. This motive characteristically coexisted with, but was not necessarily compatible with the teacher's repeatedly expressed concern for the welfare of Dan and his family. She needed to repair her relations with the child protection authorities, and she did so by offering up, as it were, a sacrificial victim to atone for her past misdeeds.

It may be remembered that we noted earlier that one of the characteristics of iatrogenic damage cases is that they strike observers as "impossible" and "absurd." One reason for this is the presence of a hidden agenda. Identifying the fact that this hidden agenda exists restores sense to an apparently absurd situation and enables us to see the conjuring trick from the correct angle. The presenting issue in Dan's case—whether a particular child or children had been sexually abused—was a superficial and distracting phenomenon. The attempts by the family and their advisors, therefore, to prove that no abuse had taken place was futile because the teacher needed to uncover an incident of sexual abuse, and this case, while basically unconvincing, was the best available at the time to suit her purpose. In this instance, the teacher may not have been fully aware of how her perceptions were being distorted by her own needs. Her hesitation in actually calling in the child protection authorities as she kept threatening to do may have meant that, at some level, she was uncomfortably aware that she might not have been acting from the purest motives of concern for the welfare of the child. She was apparently strengthened in her crusade, despite hesitation, by the prevailing ethos that encourages and even requires professionals and lay people alike to report on suspicions in order to prevent abuse—though mistakenly informing authorities may cause harm that is also far reaching. Suspicions, after all, may be composed less of realistic perceptions than of subjective needs and unconscious distortions.

☐ Hazards on the Front Lines and Shortcomings in Planning

Dan's teacher was active in this case in a role that we may call a "front-line scout." The recruiting of professionals and nonprofessionals in other fields to serve as front-line scouts of potentially pathological situations on behalf of the caregivers with primary responsibility in a particular area like mental health, child protection, and others. has probably contributed significantly to the welfare of the community. Such pathogenic issues as child abuse, family violence, and pathological psychic reactions to life crisis, if identified early enough in their course by these front-line scouts, should theoretically forestall the severe, sometimes irreversible, or even fatal damage that may be anticipated should these undesirable conditions fester unrecognized or unacknowledged. This concept, so basic to our own formulation about the implementation of preventive intervention and the delivery of care within a community mental health program, runs into trouble when it is confronted by unanticipated features of social reality. Although the efficacy of such theories can be demonstrated, there is the temptation to confuse experimental settings, which exist in idealized and privileged circumstances and tend to be manned by sophisticated and motivated researchers and selected subjects, with a routinized program manned by the general population of practitioners and clients. When subjected to the vicissitudes of random and chaotic conditions in the ordinary world, some interesting gaps in the feasibility of our theories and in the efficacy of our planning are apt to emerge.

The use of nonspecialists as spotters of potential hazards in the lives of their own clients, for example, presupposes a backup system of specialists able to assess and manage the findings of this front-line force. Unfortunately, reality seldom matches this hope that lies at the basis of plans for effective community coverage. In the first place, and most obviously, the inevitable shortage of specialized manpower means that while it is easy for other professionals and paraprofessionals to recruit and identify those potentially in need, it is far more problematic for specialists to sift and treat all these newly discovered clients. It therefore becomes a question whether procedures that identify individuals with difficulties, and procedures that raise a general consciousness of hitherto unrealized needs are serving the community's best interests if the next logistical step—that of providing appropriate follow-up treatment—is unavailable because there are too few specialists, institutional settings, and hours in the day to provide help for the newly discovered cases. All that these preventive efforts may engender is to create a larger pool of those who may feel entitled to services, and who, in its absence, feel justifiably aggrieved.

Backup systems may also fail in another, possibly less obvious respect, which will contribute significantly to the rate of iatrogenic damage. The nonspecialized front line may well identify real cases of potential risk. On the other hand, in their relative inexperience or naiveté, or because of the psychological quirks or obsessions of unselected and unsupervised individuals among this vast array of would-be helpers, they may make false assumptions about clients that misidentify them as belonging to populations at risk. Such, for example, was a high-school teacher who regularly found potential suicides among her pupils, thereby raising a flurry of dire concern around those particular youths, a flurry which usually proved to be not only misplaced, but in itself contributed no small measure of distress to the adolescents and families concerned. In theory, the specialists to whom such cases are referred should be able to winnow out the truly needy clients from those who, for whatever reason, have been misidentified. Often they do so, though clients' experience of being singled out for concern and investigation is upsetting in itself. Unhappily, as examples that are to follow in this book demonstrate, for a variety of reasons, that rectification may not occur. Once clients are labeled as being at risk, forces may be set in motion that, irrespective of the actual merits of the case, may entangle the clients in the typical Kafkaesque processes of iatrogenic damage.

Iatrogenic damage can be exacerbated, therefore, by a shortcoming of planning that is marked by a general failure to factor into any proposed social program the possibility that its attractive components may give rise to unforeseen and damaging repercussions. This can be seen on a small scale in the case of the remedial program that failed Alice, and, analogously, when so large a component of primary preventive programs as what we have here called front-line scouts triggers unanticipated damaging interventions. Such a planning deficiency means that there is then no mechanism or mind-set built into the implementation of optimistic ideas that from the outset will serve to monitor any harm that may ensue and to attempt to deal with such negative fall-out early in the course of its emergence. To guard against iatrogenic harm, therefore, the expectation that any social scheme, however beneficent its intent, may cause some damage should be factored into the design of programs from their inception. This would imply that program design should itself remain sufficiently fluid and evolving so that further information can modify it, unforeseen needs can be met, and harm to clients can be identified in time to minimize them. We will return to this subject later.

In our next examples, we will see how yet more complex, reverberating mixtures of conscious and unconscious needs of caregivers, their institutions, and the social environment led to distorted perceptions and to the consequent damaging of clients.

Professionals' Stereotypes, Premature Closure, and a Preplanned Outcome

Before we analyze our next examples, let us stress that these are not typical cases of professional practice. They are cases that demonstrate typical features and dynamics of iatrogenic harm. As such, they are not pleasant to contemplate. Let us also stress, that we do not know how prevalent such cases may be, but even if they are rare, they are instructive, providing indicators of what conscientious professionals should be on their guard to identify before harm to clients ensues.

A woman with a history of psychosis had told her neighbors that her husband was dangerously insane and was cruel to her and her child, forcing them to engage with him in bizarre rituals and threatening their lives. The husband had indeed had a brief psychotic episode 25 years earlier but had suffered no relapses. Shy and stiff, with a deceptively forbidding expression due to a facial tic, he never mixed with the neighbors. His distance from them was increased by his poor command of Hebrew, by his neighbors' ignorance of his native Spanish, and by their suspicion, fed by broad hints from his wife, that despite his Orthodox guise, he was secretly a heretical Jew for Jesus. A brisk trade in gossip was established behind the man's back as the neighbors sided with the wife, not realizing that her complaints were the product of paranoid delusions. The wife's charges energized the Welfare Child Protection officers. The latter came to inspect the household and found the mother to be ineffectual and disorganized.

The caseworker took an interest in Lily, the intelligent, charming six-year-old daughter whom she felt deserved a "normal" environment, and she tried to move her into afternoon fostering whereby Lily would spend her after-school hours in an approved family. The father rejected this offer, pointing out that his daughter was thriving and that her afternoons were already filled by a range of extracurricular activities.

☐ Penalties for Noncompliance

The father's manner, though courteous, was cold and peremptory. This was not appreciated by the caseworker, who did not find in him the submissiveness of a "good" client. In other cases we have found that clients who oppose the wishes of caregivers, and especially if they lose their temper under provocation, have this fact used against them to prove poor impulse control and social maladjustment. For example, a mother from whom a Rabbinic divorce court had removed custody of her child, granting it instead to the father who had the outer appearance of greater religious orthodoxy, was labeled "infantile" and "disturbed" because of the fuss she made. This told against her in later hearings and appeals. In fact, she was more psychologically healthy, empathic, and devoted than the manipulative father who won custody of the reluctant child. We have seen other clients who were not submissive driven into an ever more disadvantaged position, like the grandmother of a girl removed to an institution in a distant city while awaiting a court's decision on whether she was to be declared adoptable. The grandmother was permitted to visit the child for an hour once a month. Taking a day off work as a cleaner, she set off by intercity bus only to be caught behind a slow-moving military convoy. The old woman arrived an hour late for her appointment. The social worker told her off for her tardiness and permitted her to see her granddaughter for only a few minutes before the child was whisked away. The grandmother broke down in fury and grief. The allegation that she was "abusive" and "violent" in front of the child and the social worker was recorded against her in the case file.

To return to the example of Lily and her father: Before long, the mother was hospitalized for psychosis. The father hired a housekeeper and arranged for the child to have a tutor to help her with homework. He also hired a surrogate grandmother, an elderly widow who lived nearby, to read stories in Hebrew to his daughter in the evening and to represent him at the school parent–teacher meetings that took place in the language that he barely knew. Though engaged in his own activities, he freed afternoons to take Lily on picnics or to visit places of interest.

☐ Gestation Period of Continuing Surveillance

Since the mother was hospitalized, the caseworker called again, and now recommended that Lily be placed in full-time foster care. The father pointed to his efficiently run household and protested that the child was being well cared for. But the caseworker became a regular visitor, attuned to every change in the family circumstances. When a housekeeper left to get married and was replaced by another who was later fired for impertinence to her employer, the social worker complained that there were too many changes in the household and that the child should be removed to a "stable" environment. Realizing that the Welfare Officers seemed determined to remove the child on any pretext, the father asked us to certify that the girl was developing normally and was being properly cared for.

The child proved to be deeply attached to, and unembarrassed by her somewhat eccentric father. Her school progress, physical health, and social integration were all excellent. Although saddened by her mother's periodic descents into incapacity, she remained poised and realistic, deriving a sense of security from her father whose devotion to her she trusted completely. Her one haunting fear that caused nightmares and bed wetting was that the social workers would act on their threats and take her away from him. The caseworker had spoken to her about this, and Lily had cried and begged to be allowed to stay at home. In a number of cases we have seen, professionals spoke to children openly about their plans to remove them from home, thereby causing acute panic. This was all the more unfortunate since the children's fate had not yet been decided in court, so that their terror was premature and might even have been unnecessary.

The pressure increased on Lily again when her mother was discharged from the mental hospital to the care of friends, where she renewed her complaints of ill-treatment, though by now her paranoia was well documented. Meanwhile, the caseworker returned regularly, and each visit upset the child. Eventually the social worker's vigilance was rewarded. The mother began to pay daily visits to the police, claiming that her husband was threatening her life. The latter interrogated the father four times in one week. This humiliation, on top of all the accumulated anxieties associated with his wife's illness and the strain of trying to defend himself against the pressure of the Welfare Officers, proved too much. He checked himself into the local mental hospital in a suicidal state. Lily was taken in by neighbors, and by that evening, the social worker had successfully applied to the courts for emergency custody.

In several days, the father's condition improved. Lily became ill in the neighbor's house and refused to drink or to take medication and her temperature rose alarmingly. Hearing of this, her father left the hospital, went to Lily's bedside, ordered her to obey the doctor's instructions at once, watched her comply, and then returned to his ward. A few days later, the father was discharged and went home. He got a cleaning woman to tidy up, mobilized the rest of his staff, and asked for Lily to be returned. But he had now lost custody. The social workers wanted to place her in one of their shelters but were prevailed upon by the court to leave her with the neighbors for the time being.

Although four psychiatrists, a clinical psychologist, and the hospital's social worker attested to the fact that the father was able to care for Lily, the Welfare workers insisted that he endangered her. When this was refuted, they claimed that she was afraid of him because he was a raving lunatic who had tried to hang himself in the child's presence. The caseworker testified that the rope which he had used had been found in the apartment. The hospital said that no rope marks had been found on the father's neck. Lily said that the rope in question was her skipping rope that she had failed to put away, and she wanted to go home.

☐ Falsification

In this case, as in others that produced iatrogenic damage, we have seen caregivers, apparently certain of the rightness of their cause, inadvertently or deliberately altering the facts of a client's situation in order to enhance their case for removing a child from home and for recommending suspension of parental rights. For example, the drug addict mother of a child recommended for adoption was alleged to have begun seriously acting out in early adolescence as proved by the fact that she had been ordered placed in a boarding school for wayward girls. Actually, the mother had graduated normally from the local high school. It was her younger sister who had been sent to an ordinary, not a correctional, boarding school voluntarily by their parents in order to keep her away from the influences of a neighborhood that was turning increasingly nasty. The younger sister had become a nurse, married a bus driver, and was a law-abiding, upwardly mobile citizen. The family understood how the falsification of their history helped to blacken the mother's reputation, as did the false claim that she was a streetwalker. At every court hearing, they tried and failed to get the file amended to establish that, while the mother was currently an addict, which was bad enough, she was not the chronically degenerate and immoral creature that she had been painted. This false record was a crucial issue, because appeal proceedings often hinge on documented evidence, not on examination of witnesses or the presentation of new material. Thus well-calculated false material in a file tends to secure the verdict against reversal on appeal. Even if individual facts can be challenged, the preponderance of negative material reinforced by experts who support the caregiving system can still fatally influence the outcome of a review by a higher court.

In our present case, the social workers had their own version of events. For example, the caseworker insisted in court that Lily was afraid of her "lunatic father," though this was patently untrue. The social worker had told Lily that her father's brain was diseased, which apparently reflected the social worker's own phobia and communicated enough alarm to the little girl that she phoned to ask us to explain what mental illness was. She asked sensible questions and was reassured, until the caseworker upset her with more of her own fantasies. The social worker and her superiors also insisted that the caseworker was the child's dearest friend in whom Lily had confided her fears. Lily told us that she hated and feared the caseworker.

☐ Encountering the Limitations of Collegiality

We approached the Welfare Officers to discuss the case, thinking that we were dealing with colleagues with whom we could expect to pool information on an egalitarian professional level in order to clarify plans for the family's future. We were amazed, therefore, to find ourselves being interrogated police style by a tough young woman about who we were, what we knew about the case, how we had acquired such restricted information, and by what right we had dared to speak to the child and to have accepted phone calls from her without the caseworker's authorization. There was an air of menace and an arrogant display of power in this interview and the clear message that the caseworker now "owned" the child and could dictate her access to the professionals who had been designated earlier by the parents. We now experienced at first hand the bullying that clients had described to us, but accounts of which we had always taken with a grain of salt. We had been accompanied on our visit by a senior professor of social work who had taught the supervisor of that particular branch office. She was struck speechless by the attitude of the caseworker, but later recovered her voice sufficiently to berate her former student for all the lapses in the principles of correct practice that she had observed in the subordinate. The invocation of academic standards and theories, however, did not impress or alter the attitude of the branch office staff towards us or the case.

It is of great value, though an often uncomfortable experience, to feel what the clients feel, to move out of one's privileged position as a fellow professional, to expose oneself to whatever lies behind a colleague's professional mask, and to feel on one's own ego how chastening it is to be at his or her mercy. Feeling the atmosphere to which clients may be exposed can be unpleasant but enlightening, a valuable experience that can increase our understanding of the processes leading to iatrogenic damage.

☐ Delay as a Marker of Damaging Professionals

After months of delays and legal maneuvers, a court ruled that the child should be sent home, but only if the father found another adult to share his apartment in order to ensure the girl's safety. This ruling presented problems for the father, who could not in propriety hire a woman to live with him. So, after much discussion with rabbis, he found a male seminary student instead. However, the caseworker and the neighbors would not permit the child to move back into the apartment now that it was inhabited by a young man.

The neighbors, who despised the father, placed obstacles in his way when he tried to see his daughter according to the court-approved visitation schedule, and loud quarrels ensued. When asked to help, the caseworker reported that the father's ungovernable temper was a growing source of embarrassment for the child and a nuisance to her foster parents, and clearly, the child needed to be distanced from him. When yet another court-appointed expert ordered the girl home for a trial period, the neighbors blocked her way, though the child wanted to return, and the social workers refused to stop them. Periodic court hearings led to instructions to return the child "gradually," but while agreeing that the judge had to be obeyed, the caseworker, with the cooperation of the neighbors, ensured that "gradually" took forever.

☐ Phobic Projections in Damaging Caregivers

When we argued with them, the welfare workers persisted that a parent with a history of mental illness was dangerous, unfit to care for a child, and naturally terrifying. They knew this, they said, because they had taken a course in human development and mental pathology to qualify in social work. The social workers insisted that a child so clever, so pretty, and so well-behaved, "deserved" proper parents and a normal household instead of the unaesthetic father and his unconventional domestic arrangements. Ideally, they felt, she should be adopted by an approved family. This, however, had been blocked by the court.

☐ Weaned Affections and Deteriorating Relationships

In time, the neighbors and their children persuaded Lily that she should be ashamed of a father who made such funny mistakes in Hebrew, and who "terrified" the other children. They told her that she must not return home because "Who would cook your breakfast? How can you live in a house without a Mummy?" The children also told her that they would never speak to her again if she returned to her father. The foster mother, a guidance counselor, insisted both to the child and to us that Lily's father was acutely insane and therefore dangerous. She had been taught at a teachers' seminary that the definition of sanity was acting like everyone else, and madness meant being different. In this theory of pathology, and of the danger posed by mental illness, she and the social workers apparently agreed.

The relationship between father and daughter deteriorated. Though she was prepared to accept presents and treats from him, Lily began to hold her father at arm's length and to grow insolent when he corrected her. He became depressed but refused to blame her. What worried him most was that the social workers refused to let him arrange for preventive psychological monitoring for Lily, since he understood the genetic loading of a child of two mentally afflicted parents.

Meanwhile, Lily began to fail at school. She was ashamed to invite for visits friends who would learn of her altered living arrangements. She became passive, overly dependent on the opinion of the neighbor's children, and depressed, and she began to lie and manipulate like her mother.

☐ Distortions in the Caregivers' Perceptions

The social workers regarded Lily's deterioration as a proof of the correctness of their own forebodings. As so often happens in cases of iatrogenic harm, the ensuing pathology is interpreted by the damaging caregivers not as evidence that they have blundered, but as a vindication of their original dire predictions. This deterioration, therefore, can be pointed to as the expectable result of the original situation identified as hazardous by the damaging caregiver. Blame for the onset of symptoms, they feel, rests with the "abusive" parents, not on themselves who, they believe, interrupted the pathogenic situation that would have created even more havoc had they not acted.

In this case, like others we have seen, the professionals viewed the family members stereotypically, refusing to acknowledge any of their idiosyncratic but impressive strengths. In fact, objective evidence supported the father's capacity to raise the child not merely adequately, but with the advantages of a comfortable income and with the sophisticated insight gained by a high educational level and a cosmopolitan background. His own experiences of mental disturbance and its nature made him sensitive to her needs and feelings. The caseworkers, however, dismissed all expert opinions that contradicted their own bias—that parents who had been mentally ill were unfit.

☐ Privileged Position in Court

Typically, the Welfare Officers in this and similar cases were permitted by the judge to block the court testimony of witnesses who would not support their contentions. Local child protection social workers have a privileged legal position that grants them considerable power in enforcing their point of view. In court, they sit not with other witnesses but with the state attorneys. They can be cross-examined only at the discretion of the judge. When a lawyer asked to cross-examine a Welfare Officer because her report was "full of lies," the social worker countered, "Then I withdraw my report." The judge permitted her to do so, though he had already read the report and presumably had been influenced by it. Once the report was withdrawn, the opposing lawyer could not raise the points that he held to be inaccurate.

☐ Weakening of the Clients

The intervention of the Welfare Officers significantly weakened Lily's family. The father's energies were diverted from coping with the mother's illness, the need to rebuild a home, and his attempts to raise a hopefully sane child without her. Instead, an ever-growing burden of new, artificially created crises were loaded onto the father and daughter, crises that became the main focus of their lives, dissipating their resources, spoiling their relationship, and wearing down their resilience. No matter how they maneuvered, they could not free themselves from fly-paper-like entrapment. Furthermore, the court, by delaying and compromising, only rendered the circumstances more damaging by leaving the child's situation uncertain, and by allowing time and opportunity for the girl to be increasingly alienated from her father.

☐ When Does One Intervene in Members of a High-Risk Population?

There are a number of commonly occurring sources of professional malfunctioning in this case. First, the social workers betrayed a crude misunderstanding of the concept of preventive intervention. They appeared to assume that if a statistical risk of future breakdown exists for a particular subpopulation—in this case, children of mentally disturbed parents—this meant that an individual member of that population is necessarily doomed. From this, they apparently deduced that it was necessary to disrupt Lily's currently healthy and satisfying life situation in order to protect her from what they foresaw as otherwise inevitable future deterioration.

In many cases of iatrogenic damage, we encounter professional confusion about when to intervene directly in the life of a member of a high-risk population. Let us, therefore, reiterate a basic central premise: A high-risk population is one that has been exposed to a hazard as a result of which, according to empirical research, that group will have a statistically higher level of pathology than is to be expected in a comparable population that is not similarly exposed. In order to lower that higher than average risk, that statistically endangered population may be the target of a primary prevention program that has two components. First, such a program may disseminate among the entire population information about the expectably unpleasant situation and how to cope with it; and second, by influencing public policy, it may attempt to attenuate as much as possible the field of forces in the community that have been found to exacerbate the inevitable stress. Thus, if we take attempts to lower the rate of pathology among the children of divorcing parents as an example, we can first direct to all divorcing parents educational material about expectable problems that will arise, and the likely consequent reactions of children to family breakup. Second, we can attempt to modify the policies of legislators, law courts, and other institutions that mold the general climate surrounding and determining the configuration of divorce procedures, so that extraneous exacerbation of an already stressful situation is kept to a minimum. No direct interventions in the lives of individuals within this population are called for unless signs of unusual strain and maladjustment actually appear in named individuals. At that point, and only at that point, when a person stands out from the anonymous crowd that constitutes the high-risk population because, unlike the majority of his or her cohort, that individual is not coping adequately with the expected challenges of the potentially emotional hazard, only then is professional intervention indicated.

The level and intensity of that intervention must then be determined by the actual needs of the individual case, and should not constitute a standardized and forced intrusion. It should be calibrated to fit the immediate manifest situation and symptoms and must take into account the idiosyncratic situation of that particular individual, his or her emotional and physical capabilities, and the social and material resources that exist or can be mobilized to support that individual during the period of discomfort. A general profile that indicates statistical susceptibility because that individual falls into a labeled category, therefore, provides no license for direct personal intervention by professionals, unless there are empirical indicators that that person is having present, real difficulties and needs some form of active professional input. Such an ensuing intervention must be as light-handed as possible. It should take a form that is most economical of staff time and community resources, and it should promote the quickest return to self-sufficiency on the part of the individual while lowering his or her tendency (always exaggerated during a crisis period) towards dependency. The aim of the intervention, therefore, is not to recruit clients for treatment, institutionalization, or any other form of long-term care, but it should be to return those temporarily weakened to independent, autonomous functioning as quickly as possible, while keeping the expenditures of community resources as low as is commensurate with effective, high quality professional care.

Malfunctioning professionals cause considerable iatrogenic damage when they ignore a wise adage that says, "If it isn't broken, don't fix it." By confusing a statistical risk, which is theoretical, with a certainty that this prophesizes the doom of a given individual, the caregivers in Lily's case apparently concluded that, if having mentally disturbed parents endangered a child's mental health, the way to save that child was by creating a clean break from her unconventional home and removing her to a new, sanitized environment. This solution, however, ignored the fact that we, as professionals, do not know as much as we may like to think we do about which factors, acting singly or in combination, determine whether an outcome will be healthy or otherwise. In our relative ignorance, therefore, it might have been wiser to have maintained Lily, a so-far healthy child, in the hitherto successfully, nurturing environment of her own family, rather than subjecting her to the radical stress of uprooting her, and thereby turning her into a dependant foster child, fought over for years through the courts and in the corridors of her building. A more useful style of preventive intervention might have been to support the father in his efforts to raise her instead of attacking him as an incompetent and damaging parent, and to have discretely monitored Lily's progress, so that if any early signs of psychopathology were to appear, they could be treated at once.

The itch to be gratuitously proactive in cases where there is only a statistical possibility of breakdown, but where there is no present compelling evidence of disorder, may damage clients unnecessarily. First, in our relative ignorance of what forces within a complex, reverberative social, physical, and psychological system actually determine the quality of an outcome, our zeal to avert illness may inadvertently disrupt precisely those elements that are keeping a client healthy. The humbling knowledge that we cannot prophesy the results of our interventions with certainty should warn us not to try to play God. Second, if, as in this case, the professionals concentrate on "saving" only one person in a constellation, they may thereby sacrifice the rest. Whatever benefit might eventually accrue to Lily as a result of her change in circumstances, her father was left wretched and despairing and more vulnerable to psychiatric breakdowns. While the social workers concentrated their efforts on the child, they ignored the human needs of the parent. In fact, they also ignored the child's potentially damaging upset, her fear, anger, insecurity, and ambivalence. Or if they noticed it, they apparently regarded it as the legacy of her unconventional upbringing and of her "crazy" father's refusal to give her up quietly.

☐ Prejudging a Case

One of the crucial and typical aspects of this case is the fact that the professionals determined its outcome from its outset. Their subsequent efforts were directed not towards gathering information to support or correct a diagnosis or a disposition, but towards ensuring and defending their prearranged plans. From their first encounter with the attractive and charming Lily, the child protection workers had agreed to "rescue" her from her unconventional parents, though there had never been any suspicions of abuse or neglect except in the paranoid delusions of the psychotic mother. It is odd, by the way, that the influence of parents in cases like Lily's is apparently seen to be invariably negative. The positive attributes of a child, the very features that make him or her "worth" saving from the point of view of professionals engaged in social engineering, are, one would assume, the result of a good upbringing. Yet in the cases we have seen, they are never counted in the parents' favor.

When the Welfare Officers were rebuffed in their early attempts to move Lily out of her home, they characteristically kept changing the stated pretexts for her removal to fit the latest developments in the household. Though unsuccessful at first, they kept surveillance over the family for months until a crisis enabled them to act. When the opportunity offered, they were prepared to take custody at once. The "absurd" element of cases like this, as we have mentioned earlier, comes from observers being distracted from what is really happening by the social workers' mutating excuses for proposing to take Lily away from her father. In fact, all these excuses were irrelevant, and the father's attempts to disprove them by bringing evidence to show how well the child was being cared for were therefore futile.

The main thrust of the Welfare Officers' intervention involved defending their preplanned disposition of the case from any judgment that contradicted their own. Supported by administrative superiors who refused requests to review the decisions of the branch office, they were able to enforce their own position against the evidence of specialists in child psychiatry and adult psychopathology—four psychiatrists, a clinical psychologist, and two independent and senior social workers—all of whom concluded that the father posed no danger, and that the child had been thriving, and could be expected to continue to thrive in his care. While preserving an appearance of respect for the Bench, the Welfare Officers managed to neutralize the judge's decision to return Lily home. They also succeeded in blocking the courtroom testimony of any expert whose observations did not lead to conclusions that matched their own.

☐ Premature Closure

The malfunctioning professionals in this and similar cases were engaging in premature closure, thereby aborting any possibility of validating or refuting their understanding of the case as it changed and revealed itself over time and in response to fluid circumstances. There was, then, little or no possibility of correcting or modifying an erroneous diagnosis or an unsuccessful disposition. When this pattern of thinking is linked to the heavy emotional investment in their own preordained verdict on a case, as when professional judgment is frozen by a theme interference, by a personality type that favors an authoritarian or narcissistically gratifying outcome, or by a corporately held hidden agenda that subordinates the needs of a client to the practical or idealistic needs of the caregivers, then the possibility of any flexibility or reality testing and consequent corrections of the course of an intervention is reduced further.

☐ Suppose We Were Wrong

One of the issues that must be considered in defining iatrogenic damage is the timeframe in which we view results. As in the field of primary prevention as a whole, the question arises of how accurate are the various predictions of pathology in response to stressors. In any individual case, as we have noted earlier, these are educated guesses, not prophesy. For Lily, the short-term damage was obvious to us. However, it could be argued that our pessimism was misplaced, and that the eventual result a few years down the line might well justify the caseworkers' original intervention and might, therefore, compensate for short-term suffering. Perhaps, after all, the welfare workers were correct in predicting that the child would grow up happier and healthier, despite the trauma of her separation and alienation from her father, because she had been transferred to a "normal," noisy, busy, foster-sibling-filled household instead of continuing as the only child of a doting but eccentric and rigid parent and being raised in large measure by servants. It might be argued further that, despite the father's current capacity, his vulnerability to mental breakdowns might mean that his parenting would deteriorate in the future. We may answer that, once one course of action is chosen, we never know what would have happened if no intervention had occurred. We do, however, suspect that the child's genetic loading made the cost of her tolerating even short-term traumas too dangerous to chance.

Nevertheless, setting aside our doubts, let us assume that we were wrong, that, indeed, the child's best interests lay in removing her to a more "normal" environment, away from the unconventionalities, and possible periodic breakdowns of her parents. Even then, the caregivers may be judged to have malfunctioned, since because of their bias, these Welfare Officers missed an opportunity to play a positive role when they so cordially sided with the neighbors who shared their prejudice against the father, thereby polarizing the situation further. Had they instead adopted a more neutral position and bridged the gap between the various parties, each of whom in his or her way shared a genuine concern for Lily's welfare, and had the social workers been able to suspend their own phobic reactions, they might have drained much of the bitterness out of the situation. After taking custody of the child, they might have promoted a partnership and a lowering of derogatory attitudes between the father and the foster family, thereby enabling Lily to live in a "normal" household while retaining her emotional ties to her father. His opposition to her living with another family might thus have been eased. So apparently fixed and absolute were the perceptions of the social workers, however, that they could not implement such a suggestion.

☐ Ignoring Community Coverage

In their intervention in Lily's family, there seems to have been no effort by the caregiving authorities to consider the situation from the standpoint of the efficient use of scarce and expensive staff time. They seemed unaware that there was anything undesirable in the fact that so much public money and the professional time of a team of social workers, a body of attorneys from the Welfare Ministry, a number of judges, and various psychiatric and child development experts were being expended on the fate of a healthy, academically and socially successful, and well-nourished child from a cultivated and well-endowed home, when there must have been cases of genuine deprivation and abuse in their district that called for investigation. Not only was harm done to Lily and her family by aggressive professional intervention, therefore, but damage may also have been done to an unknown number of other local children whose possible suffering may have been neglected because of this dubious allocation of resources. Instead of focusing on where the needs of the population lay, the Welfare Officers concentrated on a particular case of their own choosing that appealed to them for their own reasons, as though they were an individual-client-oriented clinic answerable only to themselves, instead of being a public agency with statutory responsibility to serve and protect the welfare of an entire population.

☐ Conclusion

In this case, therefore, we see iatrogenic damage as the outcome of a series of injudicious, maximalistic professional intrusions into the domain of a family, where a more detached, watching, brief approach might have better served the clients. The caregivers appear to have been motivated by their own prejudices, fears, and possible misapprehensions about what constitutes normative professional functioning to take an unduly directive role in the lives of the clients, thereby excluding from the process of decision-making not only the expressed wishes of the child and her father, but also information, options, and the expertise offered by a number of more senior professionals. This apparent drive for exclusive ownership of the case further inhibited their collecting of data and reinforced their stereotypes, both sources of a narrowing of focus that we have identified as a warning sign of malfunctioning in other cases we have seen.

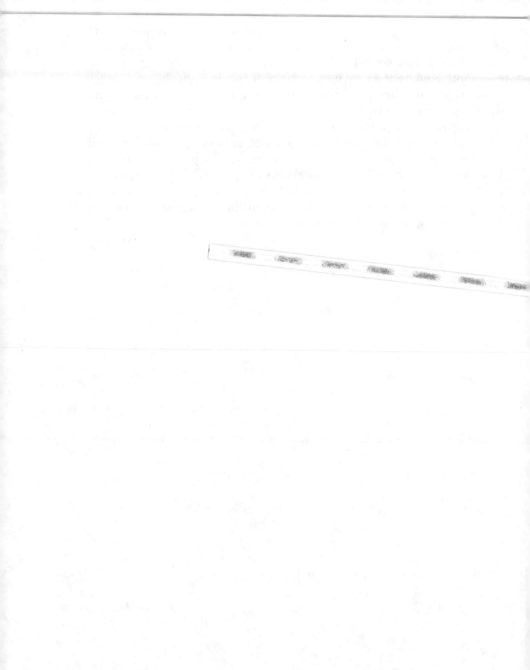

5
CHAPTER

Adoption, Secrecy, and the Hidden Agenda

Among instances of severe iatrogenic damage that we have seen were a number of adoption cases. In the discussion that follows, we will consider examples from the Israeli adoption scene during the past few years. This focus may strike some readers as narrow and of only passing academic interest because in much of the Western world, and in each state in the United States, a variety of recently enacted laws now allow a freer flow of information and contacts between the parties to an adoption than has been possible in Israel, thereby giving what is to follow a somewhat archaic feel. Nevertheless, this chapter, while ostensibly about adoption, is actually of consequence to our general discussion. Issues illuminated by such local cases have a wider implication, illustrating recurring problems that may generate iatrogenic damage in any caregiving area.

☐ A Desirable Child

Five-year-old Pearl was graceful and pretty; she was also intelligent and remarkably charming. Three years earlier, the youngest in a large, poor family of Middle Eastern origin, she had been left with her father who doted on her while her mother went to the corner grocery shop. The father was drunk at the time; and when the mother returned 20 minutes later, she found the child in shock. She rushed her to the hospital where it was ascertained that Pearl had been sexually molested. The mother cooperated in full with the child protection service and agreed that Pearl could stay in their shelter until the father's probable guilt could be established and he could be removed from home; but though he was convicted and jailed for many years, Pearl was never returned to her family. On the recommendations of social workers, judges kept extending her stay in the shelter, even though a psychologist warned that the child was pining for her mother and felt she was being punished for having been hurt. The family was allowed to visit only infrequently and was kept hoping that the next court hearing or the one after that would allow the child home.

During the next two-and-a-half years, various excuses were made as to why Pearl was being held. Her home was found to be underprivileged, and it was asserted that her mother was retarded and ineffectual. In fact the mother was of normal intelligence but culturally deprived, having herself come from a poor immigrant family and having left school early to marry the charming but feckless father of her nine children. Far from ineffectual, she was raising her family successfully despite poverty. The children were all enrolled in schools or were stably employed and married. None had inherited their father's shiftlessness and taste for drink, and none had been in any trouble with the law. The children we met were well-behaved, well-groomed, and well-spoken. They all wanted their little sister back; and they all expressed disgust at the behavior of their father and at the social workers who would not relinquish Pearl.

After nearly three years in the shelter, to the amazement and shock of her family, Pearl was placed for adoption. By the time her family learned of this plan, she had been introduced to a pleasant, warm, upper middle-class family with whom, unbeknown to her relatives, she had already been living for some time in another part of the country. The would-be adoptive parents, who were intelligent and attractive, had several children of their own and wanted another, but as the mother put it, adoption was easier than a pregnancy. They were fascinated by Pearl and showered her with attention and presents. Their own children, however, had reservations about the newcomer. The youngest child, who was barely older than Pearl, began to misbehave seriously when she came to stay. Pearl, however, shrugged off the jealousy. Tough and self-reliant, she was used to surviving rivalries after years in the shelter. The adoptive parents regarded their children's hostility with amusement and irritation; they were fascinated by this charming, talented sprite. Pearl nestled up to the adoptive mother like a kitten, self-contained and contented. Her assessment of her new life was pragmatic, "I like my bed", she told us, "and the stuffed toys, and the tape deck, and the computer." Then, after a thoughtful pause, she added, "The parents are O.K. too."

The adoptive parents, whose names and place of residence we were never allowed to know because of the laws of secrecy governing closed adoption, knew little about the child's real background, not even the details of her ethnicity. The information given by the adoption system was partial. The adoptive parents understood that the child had been systematically abused; they romanticized the adoption, believing that they were performing an act of charity by saving her and taking her in. They had no idea that Pearl's family, except for the father, was decent and caring, and that her mother and siblings were desperately trying to get her back; and we, by law, were forbidden to enlighten them.

We were permitted to see Pearl interacting with her biological mother. The mother was deeply attached to the child and proud of her cleverness. The child treated the mother with condescension, pleased to see her, but after three years of only intermittent contact, she was hardly clinging or passionate. The child also blamed her mother for "abandoning" her. Pearl had told us angrily that when she becomes a mommy, if her little girl is molested, she will never let her be taken away alone to a shelter, but will accompany her child always.

Pearl's mother brought an older daughter to the meeting who had not been permitted to see her sister for a year. When the adoption agency workers who had brought Pearl to our office heard about the presence of the older sister, they were incensed and accused us of bad faith. They refused to allow the girls to meet, claiming it would be "dangerous" and "emotionally burdensome" for Pearl. The older girl waited in the next room, with the door firmly closed and guarded by the caseworkers who made sure that she didn't peek, while Pearl, told about her sister's proximity, drew a picture for us to give to her, and sent her love to her other siblings and to a list of uncles, aunts, and cousins. When the mother begged the social workers to let Pearl phone her occasionally, they snapped that this was too much to ask. It was an ironic contrast that the convicted and imprisoned father was allowed to phone his family regularly.

Pearl was prepared to be adopted apparently because it removed her from an institutional setting, and because she was clever enough to see that it would give her a more comfortable life. Yet damage had already occurred. Intense grief had been caused to her family and upset among the children of the adoptive parents. It was also apparent that Pearl had not emerged unscathed. She had developed a cold, hard core and a calculating and manipulative manner, quite unlike the warmth of her mother and siblings. This toughness had enabled her to manage in the shelter and to adapt rapidly to the adoptive family, but it hardly augured well for her ability to sustain later long-term intimacies. Moreover, the therapy that had been provided during her years of institutionalization had born mixed results. While apparently reconciling her to the loss of her family, it had not resolved the trauma of abuse. Pearl told us that she continued to have nightmares about being attacked by her father whom she referred to as "a monster." This was invoked by the adoption workers to support their demand that the child not be returned to her mother since, in some years' time, the father would be released from prison and might return home.

☐ Corporately Held Themes

In this, as in similar cases that spawned iatrogenic damage, while the openly stated purpose was to cure and prevent further psychosocial harm, a key energizing feature appeared to be the hidden goal of social engineering that appeared to be supported by unconscious themes shared within a group of caregivers. We were alerted to this latter possibility by Pearl's strangely dramatic appearance at the doorway to our office—a tiny figure dwarfed by two adoption workers each of whom gripped the child by a shoulder and, hovering over her, looked at us with a malevolence and suspicion for which there seemed no rational reason. They had communicated this distrust to the child who at first was terrified of us. The caregivers' apparently free-floating sense of the menace of the outside world from which they felt impelled to isolate and protect the child struck us as odd. As we later interviewed them at length about the case, we found that they viewed the world in dualistic terms of good versus evil. Most ominously, they appeared to regard the sufferings of some as an acceptable price to pay in order to "save" at-risk children marked by superior attributes and graces. This mindset endangered clients because it might countenance evading strict guidelines in the service of a supposedly higher perception of priorities.

A journalist told us of an interview with a high official of the adoption service who, during a three-hour conversation, kept repeating that her service was engaged in a "sacred mission." The journalist told us that she was disturbed by this choice of words, which, in Hebrew, is far stronger than the English translation, suggesting a task of Biblical or Messianic proportions. The journalist was also disturbed by the rapt tone in which these words were spoken, which, she felt, did not conform to a professional mindset.

☐ Social Engineering

In Pearl's case, it became clear that adoption had been proposed in large part to provide a superior child with an appropriately superior environment—this despite the fact that it would deprive the child of ties to her extended kinship network whose supportive value we have found to be unappreciated by many modern caregivers. In fact, social engineering might have been better served by leaving so intelligent and talented a child in situ, while enriching her environment and using her development to raise the aspirations of her surroundings.

By the time we saw the case, however, the facts had been established. The child had been weaned away from her family and had formed a willing bond with the warm, caring adoptive parents and their comfortable world. Uprooting her again and sending her back to the relatively deprived surroundings to which she no longer expressed interest in returning would have generated more problems for her. The least detrimental alternative would have been an open adoption, then almost unheard of in Israel. Pearl herself suggested that she would like her "two mothers" to meet and get to know each other. The adoptive mother was prepared to cooperate with this wish, but the adoption laws at the time precluded it.

☐ Timeframes

As in the case cited in the last chapter, the handling of Pearl's situation raises issues about timeframes. First, there is the question of how much present suffering can be countenanced in the hope of a necessarily theoretical future gain. It can be argued plausibly, setting aside our concern for Pearl's biological family, that the child herself would benefit from her incorporation into a loving, upper middle-class home with all the attendant advantages for social and educational advancement and economic security that such a placement might be expected to produce. Yet, if we look at the longer term, we may ask what possibly pathological consequences may be expected to arise not only to Pearl herself, but for her future offspring, from the girl having been unnecessarily deprived of warm, empathic mothering during so critical a period of her own development.

Another time-related issue, as in Lily's case, involves the tendency of the courts to procrastinate and temporize in cases involving children. This not only leaves children in an insecure legal limbo, but it enables facts to be created that eventually are best not reversed, however undesirable they may have seemed to most of us at an earlier stage of the case. Therefore, due to a sort of lethargy and passivity built into the legal system, welfare and adoption workers in the cases of Lily, Pearl, and various other children we have seen, by waiting, have been able to achieve the preplanned ends that appeared so undesirable and even absurd at an earlier stage. In Pearl's case, moreover, they achieved this with the reluctant concurrence of people like us, who were well aware of the damaging aspects of the case, but who, by the time we saw it, could find no other solutions within the law that would offer any more satisfactory outcome. We were in sympathy with Pearl's mother's lawyer, who asked, "How rational is it to redeploy children in order to provide them with 'better' families than they were born into? These adoptive parents are rich and nice, while the child's mother is also nice but poor. What is the legitimate professional point of this whole exercise? It seems a frivolous exercise to me."

☐ Sources of Malfunctioning Stemming from Normative Practice

In this example we can see three distinct but interacting sources of possible professional malfunctioning. First, there is an apparent corporately held hidden agenda of social engineering. Second, there is a suggestion that particular personality types were drawn to Pearl's case with unconscious elements of free-floating suspiciousness towards the outside world and a fervor to "save" certain individuals at the expense of others. Third, there were elements built into normative professional functioning that, irrespective of the personalities of individual staff, could damage clients. An example of this may be found in general medicine, where there is a style of conducting ward rounds in which senior doctors behave as though patients are deaf. In the patient's presence, they may describe his or her condition and prognosis to colleagues in terms that may be shocking and injurious to the subject of the discussion. Such doctors are not necessarily uncaring; they are merely behaving the way their teachers and colleagues have always behaved, with no apparent realization of the damage this insensitivity may cause to patients. In a similar way, the almost routine use of police to seize children whose custody has been awarded to child protection workers is a traumatic and potentially damaging experience for the children. An adoptive mother told us, for example, how her new daughter, aged nine, compulsively replayed the scene of being removed from home by police and social workers amid hysteria and violence. This form of taking possession of possibly endangered children is a routinized professional tool; and the harm it may cause is irrespective of the personalities and unconscious themes of individual caregivers who use it. In the same way, certain aspects of Pearl's case illustrate system-generated iatrogenic damage that is built into long-held traditions of professional practice.

One of these traditions is the confining of children to shelters for long periods, isolated from their families. The child's sense of parental abandonment when removed to a shelter and residential care may be deeply upsetting, as Pearl's example shows. Children already traumatized by possible abuse, and perhaps by being seized by police, are separated from their familiar world in an institutional setting, and may consequently feel, like Pearl, not rescued, but doubly punished.

A further potentially damaging element for all the parties involved was built into professional functioning by the rule of secrecy governing closed adoption. For, though vulnerable to other causes of malfunctioning by caregivers, the parties to local adoptions are particularly endangered by laws of secrecy. Such laws, while governing all issues involving juveniles, have added stringency in adoption cases. The secrecy originally intended to guard the interests of clients, has, in more recent times, and in other instances of community caregiving besides adoption, enabled malfunctioning professionals to avoid scrutiny, and has given them the power that comes from holding forbidden knowledge.

☐ Legacy of the "Poor Laws"

Adoption in Israel remains largely secret. From the moment a court declares children adoptable, a wall comes down between them and their biological family. No further contact is possible until children reach the age of 18 and take the initiative to search for their roots. It is a criminal offense to transmit identifying information about the adoptive family and the child's family of origin to either of them. No notification of any change of circumstances can be exchanged.

Until recently, this secrecy, or "clean break" as it is called in England, or "sealed papers" in the United States, was normative in much of the western world, a vestige of English and American Poor Laws, which for over a century had governed the illiberal custody and control of the "undeserving poor." The latter constituted an underclass whose poverty was seen to emerge inevitably from their racial inferiority, degenerate and immoral life style, mental incapacity, and willful failure to live by the norms of society—to be clean, honest, punctual, diligent, thrifty, temperate, sober, and God-fearing. The poverty of these people was understood as a sign of Divine displeasure with their shiftlessness and lack of social conformity. In consequence, it was felt that to break the cycle of poverty with its attendant crime, disorder, mental illness, idleness, and "primitive" customs, children should be rescued from their parents in order to instill in them the values and decencies of the middle class. In the nineteenth century, this led to restricting, or altogether stopping contact between children who came to public notice and care and their impoverished parents, because the latter were considered a bad influence on their children (Triseliotis, 1993).

This philosophy, which survived well into the twentieth century, led to the deportation of British pauper children to the colonies, particularly to Australia, in order to ensure permanent separation from their families. It also led to children being shipped out of the slums of the eastern United States to the western frontier, often without the parents' consent or knowledge, and to children of various indigenous populations in North America and Australia being forcibly taken from their tribes to be institutionalized and adopted in an effort to stamp out their "primitive" cultures and languages. Dr. Thomas J. Barnardo, of the famous Barnardo homes for abandoned children, the first of which he established in England in 1867, called this process, of which he enthusiastically approved, "Philanthropic Abduction" (Barnardo & Marchant, 1903).

The twin elements of total separation and secrecy became intrinsic elements of adoption, and the belief that the welfare of deprived children was best served by preventing their contact with their family remained, until recently, largely unchallenged. These vestiges of the old Poor Laws integrated easily into twentieth century social and psychological theories as times and customs changed, for they appeared, at first sight, to serve the best interests of all concerned.

☐ Twentieth Century Rationales for Secrecy

Because most adoption in the early and mid twentieth century involved infants, most of whom were the product of unmarried or adulterous unions, it was felt that the biological mother needed secrecy to hide her shame and to enable her to take up her life again unencumbered by the burden of past indiscretion. For adoptive parents, secrecy was seen to be desirable since it preserved the fantasy that the child was truly their own, and it hid from casual eyes the stigma of possible infertility. Furthermore, it reassured them that they could raise their child according to their own views, without fear of interference, contradiction, or sabotage from another, possibly disgraceful parent figure. For the child, secrecy was seen to be imperative. It was felt that it enabled him or her to be "reborn," to have a "fresh start," rescued from the bad influences of the family of origin. In some cases, this even led to the issuing of new birth certificates that expunged the names of birthparents and replaced them by the names of their adoptive parents (Jaffe, 1994).

The psychoanalysts, J. Goldstein, Anna Freud, and A. J. Solnit (1973, 1979), whose work influenced the Israeli adoption service, provided a theoretical basis for total separation and secrecy that fitted twentieth century ideology, holding that it enabled the child to achieve a permanent relationship, or bonding with a good "psychological parent." They claimed that children have no psychological conception of relationship by blood-tie until quite late in their development, and that continuing an existing relationship with birth relatives was less important than ensuring the uncomplicated development of new attachments within the adoptive family. The adoptive parent was to enjoy an exclusive relationship with the child to avoid the latter's being confused or feeling a conflict of loyalties by having to relate to more than one set of parents.

This rationale for secrecy was based on a theoretical model whose validity was called into question by the findings of later empirical research. Recent studies, for example, do not appear to support the contention that a child will be "irreparably damaged" if he or she does not have an exclusive relationship with a caregiver. In fact, while bonding indeed appears to be decisive, studies of kibbutzim (Fox, 1977) have shown that children can attach themselves to several caregivers at the same time and can differentiate between them even at a very early age without detriment or confusion. Scheffer (1990) showed that even very young children are capable of differentiating between more than one set of caregivers:

> The fear that the relationship is in some way going to be "diluted" by the simultaneous existence of other relationships is quite unjustified. A child's attachment is not some limited quantity that has to be divided up amongst people. Moreover, it has also become apparent that children are able to sort out the different roles of people at much earlier ages than they had been given credit for.

In confirmation of this, experience in divorced families has shown that children can relate positively to a noncustodial biological parent as well as to a stepparent, and can differentiate between the relationships. A three-year-old, for example, was in no doubt about who was who. He called his stepfather "Daddy" and his biological father "*my* Daddy."

It is ironic that while certain professionals enforce continued contact in cases of divorce between noncustodial parents and reluctant children even to the point of legal and physical coercion, in closed adoption they take what amounts to an inconsistent position. Differences between the various professional groups appear to have obscured the fact that children's needs and reactions in both types of family disintegration share a common ground. A number of recent studies of both divorce and adoption have shown that, contrary to traditional theories, children generally adjust better to a stepfamily if they have a continuing relationship with a noncustodial parent, and that they adjust better to foster and adoptive families if they maintain links to members of their biological families. These studies suggest,

> . . . that the stability of a placement is not threatened by the maintenance of links with meaningful figures from the past. In our studies involving the adoption of older children we have come across children who were secretly pining for contact with a birth parent, something that was posing a threat to the stability of the placement. In contrast, children who maintained contact with a birth parent, sibling, or grandparent appeared more satisfied. . . . On the basis of these studies the hypothesis could be put forward that severing children's meaningful emotional links with members of their birth families limits their capacity for full attachment to their new families. (Triseliotis, 1993, p. 42)

As another researcher put it,

> There is no evidence that continual family contact impedes the growth of attachments within the substitute families in the generality of cases. There is some evidence that the child is helped to settle if he or she does not feel disloyal to the first family, and is reassured on seeing them that nothing too awful is happening to them. (McWhinnie, 1969, p. 153)

In other follow-up studies of closed adoption cases, it was found that secrecy and the clean break had often produced results that contradicted optimistic expectations. Instead of forgetting their child and getting on with their lives unencumbered, many biological parents were found to have continued to mourn the loss of the child, to feel guilty about giving it up, and to worry about its welfare in an unknown family. Many adoptees, even those with excellent relationships with their adoptive parents, were found to search for lost roots. Rather than expunging a child's history and wiping the slate clean, for some adoptees secrecy made the unknown past the object of obsessional rumination. Because what lies behind such secrets is undefined, they can become screens on which to project often painful fantasies.

Furthermore, because of changing demographics, enforced secrecy and the clean break may now have a certain artificiality. Once, most adoptions involved infants, but nowadays, because of changing attitudes to out-of-wedlock pregnancies and the availability of birth control and legal abortion, babies who once would have been released for adoption are either not born at all, or are kept by their single mothers. In the virtual absence of locally available babies, the pool of adoptable native children in Israel is now filled with older candidates. These, unlike infants, have not only a life history of possible deprivation and abuse often consciously remembered, but also of warm relationships, the memories of which are not obliterated by the professionals' fantasy of rebirth by legal fiat, or even by the love of nicer parents and the comforts and orderliness of middle class life. Such children may not only be haunted by conscious and unconscious memories of suffering, they may also be silently mourning the loss of loved family members. One child told us, "I dream over and over that my grandmother is ill and nobody has told me." Another told his adoptive mother glowing stories about an uncle whose computer he had been encouraged to use, and about the cousins he missed. Another child told us, "I want to see my mother's face again. I want to see what she looks like now."

☐ Resistance to Giving up Secrecy

Since empirical research has called into question the traditional assumption that secrecy, a clean break, and a "new birth" will necessarily encourage a positive emotional outcome in adoption, we must consider why certain professionals caution against changing laws and practices that embody the old, closed approach.

Part of this professional opposition can be understood as the outcome of legitimate scientific reservation about the possibly overenthusiastic, untested, fad-like reversal of an established framework. For, while nowadays prevailing professional and lay opinion in many western countries favors nonsecret adoption, there are also informed, judicious researchers who reason that the pendulum of professional and legal theory and practice has swung too far too fast. They argue that opponents of closed adoption have based their conclusions on problem cases, while not giving sufficient weight to others where everyone involved was satisfied with the traditional secrecy and isolation. They fear that the new order has been applied with uncritical enthusiasm before follow-up studies have tested the long-term results, just as the long-term consequences of the clean break were not rationally and empirically monitored in the past. While they support the end of secrecy in theory because it seems more humane and it benefits many, they hesitate to agree to the wholesale shift that has so rapidly overtaken the field (McWhinnie, 1969).

Professionals may also legitimately worry that disruptions to successful adoptions may be caused by continued access to children and their new families by unfit biological parents if communication between the parties is allowed. However, experience in the United States, Canada, New Zealand, and Australia has shown that, if necessary, transfer of information can be carried out by the adoption agency or by other community welfare workers without divulging identifying information about the parents to each other. Despite the fears of those who oppose modification of rules of secrecy, it has not proven difficult to transfer information without destroying anonymity, which may be considered essential if there is fear and hostility between children and abusive birth parents. In practice, once legal prohibitions have been removed, the patterns of information transfer, personal communication, or face-to-face contact can be subject to the wishes of the parties themselves and to their mutual consent. The actual arrangements may be carried out by welfare workers or may be left to the personal initiative of the parties.

Another source of opposition to a free flow of information between the parties to an adoption may be due to the burden for veteran caregivers of so fundamental a restructuring of their accustomed ways of practice. This may hinder acceptance of radical innovation in any service field. But on a deeper level, the end of secrecy may insidiously threaten professional identity, because it removes a source of power—power that sometimes may have been used to serve not the best interests of clients, but of professionals themselves.

☐ Secrecy Versus Confidentiality

Secrecy is not to be confused with confidentiality, which operates for the benefit of clients. Confidentiality has a voluntary component; it restricts secrets at the will of the client, but it can be waived at the client's discretion. Secrecy, on the other hand, removes the client's ownership and control of information about his or her affairs and restricts it to the hands of designated professionals—the courts or other categories of caregivers. This sealing of information can generate damage, because the client can no longer freely disclose precise data about his or her own affairs. This may effectively limit his or her ability to publicize grievances and rally public support. While barring disclosure may indeed protect certain parties to an adoption who may be too young to realize any need for confidentiality, or who may be ashamed of the circumstances that led to the adoption, it may also bar clients from using all normal means to gain a reversal of judgments against them. In a later chapter, we will return to the subject of secrecy inhibiting clients' redress against damaging professional behavior, especially when coupled with false official data.

Secrecy carries another set of dangers that are highlighted in adoption cases, though they are not exclusively confined to this social service area. It creates a monopoly on sources of information. The professionals who control the knowledge can not only withhold it, but also disperse it in a partial form or in one that is distorted by their own limited understanding, prejudices, or needs, and which cannot then be tested against other sources of information. The implications of this for creating iatrogenic damage can be seen, for example, when adoptive parents have been furnished with insufficient information about a child's history.

One of the rationales for adoption has been the belief that if traumatized children are given stable, healthy, loving parents, and are separated from their unhealthy past, the trauma will be eased, and they will be free to grow into well-adjusted adults. Unhappily, experience has shown that parental love does not always compensate for past suffering, and sometimes secrecy has prevented the adoptive parents knowing enough to adequately understand and help their children. The adoptive parents of a child who required intensive and expensive therapy as he grew older and ever more antisocial, complained of the lack of any credible background information. "They wouldn't tell us the full story of what happened before we got him. Whether the mother drank or took drugs. Whether she was ill during pregnancy. Whether she or other family members were mentally or physically sick. We are working in the dark."

A monopoly on knowledge can also lead to damage when professionals communicate insufficient or prejudiced information, so that adoptive parents are left to fantasize about the "monsters" that mistreated or neglected their child. Pearl's adoptive parents, as we have seen, knew little that was authentic about her background, but at least they did not demonize her family of origin. In another case, a would-be adoptive father greeted our suggestion that he consider allowing the child to have contact with the biological mother with, "Certainly not! I would never allow people of *that sort* into my house! I will have to call in my lawyer if it is mentioned again! In fact, I will refuse to go through with the adoption!" We were unable to convince him that his fantasy that the mother, whom the child kept begging to see, was some sort of demon was inaccurate, but could contribute to future problems if the would-be adoptive father's prejudice spread to include the child as partaking of some supposed inherited inferiority or perversity. Some years later, our prediction was unhappily proved correct when the child contacted his mother, whose phone number he remembered, and begged to be rescued from the adoptive parents whom he felt hated and looked down on him. In such cases of stereotyping of the family of origin, the child is not only seen as the victim of supposed demons, but since he or she also shares their blood, the child may be seen also as partaking of their "monster" nature. Thus when problems and conflicts arise, real knowledge about the family of origin can help to ensure that there will be less of a tendency to identify the child's behavior as a throwback to an imagined evil genealogy. Such a prejudicial characterization communicates to the child and can be absorbed by him or her, promoting a further weakening of self-image. It can also constitute a possible spur to antisocial behavior, fed not only by rebelliousness, but also by a sense that he or she is doomed to relive the supposed degradation of the family of origin.

☐ Shame and Secrecy

In most of the cases of iatrogenic harm associated with adoption that we have seen, not only did the system demand secrecy but so did some of the biological parents who, even if objectively innocent, were humiliated by being accused and convicted of the charges of abuse and neglect. This collusion in secrecy that served to isolate them from social support and practical help is akin to the secrecy practiced not by the guilty, but by beaten spouses and abused children—the humiliated victims who have identified with their aggressors and for whom the fact of abuse itself indicates a measure of culpability which must be hidden from the eyes of the community. Pearl's mother, for example, told us how she dreaded the questions of her friends and extended clan about the whereabouts of the little daughter whom nobody had seen at family gatherings for years. She had always turned away inquiries by saying that Pearl was staying with friends in another town, a story that was proving hard to sustain for so long. She dreaded having to admit that she had been judged unworthy to bring up her own child. So, along with the fearful prospect of losing Pearl through closed adoption, there was the accompanying fear of how to keep up this deception permanently. Other victims of iatrogenic damage shared this inhibition and sometimes refrained from asking for help from influential people who might have interceded for them, cringing because they needed to hide their irrational sense of shame.

As they currently stand, laws of secrecy, not only in adoption cases, but also in other areas affecting children, may not distinguish between confidentiality that serves the interests of the clients, shielding their privacy and protecting their feelings, and the laws that enable caregivers to keep their malfunctioning and misrepresentations hidden from public view. Such caregivers may indeed be quite satisfied with the traditional secrecy in adoption and in other areas of professional practice, and may be threatened by any weakenings of its walls and especially by the termination of their agencies' powers of surveillance and control, weakenings that are likely to be associated with greater openness.

☐ Openness May Help to Reduce Iatrogenic Damage

The end of secrecy in adoption is not appropriate in every case, but it seems to be helpful in many. Further investigation will show the extent of its applicability and whether or not it alters the prevalence of iatrogenic damage. In those countries where nonsecret adoptions have become the norm, it has been found to help relieve the anxiety and guilt of birth parents, and reassures them that the child is well cared for. In cases where parents had fought adoption, suspension of secrecy and the possibility of continuing contact tended to reconcile them to the situation and reduce their opposition. An end to secrecy might console one of our clients, whose only daughter had been taken away from her for adoption, and who told us, "I look at windows in the streets I walk through, and I wonder, is she behind that one, or that one? Whenever there is a child hurt in a car accident, I wonder whether it's my child."

Studies in Great Britain, the United States, Canada, Australia, and New Zealand have shown that direct contact between adoptees and biological parents have helped reduce the sense of rejection that is endemic among such children by reassuring them that they were, and still are, loved by the birth family as well as by the adoptive parents, thus strengthening their self-image. It was also found to reduce the guilt of children who feel that they are betraying their biological family by enjoying the warmth and comfort of the adoptive relationships, because in such an open system, their birth family may provide sanction for the new order.

Whatever its impact may be on the specific process of adoption, secrecy has implications for the functioning of caregiving profession-als in many other areas that affect clients' emotional well being, since by its nature it casts shadows behind which malfunctioning practi-tioners can shelter. In attempts to avoid iatrogenic damage, therefore, professionals should differentiate confidentiality, which serves the in-terests of clients, from secrecy that implicitly makes it easier for mal-functioning caregivers to perpetrate unhelpful practices.

A Loss of Professional Objectivity

Mr. and Mrs. N. and their five children had emigrated from Australia and settled in a desert community in the south of the country. Their daughter, 12-year-old Leah, was a dominant and domineering force in the family. Significantly overdeveloped physically and sexually for her age, she towered, Junoesque, over her diminutive mother. She looked like a woman in her twenties, and had so much the manner, as well as the appearance of maturity that it was difficult to relate to her as the child she was.

The N.s had been worried about Leah for some time. In public demure and deferential, recently, after certain of her demands had met with disappointing rebuffs from her parents, Leah had begun to make the private life of the family difficult with tantrums, rebellion against her parents' rules, pilfering her siblings' money, and wearing clothes more suited to an adult than to a 12-year-old. Since she was developmentally out of step with her contemporaries, she began to keep company with a much older, rebellious group of teenagers who hung out in a local pizza parlor, and were suspected by the local children of engaging in illicit activities, including sex games. Leah's behavior at home became such an embarrassment to her siblings that the younger children never mentioned it to outsiders, and they referred to her as the "family secret."

Mr. and Mrs. N. took Leah for treatment to a psychotherapist to whom Leah reported that her parents forced her to do chores at home, and that her father repeatedly beat her savagely. At this time, she often skipped school to go shopping and to attend restricted movies, entrance to which she effected by claiming to be much older than her years. When the school asked Leah why she was absent so often, she said that her mother forced her to stay home to clean the house, a claim that the family cleaning lady later scornfully denied.

Meanwhile, Leah was frightening her friends with tales of beatings by her father who she said broke her bones, a story that resembled the plot of a book about the Holocaust that her classmates reported she had taken out of the local library. They also reported that she had a particular preference for lurid reading matter.

When the attention of friends began to flag, Leah complained of various bodily symptoms and was hospitalized for tests. No physical illness was found, but the hospital noted that the girl behaved oddly and made "strange" relationships. After discharge, Leah approached the local social worker and talked vaguely about suicide. The social worker was sufficiently concerned that in collaboration with the therapist and the parents, she had Leah admitted to the regional mental hospital.

Leah puzzled the mental hospital. While she talked of suicide, she was not depressed, but rather seemed angry and hysterical. She told a variety of stories that could be easily disproved—that she had been adopted, that she had been placed with foster parents as a toddler because her parents had abused her, and that there was a baby with cerebral palsy hidden in the family. She was found to have a poor perception of reality and a low ability to accept social norms, and she invented so many stories that some psychiatrists felt that she was suffering from "pseudologia fantastica" (pathological lying).

The head of the regional Welfare Office began to visit Leah. She told the hospital staff improbable and easily refutable stories about the family that she had learned from the girl. The hospital records noted that "the Welfare Officer tends to believe Leah's stories." In subsequent court testimony, the Welfare Officer said that she had not agreed to the medication prescribed by the hospital for Leah and had urged the girl not to take it. When Leah demanded to be taken home for a holiday, the Welfare Officer advised the parents not to return her to the mental hospital because "it was not doing her any good."

After spending considerable time closeted with Leah, the Welfare Officer approached the court to inform it that a youth investigator from the juvenile probation service had questioned Leah, because the girl had accused her father and an older brother of rape. The Welfare Officer was granted temporary custody, and she removed the girl from home. At 6 a.m. the following day, armed policemen arrived at the N.'s home and in the presence of the younger children, arrested Mr. and Mrs. N. and their 15-year-old son, Benny, and took them away in handcuffs to prison where they were interrogated for the next two weeks. Mrs. N. was arrested because it was claimed that she had held Leah's legs apart while Mr. N. and Benny raped her repeatedly. This took place, it was said, in the bedroom that Leah shared with three sisters, all of whom were sleeping there at that time. When their elders were arrested, the younger children were left with nobody to care for them, since the oldest brother was abroad on a study program. Neighbors found them wandering about the street, panic-stricken, later that morning and cared for them until a grandmother arrived from Australia to take charge of them.

Under intense police interrogation, Benny admitted that two years earlier, he and Leah had undressed together and had fondled each other, but he denied any rape. Tried and convicted of indecent acts, he was sentenced to "treatment" and community service. Mr. and Mrs. N. denied all charges, and in the absence of any corroborative evidence, were released.

Some days later, the Welfare Officer got another court order to place Leah again in a psychiatric hospital for "occasional depression as a result of her trauma." She claimed that according to Leah, Mr. N. beat all his children savagely, and there was a suspicion that he had sexually abused them. Mrs. N. was described as impulsive and lacking the emotional strength to deal with her family, whom she was said to govern by fear, violence, and outbursts of anger. According to the Welfare Officer, Leah was intelligent, sensitive, emotionally mature, and sexually abused.

A few days later, Leah ran away from the hospital and returned to her parents. That night, the parents and their lawyer brought Leah to us, and we interviewed her and watched the interaction of the supposed victim and victimizers. In this, as in subsequent observations, we saw an affectionate family, relaxed in each other's presence, with no signs in Leah of any fear, repugnance, or anxiety towards her parents. Leah told us that she had run away to escape the pressures being put on her to incriminate her father. She said that the Welfare Officer and a youth investigator from the probation service had spoken with her repeatedly, pressing her to tell a false story. "They put words in my mouth and insisted that I accuse my father of rape. I knew it was untrue, but in order to get rid of them I agreed to what they wanted." Leah said that she had in fact been raped repeatedly by an unknown man who had blindfolded her and had dragged her into a vacant lot.

The following morning, Leah stood up in court and with great self-possession denied all the charges against her family and told about the unknown assailant whom subsequently nobody tried to trace. Later, she and Benny met in our office. Her manner to the brother who had just been released from two weeks of imprisonment and interrogation because of her charges against him was unexpected. She was not embarrassed, apologetic, fearful, or repelled. On the contrary, she greeted him effusively and flirted with him in a most unsisterly way, like a temptress in a film, while the boy became shy and uncomfortable. When, however, he began to describe the late night illicit activities of the teenagers in the pizza parlor and how he had seen them touching Leah, she rose in majestic fury, and stalked theatrically out of the room. Later she returned and, like an angry child, expressed hatred for the brother who had dared to tell such stories about her.

Still later, when we saw the entire family together, we found them to be a normal group of loving parents and children joined closer by their fear of a common threat. The younger children were traumatized. Since their parents' arrest, some of them had begun to sleep barricaded under their beds. They clung to their parents in paroxysms of terror, begging them to promise not to leave them again. Mr. N. was depressed and unable to concentrate on his business. Mrs. N. kept the family functioning and got herself an extra job in a vain attempt to stave off the financial ruin that was fast approaching because of legal fees. She proved to be a warm, caring mother whose children were deeply attached to her.

As in our earlier examples, we can see here an early signal of professional malfunctioning in the exclusive concern of the caregiver for certain supposed victims and her obliviousness to the fact that her interventions were creating disturbances in the lives of other family members. The attention of the Welfare Officer in this case was so narrowed, that she could not assess or apparently deal with the larger picture in which the welfare of children and adults was now at increased risk because of the nature of the professional intervention.

A series of court-ordered placements for Leah—educational, therapeutic, and custodial—proved unsatisfactory. The professionals involved all agreed that the girl was too ungovernable and disturbed to manage in their frameworks. This diagnosis was steadily denied by the Welfare Officer who kept in frequent touch with Leah, and insisted that she was normal. One such meeting was witnessed by a foster mother, who told us how shocked she had been. "I wish I had had a video camera," she said. "It was one of the most perverted things I have ever seen. The social worker kept telling Leah in a whining tone how much she loved her, and that she could have whatever she wanted if she would only tell her dear friend what it was. Leah played all helpless and pathetic. If Leah was not disturbed already, the relationship with that Welfare Officer would soon make her so. It was sick!"

Despite court orders forbidding it, Leah found frequent excuses to return to her home town, ostensibly to see her family, but also to spend time with the older teenagers. She confided to a neighbor that she had told so many lies that nobody believed anything she said any more. The Welfare Officer, however, believed her implicitly, and began to press for three younger siblings to be removed from the family. Though she approached the court for an emergency order for custody, alleging deterioration in the children, the latter denied ever having spoken to her. They had been questioned extensively by a youth investigator, however, as a result of Leah's periodic claims, later denied by her, that they too had been sexually abused. The youth investigator had got them to admit that there was a "secret" in their family. This is a code word among child protection workers for sexual abuse. Unfortunately, the children did not know the official terminology. They were talking about the "secret" that while Leah behaved like a paragon in public, she was quite different inside the family. The judge, however, refused to remove the younger children for the present.

Mr. N. was arrested again. This time it was said that there was irrefutable evidence and independent witnesses to prove that he had indeed sexually abused Leah. After Mr. N. had been in prison for a week, a court hearing was held to extend his remand. The neighbors turned out to support him, ready to testify that in a community where doors were left open and neighbors knew each other's business, the warmth of relationships in the N. family was common knowledge, as was Leah's tendency to tell improbable stories. Oddly, no social worker or policeman had ever questioned any of the neighbors nor were any of them allowed to testify in court. The entire case rested exclusively on the words of Leah and the Welfare Officer.

Mr. N.'s remand was extended, but some days later, he was unexpectedly released. We then learned that Mr. N. had been rearrested because Leah had told the Welfare Officer that her father had stuffed objects into her vagina. When she was rushed to hospital and examined, indeed various foreign objects were found as specified. When Mr. N. did not admit that he had inserted them, the police, who had their own doubts, questioned Leah who admitted that she had pushed an eraser and a pencil sharpener or two into herself.

When Mr. N. was arrested for the second time, Mrs. N. felt that her younger children had suffered enough, and she quietly sent them all abroad to their grandparents. Not knowing that the children had already left the country, the Welfare Officer applied for an emergency court order for their custody that, this time, was granted, and for a week she searched for them. When the court was eventually told that the children had been sent to Australia, the judge demanded that they be brought back. The court gave the parents permission to travel abroad after posting bond, and they were ordered to bring their children back within a month.

The Welfare Officer, acting independently from, and without the knowledge of the judge who had decreed a month's grace period, collaborated with a State Attorney in sending affidavits under the Hague Convention, claiming that the children had been kidnapped and that the father had been found guilty of sexual abuse of the younger children, and requesting the help of local social workers and police in returning the family to Israel. The Australian social workers asked their court to issue a warrant for the family's arrest. The parents threw themselves on the mercy of the court and asked for sanctuary for themselves and their children. The judge read a report that we sent, and after investigations by the court clinic, dismissed all charges against the family and granted them asylum.

☐ Two Interpretations of the Case

In this instructive example, there were two interpretations of the case. According to one body of professional observers, the N.s were a psychologically normal and loving family with parents who had been shown by exhaustive testing to be mentally healthy, whose good characters had long been known to their neighbors, and whose excellent relations with their other children were supported by corroborative evidence. They were having recent difficulties managing a rebellious 12-year-old, who because she was so developmentally precocious, did not fit easily into her own age group, nor into the older, more sexually experienced one to which she aspired. Being histrionically inclined, she seemed to relish occupying center stage and striking poses, which is hardly unusual at that age. She alternated roles, either being a model of rectitude (the perfect daughter), or by playing a series of victimized heroines in her own adaptations of books, fairy tales, and stories she had encountered. An analysis of her tales revealed not only similarities in theme to some of her more lurid reading matter and to the plots of restricted films she had managed to see, but the central story of being raped while her mother held her legs apart bore a striking resemblance to evidence that had lately been given in a then much publicized trial for torture and murder in another country. What certain observers came to see, therefore, was an overimaginative, histrionic adolescent, suffering from probably temporary, if marked, difficulties that, while requiring therapeutic intervention, would, one hoped, pass with growing maturity. However, it was also clear that the pressure engendered by the Welfare Officer and the systems she had activated were leading to deterioration.

The second version of the case was the one the Welfare Officer saw, one in which an innocent young girl had been repeatedly raped by a perverted father and brother with the mother's active collusion. The heroine of this drama was seen to be doomed to a tragic end unless the Welfare Officer could rescue her from the monsters who continued to threaten her. This view, it will be noted, filtered out all but selected bits of Leah's behavior and stories, as well as such circumstances of her family's life as the suspicious proximity in time between Leah's charges of various forms of parental cruelty and her having been denied privileges that she had set her heart on. It would seem that, triggered by some aspect of the girl herself or by certain of her stories, the Welfare Officer had unconsciously created a melodrama in which she had assigned members of the N. family to stereotyped roles, and in which she might even have been influencing the dialogue, as Leah kept insisting when she said that the Welfare Officer was putting words into her mouth that the girl knew to be false.

☐ Uncharacteristic Professional Functioning

This case, therefore, appears to be a particularly vivid example of a loss of professional objectivity caused by a theme interference that impelled the Welfare Officer to act in a way that was uncharacteristic of her normal working practice. We knew that her actions in this instance were an aberration because we had worked with her and seen her functioning well in earlier and even more psychologically complex cases. None of the earlier cases, however, had involved suspicions of sexual abuse. Therefore, we knew that her mismanagement of Leah's situation was not due to any lack of general professional knowledge or skill. It did, however, bear the hallmarks of an unconscious theme building up and being displaced onto the client. In psychoanalytic terminology, her professional shortcomings in this case may have been caused by a type of unconscious interference termed "acting out." Acting out implies that a person is dealing with an emotional problem from earlier in life that was so hard to handle that all memory of it was repressed. When its arousal is stimulated, it returns in the form of action. "We may say that the patient does not *remember* anything of what he has forgotten and repressed but *acts* it out. He reproduces it not as a memory but as an action; he repeats it without, of course, knowing that he is repeating it" (Freud, 1911–13).

This theoretical construct would explain why the Welfare Officer, normally effective and sensitive in her perceptions of real life, in the present case behaved irrationally and misperceived the reality of Leah's situation. Whenever she looked at Leah, she apparently saw in her mind's eye the stereotyped picture of a daughter caught in the clutches of a sexually abusive family in which a father and a brother repeatedly raped her while her mother acted as their accomplice. She had no insight into the fact that she was seeing a projection from her own unconscious. We have no idea why this picture was so meaningful to her, but it appears that she was compelled to keep trying to rescue the girl, as if in some way she was identified with her.

The source of the theme or acting out, and hence the reason for the linkage, we must emphasize, are none of our business to speculate about nor to probe. They lie within the private world of a colleague into which we have absolutely no right to trespass. Our concern must remain within the purely professional sphere, identifying the fact that this process is taking place and adopting measures to extract both the clients and the caregiver from the ensuing morass. We should further emphasize that, while it may be tempting to blame the Welfare Officer for her professional misconduct, for the severe psychological, social, and financial damage that this caused to the N. family, and for the waste of public resources that the case created, in fact, she was also a victim both of her own unconscious demons and of the failure of the various authorities with whom she was working to notice that something was awry that required urgent corrective intervention.

☐ Paralysis of Critical Faculties

The signs of lost professional objectivity could be seen in the Welfare Officer's tormented and obsessive preoccupation with Leah and in her inability to see any aspect of the case that did not conform to the preexisting melodramatic script. Her ability and motivation to collect additional data appeared effectively paralyzed, for it will be remembered that she had built her case principally on Leah's stories, or perhaps, on the stories that she had unconsciously manipulated Leah into telling. She did not collect information from the neighbors, the school friends, siblings, or even the teenagers in the pizza parlor, all of whom had, or may have had, insights into Leah's situation. Moreover, nobody followed up on the girl's story of an unknown rapist who had allegedly attacked her. The Welfare Officer was fixated on a particular, unchanging vision of what had happened, even when the central story itself was so illogical as to raise immediate doubts in others. For how could a child be raped repeatedly by so many actors in the presence of three sleeping sisters, none of whom was disturbed by what was allegedly taking place? This blocking out of data that might have cast doubt on the melodrama extended to court hearings in which the Welfare Officer, because of her official and privileged position and with the help of the State attorneys, was able to prevent the witnesses supporting the family from being heard. The paralysis of her critical faculties was all the more noteworthy for occurring in a senior and energetic caseworker who in our earlier joint cases had never shown signs of being similarly inhibited. It was understandable, however, as a feature of an unconscious defensive maneuver, to block out discrepancies in the world of reality that would have disrupted the tenuous match between the irrational theme and Leah's actual circumstances.

☐ A Sense of Doom

Another aspect supporting our conclusion that we were seeing a theme interference was the atmosphere of doom that the Welfare Officer appeared to find in the case. This is a typical and recurring feature in such instances. There was a consequent sense of desperation and urgency in the Welfare Officer's attempts to cling to and rescue the girl. Typical also was the way in which her frantic efforts were unconsciously bringing about the very ruin of the child that she was trying to save.

This desperation grew even more urgent as institutions and other professionals increasingly failed to support her foreboding and her need to punish the father. On several occasions, for example, the Welfare Officer complained publicly about Professor Caplan's support for Mr. N.'s claims of innocence, saying, "I do not understand how a mental health expert of Professor Caplan's status can accept such a distortion of reality." When discussing the case with the lawyer representing the child's family, she said, "It is a pity that Professor Caplan did not retire from practice before he became senile." We realized that the intemperate language of the Welfare Officer was an expression of her complete incomprehension that so erstwhile respected a colleague could doubt the guilt of a father whom she was certain had repeatedly raped his daughter, and could impede the caregiver's efforts to bring this monster to justice.

The Welfare Officer cannot be condemned for suffering from, and displacing unconscious terrors. But her supervisory system failed in its role to be vigilant and to monitor what was happening in the interests of client safety. Eventually the court, police, and others felt that the case, as the Welfare Officer had presented it, made little, if any sense. But by the time the various authorities had begun to wonder, great harm to the family and to Leah had already occurred. If these various agencies had been sensitive to the possibility of such lapses occurring in even an experienced and otherwise competent professional, the damaging process might have been interrupted earlier.

☐ Collusion Between Client and Damaging Professional

One of the many interesting elements in this case was the unconscious collusion between the damaging caregiver and the child. Often, we see iatrogenic damage cases in which the caregiver finds a hook for stereotyping and imposes a prefabricated categorization on a bewildered client who repudiates his or her place in the ensuing picture. In this case, however, we see a kind of folie à deux, in which the child and the Welfare Officer were linked in their theatricality, helping each other to create and act out a phantasmagoric drama that was indeed Kafkaesque—the concrete embodiment of a nightmare. The foster mother apparently sensed this when she watched the interaction between the two, what she referred to as a "sick" and "perverted" interrelationship. The rest of us never had an opportunity to watch this in action. It is unfortunate that in iatrogenic damage cases, while the clients can be tested and their interactions observed professionally, few except for psychoanalysts consider it appropriate or necessary to study the client–caregiver interaction explicitly to see whether it itself may be a contributory factor to the problem.

What is most fascinating from an intrapsychic point-of-view was the way their defensive structures imposed blindness on both the actors. Though what they were doing together in mutual stimulation and arousal was quite obvious once one had gathered enough evidence to see the clearly emerging pattern, they themselves were unable to see it. The foster mother, who was not a mental health specialist, could not believe that a situation that she could see so clearly was not equally obvious and, hence, intentional on the part of the Welfare Officer. She, therefore, saw the relationship as not only "sick," but also exploitative. Those of us who are more accustomed to studying the psychopathology of everyday life will be less surprised by the fact that an experienced professional could be completely unaware of what she was doing. The essence of the defensive mechanism against unconscious intrusions into waking life is precisely this obliviousness of the individual to what he or she is actually doing or saying.

A further generally applicable point should be added here. Professionals must collect data not only to test the reality of an initial impression and to establish the appropriateness of any eventual disposition, but also to enable those in charge of the case to make a credible diagnosis based on what may be only a gradually emerging pattern. The pattern, as in this case, may be surprising and unexpected. Until one had enough dots, as it were, to join into a detailed picture, one could not guess at the central significance in this case of the theater of the absurd, both for the unconscious dramatist and for the actress whose remarkably poised demeanor in court appearances, despite her youth, bespoke her pleasure in any starring role. The basic falsehood of that starring role was not immediately recognized because a third party colluded in the drama. That party was the audience, composed of the rest of the caregiving system and stimulated by the dread words "sexual abuse." It took months, and even years, before the various agencies involved dared to accept that no sexual abuse of the child, certainly by the father, had ever taken place.

☐ Iatrogenic Damaging Behavior Versus the Models of Support During Crisis

Like the instances cited earlier, Leah's case was protracted, lasting several years. Professionals expended a disproportionate amount of their own effort and that of the legal system, and spent considerable sums of public money in pursuit of an inappropriate, preordained end. That such processes are destructive is intuitively obvious. If, however, we recall the characteristics of crisis cited at the beginning of our study, and the determining role that support systems have been seen to play in ameliorating the psychic disequilibrium that such crises induce, we may see more clearly that these harmful, system-induced factors precisely oppose the positive model and thereby increase the risk that the malleability of the crisis state will tend towards a negative pole with corresponding long-lasting repercussions for the client's mental health. It will be remembered that psychosocial support that has been found to lower the risk to mental health (a) lowers the level of emotional reactions such as anxiety, anger, shame, guilt, and others, (b) helps the individual deal with cognitive burdens by guiding him or her to overcome possible confusion and work out effective ways of solving the problems raised by adversity, and (c) helps with the tasks involved in coping with the predicament and provides extra material and financial resources. Iatrogenically harmful caregivers, in contrast, stimulate negative emotions and cognitive confusion and create ever more disequilibrating and exhaustive demands for immediate decisions and actions in people who may already be unable to plan or think clearly because of the pressure under which they already labor. Clients are deprived of resources, both social and material, and the social feedback that is required urgently during a crisis to remind the client of, and restore him or her to a precrisis sense of identity, competence, and worth—the memory of one's own personality is typically and temporarily lost during such upheavals—is here distorted by the negative feedback of damaging caregivers. This further weakens and deprecates the client's sense of his or her historic self. As Leah's mother, reeling between blows, said, "Tell me, we are not the sort of people who beat and rape our children . . . are we?"

If any doubts remained about the N. family, they were resolved by time. Freed from system-induced pressures, the family members recovered. The children gradually adjusted to their new environment. After further legal efforts by her parents, Leah was released to join them. She was later reported to have succeeded particularly well in the local school system and to have renewed a cordial relationship with her family. She repudiated all accounts of mistreatment by her father, saying that the story had been forced on her by the persistent questioning of the welfare worker.

7

Kafka's World

Our next example not only illustrates causes and processes that lead to iatrogenic damage, but also demonstrates why a prominent lawyer who has dealt with scores of such instances told us flatly that no case of this type can ever be won. It illustrates the characteristic Kafkaesque atmosphere of absurdity and blocked exits that is a major feature of institution-sanctioned malfunctioning by damaging caregivers.

Eight years before we encountered this case, Mr. B., a middle class professional of European descent, underwent a radical personality change that, we were told, was never diagnosed or treated, becoming moody and violent towards his wife and child. One evening, Mr. B. suddenly attacked Joe, then aged 7. When his wife, of Middle Eastern descent, interposed herself between them, Mr. B. allegedly tried to kill her, and she was hospitalized with broken bones and concussion. Mr. B. was driven from the house by neighbors, but returned and tried to kidnap Joe, dragging him out of the building. The boy was rescued subsequently by passers-by.

Mrs. B. got a court order distancing her husband from the family. Mr. B., however, continued to harass her by bringing a stream of suits against her in religious and secular courts, demanding access to the boy, and claiming that Mrs. B. was an unfit mother. Every suit swelled the case file, which grew monumental over the years with his charges and her refutations. Although he pleaded guilty to the attack on his wife, Mr. B. was never imprisoned and, as was apparently customary some years ago, before the issue became one that roused public and judicial outrage, he was ordered only to participate in group therapy for those who had committed acts of family violence.

Mr. B., tall and handsome, won the sympathy of Helen, the local child protection and welfare officer. She championed him in repeated court suits, all of which were denied by local judges. When Joe was 9, he contracted mononucleosis, and remained run-down for some months. Helen now attempted to remove him from his mother's custody on the grounds that Joe's lingering malaise was proof of Mrs. B.'s negligence. Mrs. B. managed to mount a successful defense, and subsequently entered an official complaint against Helen and her agency for their handling of the case, a complaint that was officially acknowledged as justified.

Mr. B. and Helen continued to demand that the father be given access to the boy. Helen brought in specialists to say that Joe needed therapy to overcome his reluctance to see his father, and to affirm that his hatred of him and his closeness to his mother constituted a threat to the boy's future mental health. The child refused to engage in any therapy, and since he was above average academically, well-integrated socially, and seemed otherwise to be thriving, the courts let the matter rest.

Mr. B. and Helen, however, remained vigilant, and were rewarded five years after their first attempt to seize him when Joe again became ill. He had recently gained weight and when told by a specialist treating his chronic allergies that he should control his eating, he began to diet. He then contracted a stomach infection and lost his appetite. Alarmed by Joe's weight loss, Mrs. B. took him to the local general hospital to which he was admitted for tests. After a thorough review, the hospital concluded that the weight loss was due neither to any significant physical nor to any psychological abnormalities. He was discharged and ordered by the hospital dietician to eat properly and to report to the outpatient clinic for follow-up. The hospital psychiatrist attested that he suffered from neither anorexia nervosa nor depression caused by tension due to his parents' chronic fighting.

Meanwhile, Mr. B. and Helen had learned of Joe's hospitalization, and Helen had applied to a recently appointed judge to rescind the original order forbidding Mr. B. to approach his family. This the judge did unilaterally, reportedly without informing the family or allowing them to react to Helen's request. Mr. B. then went to the general hospital, where his appearance so upset Joe that the ward staff, who did not like the man's manner, hid the boy and persuaded the father to leave. Helen then appeared and insisted that Joe meet his father, voluntarily or else. Joe refused. When Mr. B. learned that Joe had been discharged, he informed Helen, who visited the boy at home and again insisted that he see his father or be removed from his mother. Mrs. B. was summoned to a court hearing at which the judge announced, "In my court, *all* fathers see their children." Joe became agitated and lost his appetite again. Helen got an order from the judge granting her emergency custody of the boy on the grounds that his weight loss endangered his life. The next night, she arrived at Joe's house with a police escort who dragged the by now hysterical boy away. As they were leaving, Helen returned and allegedly said to Mrs. B., "Don't you dare complain about me this time!"

The police and Helen drove Joe to a mental hospital in a distant city where the admitting psychiatrist interviewed Joe and then told the police that the boy was not mentally ill and he would not authorize hospitalization. Helen tried to force Joe to sign a voluntary admission form although this would have been invalid because of the boy's age. Valid or not, Joe refused to sign. Then Helen phoned the judge, who arrived at the hospital an hour later. By then it was past midnight. A consultation took place behind closed doors, and Joe suddenly found himself hospitalized. The judge assured him that he was only there for tests and would go home the next day. The judge is said to have told the hospital personnel that Helen was in charge of the case and that from now on they were to obey her. In response to later questions, the judge insisted he had only come to the hospital to tell Joe that he was there for his own good.

Joe was kept in a locked ward for the next five months despite all the safeguards enacted to prevent mental hospitals from being used as places of incarceration. He was the youngest child among a group of severely psychotic patients. His stay in the hospital was periodically extended, but always for a different reason—once for "depression;" another time "to prevent the depression that would have occurred had he not been hospitalized;" another time it was "to complete testing;" and another three months extension was for his parents to be tested for "parenting capacity." Some members of the staff told him that he was being held because he was "mentally unstable," and he was told by others that he was normal and would soon be sent home. At no time did he receive any treatment, but he did have regular visits from Helen and from the judge, who tried to persuade him to see his father. According to Joe, the judge told him that his father had never tried to hurt him, but when Joe countered that he certainly had, the judge said that the father had changed and now really loved his son. Joe pointed out that the harassment of himself and his family did not look like love to him. On occasions, Joe was tricked into meeting Mr. B. in the psychologist's office on the pretext that he was going to have yet more psychological tests, but the boy steadfastly refused to speak to his father.

Meanwhile, Helen had returned to the general hospital and had interviewed the psychiatrist who had originally said that Joe was not mentally disturbed. On second thoughts, however, the psychiatrist now provided Helen with a document saying that Joe and his mother had a "harmful symbiotic relationship," a diagnosis that sounded impressive to anyone who did not recognize its absurdity. According to DSM IV, 313.89 (Diagnostic and Statistical Manual of Mental Disorders, 1994), this very rare form of relationship is found among mothers of infants and young children who suffer from "reactive-attachment disorder of infancy and early childhood." Such children usually do not recover and their mothers also suffer from major mental disorder. It is unheard of for a well-adjusted 14-year-old, or for a healthy woman, as Mrs. B. was found to be after exhaustive psychological testing, to be suffering from such a condition.

After Joe had been hospitalized for some weeks, and after Mrs. B. had found that lawyers, journalists, and even members of Parliament were reluctant to get involved—for apparently, like the veteran lawyer cited earlier, they saw the signs of an unsolvable case—she was referred to us. The hospital had agreed that the family could appoint an independent psychiatrist to interview the child, and a time was arranged officially for Professor Caplan to travel to the distant institution. Mrs. B. also found a lawyer who was prepared to represent Joe. When the judge was formally asked to appoint him guardian ad litem, he hesitantly agreed to tolerate his presence but did not make the appointment formal. When the lawyer made himself troublesome with appeals and challenges, the judge removed him from the case and appointed another, more compliant lawyer in his place.

In preparation for his visit to the mental hospital, Professor Caplan had a number of telephone conversations with Joe at the latter's request. In these conversations, Joe asked for help and described the conditions of his incarceration. Professor Caplan was able to ascertain that Joe was well oriented in time and space, and had no impairment of memory, nor did he display any lapses in logical thinking. On the morning of the planned visit, the mental hospital authorities cancelled the appointment, on Helen's orders. The Welfare Officer had forbidden any outside intervention. Later it appeared that Joe had not been told that this anticipated meeting had been cancelled, and he had been left wondering why he had been let down.

Whatever scanty material now existed about Joe's mental state was brought to an Appeals Court that refused to intervene.

As a result of this abortive attempt to free Joe, the conditions under which he was held were restricted further and the treatment to which he was now subjected was punitive. He was denied access to a phone for some time, and his mother's visits were reduced to one hour per week and allowed only in the presence of a member of staff. While the other, severely disturbed patients were allowed visitors and trips home for weekends and holidays, Joe was confined to the ward. When Joe demanded to know why he alone, among all his roommates, was not allowed home for a religious holiday, he was allegedly told that if he were to cooperate with the tests he might be let out for the next holiday in a month's time. He was also told that his situation would improve if he would agree to see his father. When he asked his mother why his family, unlike those of all the other patients, had not attended a ward party (the family had been forbidden to visit), Joe told her that apparently the people in the hospital were correct when they said that he had better cooperate with those who had his true interests at heart, because, they had told him, his mother's absence proved that she did not love him enough to visit him at a time when he needed her so badly.

Like most local children, Joe was ashamed of being associated with a psychiatric diagnosis and was afraid that his friends would learn of his plight, which further isolated him and protected those holding him. His severely ill roommates advised Joe that if he were to attempt suicide, as some of them had done, the hospital might let him visit his family, as they were allowed to do. Joe reported this to his mother as a possible option, but she was able to dissuade him from taking any rash steps.

By then the conditions under which Joe was being held could have been expected of themselves to cause depression and other forms of mental disorder. The fact that no outside experts had been permitted unrestricted and ongoing contact which would have allowed systematic monitoring of Joe's condition provided those holding him with a measure of defense against claims for malpractice and damages of which they had already been notified by Joe's lawyer, since if the boy had become depressed no date of onset could have been ascertained. There was also an attempt to impugn the validity of, and to mock, the earlier telephone contacts by means of which Joe's mental capacities had been assessed as probably normal by outside psychiatric and legal experts. In this way, Joe had been rendered progressively more isolated and hence more vulnerable to manipulation by those incarcerating him. If he had broken down, he would have been further weakened in his capacity to test reality and to maintain hope.

According to some children we have seen who were awaiting adoption and who were old enough to describe their experiences in the secret shelters in which such candidates are kept, some elements in

Joe's incarceration were not unusual. These children reported the same isolation from relatives, and the same insinuations that longed-for visits from parents did not take place because the family did not love them. They also understood that they were expected to comply with the demands of powerful adults to wean the child away from earlier attachments in order to create for him or her a new future. In this case, Joe proved to have more ego strength than most, and refused to give in.

The hospital staff showed increased discomfort with the situation, and there were those among them who privately admitted to Joe and his mother that there was no reason to keep him. Nevertheless, with Helen's insistence, the regimen of "testing" continued. The hospital then allowed Joe an overnight visit home for a holiday. He was told to report back the next afternoon. At 7 a.m. on the morning of the day he was supposed to return, Helen called the family in fury. They were to return the child at once or face imprisonment for contempt of court. Joe returned, heartbroken at having his first visit home in months suddenly and arbitrarily cancelled. Gradually, however, more visits home were allowed by the hospital authorities. During one such trip, he came to our office for a 2-hour diagnostic session that showed that the boy was indeed mentally stable, even after all the trauma he had endured. Transcripts of the session were submitted to an Appeals Court, but since the case was still pending in the lower court, the superior Court refused to act.

After five months of vain attempts on one side to force the boy to see his father, and on the other to gain his release by appeals to every court and agency that could be approached, Helen decided to move Joe to a boarding school for problem children. During the time of hospitalization, Joe had received no formal schooling, except for the assignments that his mother was able to bring him from his classroom teacher. Joe refused to go to the boarding school and said that he wanted to go home. Helen told him that his protests were irrelevant; he would be taken by force. On his next visit home, he ran away. His mother insisted that she did not know where he was. She was jailed twice and told that she faced long-term imprisonment for kidnapping unless she divulged her child's whereabouts.

☐ Typical Features of This Case

So far, this case synopsis raises a number of crucial issues, not only about the nature of those forces which promote iatrogenic damage, but also about the difficulty of combating it. We see here, as in the earlier examples, a preexisting intention to seize a child, irrespective of his or her actual situation. Typically, there was a long gestation period when the family was watched for any changes in their circumstances that could be turned into grounds for official action. When the child was taken, the family attempted to refute the immediate grounds for the seizure, not realizing that they were basically irrelevant, since the reason lay elsewhere. This lends to these cases their typical absurd, Kafkaesque quality, as we have seen in cases cited earlier. The grounds for seizure present themselves deceptively as being due to the child's weight loss, or the mother's incompetence, when, as the social worker admitted to Joe's lawyer during a court recess, she knew perfectly well that the boy's life was in no danger and that he was not disturbed. She wanted him institutionalized only because she did not feel that his relationship with his mother was healthy. The other Kafkaesque feature is that there is never any exit, only mirages of escape in the next court hearing or the next meeting of experts about the case. Effectively, these serve no purpose except to wear down resistance, create appearances of due process, and exhaust with false hopes until resources are used up and the clients capitulate.

An obvious element in this case is that the actual welfare of the child and his family was disregarded. At the outset, when the court granted custody to the Welfare Officer, the boy was mentally healthy, socially and academically successful, and well integrated into a mutually supportive extended family. The result of the intervention was to stop his educational progress, disrupt his social ties, subject him to protracted humiliation and isolation, and to eventually leave him a fugitive hiding out in situations of possibly real danger and privation. His family was financially ruined and subject to repeated and arbitrary police questioning and arrest. This havoc was created with considerable official effort, in part by influencing professionals to revise earlier opinions so that they would fit with the requirements of the social worker's case.

It is characteristic of such cases that the negative assessment of the child and his situation was supported by experts chosen by the Welfare Officers, since the latter apparently exercise the power to veto the appointment of witnesses of whom they do not approve. A judge who had sat on many adoption and child protection cases told us that long ago he had been struck by the fact that social workers always insisted on evaluative reports from "our" psychologists and "our" psychiatrists. By coincidence, the judge said sardonically, "our" experts invariably supported the conclusions of the social worker in every respect, a fact that had raised the suspicions of this judge, though, not apparently, of some of his colleagues. Once a body of "our" experts have answered every challenge by the family by coming to the same conclusions as the child protection or adoption workers, the file becomes a heavy, unassailable weapon that can convince even skeptical appeals judges by its sheer volume. These experts have an incentive to collaborate with the authorities, because they may then have a lucrative practice from a steady stream of referrals. If they do not produce the "correct" assessment, they will be blacklisted and their reputations may be impugned. The reports of experts that bolster cases of iatrogenic harm are commonly marked by jumps in logic. The conclusions flow not from the material described as gathered in the investigation, but from the requirements of the agency. We have been in cases where it was made clear to us in advance what findings were expected, and there was considerable chagrin when we did not oblige.

In Joe's case, the formalities of the boy's hospitalization ran counter to an entire body of legislated safeguards of the civil liberties of those committed to mental hospitals. When the child ran away, the mother was incarcerated, and then threatened with kidnapping charges which, according to a very senior judicial figure, was absurd. The use of various gagging methods to silence and mislead the media and anyone else who tried to intervene was systematic. As long as the case was continued, laws of sub judice and the secrecy prevailing in all cases involving juveniles made it difficult to discuss openly. Furthermore, power resided with the court of first instance. As long as the judge continued the case interminably, the senior appeals judges would not intervene because their colleague was still deliberating and there was no final judgment that could be reviewed. As a retired justice told us, "You are stuck with the judge."

☐ Judges and Welfare Officers

The judge was apparently a compliant partner in the tidying of untidy ends until the case began to have an outward coherence. For example, a glowing report about the boy by his school was concealed by court order. The teachers and principal told the mother secretly what they had written. When a psychologist gave her opinion that as a result of testing the father, she felt that he was so problematic that she recommended that the child not be forced to meet him, the evidence was deprecated. From the start, when the judge, himself divorced, declared, "In my court, *all* fathers see their children," he, like the social worker, had predetermined the outcome.

His original common cause with the social worker was not unusual.

In a survey of hundreds of files of cases involving children, a lawyer examined the relative weight given by judges to expert testimony from psychiatrists and psychologists and from welfare officers. He found that the welfare officers' testimony was overwhelmingly preferred because the judge concluded that the social workers were the real experts about the realities of the particular case. While other experts might have more and broader theoretical knowledge, judges reasoned that the social worker had direct knowledge of the individual family members, their physical and social environment, and the changes in their patterns of life over time. This would have been valid if the social workers had actually covered the field in a fair and comprehensive manner. However, in case after case, we have heard clients say, "The social workers wrote lies about us. They never bothered to talk to us or visit us. Let them ask the neighbors whether we did thus and so. . . ."

Even independently minded judges may be worn down by the weight of their caseloads, which in family, divorce, and juvenile courts at least are backbreaking. When faced with piles of complex, ambiguous files of highly fraught relationships and emotional charges and counter-charges, an unambiguous pronouncement by a welfare officer can be enticing.

The tendency for judges to trust the evidence of social workers may be increased in courts that specialize in juvenile and family cases, since these judges may have regular contact with the same group of welfare officers to which they may then become accustomed and whose style and values they may come to accept as normative. Especially if the social workers are experienced and the judges are either newly appointed or have been chosen from the ranks of state attorneys with a history of working cooperatively with welfare officers, the chance of judges and social workers sharing a point-of-view may increase and may endanger the impartiality of the legal opinion. A tendency to be unduly swayed by welfare and child protection workers may be enhanced, as a famous American civil liberties lawyer told us, by the worry of some judges that they may be vulnerable on appeal or may be held responsible if the child's situation deteriorates. If they accept the opinion of the social workers, they can counter criticism by pointing out that they had no reason to doubt the word of the person whose official role is to serve as the direct investigative instrument of the state in such cases. The judge could then legitimately claim that he or she had no means to check the data that the social worker was presenting. If, however, the judge were to overrule the social worker, and the case were to deteriorate, he or she might be directly criticized.

☐ A Failure to Find Help

To return to Joe. No judicial appeals could reverse the situation, so we turned to a number of other agencies. The governmental mental health establishment, when asked to intervene, said that the hospital was obligated to obey the court and should be permitted to conduct their tests of parenting capacity at their own rate. In fact, after Joe's disappearance, the hospital did produce a report that concluded that Joe was sane and that he should not be forced to associate with his father.

This case eventually became notorious in legal and psychiatric circles. While many professionals examined the documentation and expressed shock and disapproval of the handling of the case, nobody was prepared to speak out. Lawyers either said openly that it was so tangled that it was beyond their capacities, or they excused themselves by saying that they did not practice in the town where the court sessions took place. Psychologists and psychiatrists of recognized status expressed outrage over the diagnosis of a "harmful symbiotic relationship" and the hospitalization of Joe, but they were not prepared to state their opinion openly. Apparently, nobody wanted to challenge conspicuously the tacit alliance of colleagues, the Welfare department, and the judiciary, whose combined power was daunting.

☐ An Unexpected Continuation to the Case

Strange and damaging as was the treatment of Joe and his mother up to the time the boy ran away, the development of the case grew ever more Kafkaesque. Some months later, the quarry was found, not by the police, but by a private detective hired by the welfare officer herself. When Joe was detained, it turned out that his mother had known of his whereabouts all along, and she was promptly imprisoned again for contempt of court and for "interfering with a welfare officer in the execution of her duty." The judge then ordered the boy to move into his father's home until he could be admitted to the closed institution for problem children that Helen had designated. The guardian ad litem chosen by the judge told the boy to do as he was told, and Joe was moved to his father's house. To Joe's surprise, his father did not attack him, and a measure of contact was established between them. Joe was later transferred to the boarding school by order of the judge, who was reported, by Joe, to have told him, "Unless you do as you are told, I will use my power to force you; and I have a lot of power." From the boarding school, he was sent periodically to visit his father, and he now complied.

At this point, the judge and welfare officer could claim that their intervention had succeeded. During a court recess, Joe's mother overheard the social worker on her cellular phone telling the apparently skeptical psychologist at the mental hospital about her success. "I know it's unbelievable," she said, "but I have actually managed to get the boy and the father together. I know you thought it was impossible, but I've really done it." Apparently, Joe no longer regarded his father as an ogre, and the wall separating father and son had been breached. The social worker and the judge could now announce that their methods of forcing the boy to relate to his father had succeeded, and their questionable methods might therefore inspire imitation among colleagues.

☐ The Price of "Success"

However, this apparently heart-warming ending had been accomplished at a price so high that we might ask how much had been gained and how much had been lost. The mother was imprisoned, and later put under house arrest. She and her family were forbidden, on pain of massive fines, to communicate in any way with Joe or to discuss the details of the case with any outsiders. She was already heavily in debt and unable to work. Joe was now a public charge, institutionalized among problem youth. He was still cut off from extended family and friends, humiliated and angry, with a major shadow over his educational, social, and occupational future because of this "shameful" episode that documented doubts about his sanity.

Joe suffered from the disturbed population of his classmates, and after some months, he wrote a letter to the judge, at the latter's instigation, begging to be sent to live with his father because he found conditions in the boarding school unendurable. According to the boy, the judge had instructed Joe to write the letter if he wanted the judge to consider releasing him from the institution. Joe complied, thinking that once he got back to his home town, he would soon be reunited with his mother and the extended family. In fact, Joe now found himself permanently domiciled with Mr. B. At the next court hearing, Helen petitioned the judge for an extension of her emergency custody of Joe until he was eighteen. Joe asked his guardian ad litem to say that he wanted the custody terminated and wanted to return to his mother. The guardian stated his request in the briefest terms, and then remained silent for the rest of the hearing. The judge postponed ruling, thereby freezing the situation. Joe concluded that the judge had realized that he had made mistakes in the case and was not sure how to extract himself.

☐ What Lay Beneath the Surface

Beneath the carefully erected facade of the heart-warming reunion of father and son, Joe's situation, as he described it to us, failed to fit the normative picture of a child's best interests. According to Joe, Mr. B. left for work at 7 a.m., and returned at 6 p.m. After a short time at home, he went out again for the evening, where or with whom Joe neither knew nor cared. For the whole day, Joe was unsupervised. He truanted from school because he was ashamed of his experiences and dreaded the questions of schoolmates about his unaccountable absence. His father could not enforce his son's attendance and worried that he would be declared guilty of not sending the boy to school, which amused Joe. However, since only a few months remained before his compulsory schooling ended at 16, the authorities may have decided to overlook this breach of law. In the absence of a formal framework, Joe spent his days as he liked, wandering the town vacantly and watching television. Nobody cooked for him. Father and son picked up what each liked to eat in the local supermarket and each fended for himself. Joe associated with no friends. He knew the neighbors in his father's building only by sight. Had he become ill during the day, he had nobody to turn to. As he said with a shrug, "I would manage; I'd take an aspirin."

Although they occupied the same dwelling, Joe said that he and Mr. B. led separate lives, and barely communicated. Joe despised his father whom he now saw as a weak, vacillating bully, who was unable to take any action without consulting authority figures like Helen. Joe, however, was careful not to reveal his hatred for Mr. B. openly, because he was afraid that, were he to do so, in some way retribution would be visited on his mother. On the whole, he remained optimistic, since, as he said, he was no longer locked up, and with time, his situation could only improve. Others, however, worried about what might happen to a naive, unsupervised adolescent who might be taken advantage of by vagrants, or who might become an opportune suspect of street crimes in which he had no part. Ensuring his safety and welfare, the job of the child protection system, was in default. A possible solution was suggested, however, after analyzing the mechanisms that had led to professional malfunctioning.

It was clear that no further appeal could be made to the legal system based on the present neglect of the child. The probable outcome could not be the boy's return to his mother or to another relative, because Helen and the judge were too invested in supporting the father's claim to Joe. The only option would have been to return him to a closed institution, which he opposed. Analyzing the situation, it was realized that one of the reasons for the intractable and apparently illogical position of the social worker and judge in this case was the noncompliance of Joe and his mother. As we have already noted, noncompliance by aggrieved clients is apt to polarize the position of caregivers. The more determined Joe and his mother were to get free and to seek redress, the more threatening the social worker and judge became, apparently to assert their own power against opposition, but also, perhaps, to protect themselves against appeals to higher authorities. Recognizing this issue of noncompliance, and remembering that the only redress in extreme cases is escape from the system, since the system's own safeguards had failed, led Joe and his mother to consider pretending compliance by stopping open opposition to the judge and the social worker. Instead, it was suggested, Joe could be helped to create a secret life within the vacuum left by his father's neglect. A cousin could rent an apartment to which Joe could be given the key, and where clean clothes and cooked food could be left regularly. It could be arranged for him to be enrolled in a make-up program for school dropouts in a neighboring city so that he could matriculate and have social contacts. As far as Mr. B., the judge, and the social worker were concerned, Joe could be idling away his time harmlessly in his father's house. In fact, he might now take advantage of the freedom afforded by neglect to reestablish a substitute life. There were serious constraints, however. He could not communicate with his mother or her family because of the danger of discovery that would lead to her imprisonment and to massive fines.

This possible solution meant leading a double life, hardly an optimal educational experience for any adolescent, though it no doubt had its age-appropriate attractions as an adventure and as an exercise in self-sufficiency. It would not be unique. We know of an adoption case in which a child old enough to remember the phone number of a supposedly abusive parent secretly initiated contact because of the child's dislike and distrust of the adoptive family. For years, mother and child met secretly, behind the backs of the adoptive parents and the authorities, none of whom could have been expected to react positively to such a situation.

A year later, we had holiday greetings from the principals in Joe's case. The plan for a secret life had not materialized. Joe had dropped out of school and was roaming the streets. He was still domiciled with his father. The judge had made no final rulings that could be appealed. The case lay in limbo until Joe should reach the age of 18.

☐ Lessons to be Learned

As in the case discussed in the previous chapter, it would be easy to dismiss Joe's situation as an example of the child protection system acting as a source of child abuse. That, however, would be a simplistic and sensationalist conclusion that would prevent our noticing the important lessons to be derived from this case.

In the first place, we must note that unlike all the other cases cited, though we were intensively involved with the child and his family, we had no personal contact with this social worker or with this judge. Consequently, we had no opportunity to formulate our own impressions of why they were acting as they did. They fended us off very effectively, and although we submitted diagnostic reports, they refused to accept them or to allow us to testify in court. Since Family Courts, juvenile courts, and Rabbinic courts are closed to outsiders, we could not even attend the proceedings as spectators to draw conclusions from watching their demeanor or style of acting. All our impressions of the two principal movers of events, therefore, were derived or extrapolated from the actual unfolding of the case as we watched it from afar, and from the accounts of lawyers, family members, and the boy himself.

Therefore, we cannot discuss the possible source of the malfunctioning of the social worker. We can, however, question the role of her supervisory system. It may be remembered that some years before the present episode began, the mother's complaints about the agency's and the Welfare Officer's earlier handling of the case had been officially upheld and a reprimand had been issued. We may wonder what internal conclusions were drawn from this, and what, if any administrative consequences or investigation had taken place around the individual social worker. Why, we may wonder, was the same social worker permitted to handle the same case again, and with apparently little or no oversight (at least, none was visible or accessible to any of the highly perturbed observers who tried to interrupt the damage)? Agencies may shrug off even official rebukes, feeling that they are under such intensive pressure from a flood of cases and from unfair detractors that they cannot take the time or effort to follow up on even official reprimands, let alone the complaints of private individuals. This, however, would be a most shortsighted policy, since it would guarantee that no lessons would be drawn to improve agency functioning or to upgrade the quality of staff performance. In the long run, agency efficiency, let alone the quality of service to the public, would only be improved by, for example, eliminating the wastage caused by compulsively pursuing cases that do not merit intervention.

As for a system that does not monitor caregivers who fail in certain types of cases, permitting them to return to already documented damaging behavior; that is not as unusual as we may want to believe. Even the British General Medical Council has found to its cost and that of countless unfortunate patients that some physicians who have been struck off the rolls for a certain period have managed to be reinstated, to cover up their past history, and again to perpetrate damaging actions. A large, nationwide institution may have understandable difficulties keeping track of thousands of individual members, especially if the latter actively hide their tracks. It should not, however, be beyond the capacities of a local or regional welfare office to know its core staff and their performance records well enough to avert such situations, as long as they regard it as a worthwhile and rational administrative priority.

The second principal in Joe's unhappy fate was the judge, whom, once again, we never encountered personally. We gathered from others, however, that the latter was new to the bench and, depending on how one interprets "In my court, *all* fathers see their children," either biased (being himself divorced), idealistic, or naive. Joe's assessment was that the judge was not a bad person at all, only an inexperienced one who had been influenced by the more senior and plausible social worker who "knew the ropes" as the new judge may not have done. Once the judge had begun to make mistakes, Joe concluded, he did not know how to extract himself, and made ever more blunders in an effort to compensate for, and cover the ensuing mess. Certainly, the judge is alleged to have acted in unorthodox ways that alarmed senior jurists whose advice was asked, as when he went to the mental hospital and to the boarding school to see the boy. These veterans on the bench were startled to learn that any judge was acting outside his courtroom and off the official record of the court protocol. However, while this might be seen as flouting necessary judicial conventions, it could also be seen as a genuine concern for Joe, or possibly as a sign of lost professional objectivity.

The plight of the judge in this case may have been a function of the fact that he sat alone, apparently with only the social worker to advise him. Such isolation would not have occurred in the Rabbinic court, for example, where panels of three judges sit, supporting and challenging each other, and where the membership of these panels is often mixed by age and experience. Thus, younger judges, while having an equal voice in deliberating, are nevertheless serving an implicit tutelage under more senior rabbis who have long ago internalized the rules, procedures, and workable methods of evaluating conflicting evidence. This mixing of levels of experience can have a paradoxical effect from our mental health point-of-view, for we have noticed that these younger, less experienced Rabbinic judges can be more open to the psychological suffering of clients than are the veteran judges, who may have been desensitized by years of exposure to cases. The latter's professional distance, therefore, may be offset to the benefit of clients by the still raw sensibilities of the younger men. Thus, the system often has a fortuitous internal balance that may foster positive features not necessarily anticipated by the formal rules.

In this respect, it may be instructive to mention an episode that occurred many years ago, a discussion overheard in the staff dining room of the Children's Hospital in Boston. A group of young physicians had just been watching Robertson's landmark film, *A Two-Year-Old Goes to Hospital*, which shows the suffering of the child so poignantly that it caused a revolution in the treatment of hospitalized children in Britain. The young doctors were engaged in a heated debate. One group had been deeply upset by what they had seen. Another group apparently had been unmoved by the child's misery, but were angrily denouncing those who would draw general conclusions and advocate changing established hospital procedures because of a single, unrepresentative case. It gradually became clear that the first group was composed of pathologists who worked in the laboratories and had little contact with patients on the wards. They reacted to the film with normal sensitivity and vulnerability. The second group were ward pediatricians who had developed a professional distance that had enabled them to function effectively despite the sufferings of their patients. Their normal human sensitivities had been anesthetized by constant exposure and by the necessity of overcoming inhibitions to causing pain that might have interfered with their operational effectiveness. Many categories of caregiving professionals have to maintain a balance between these emotional poles if they are to function effectively, while also maintaining sufficient empathy to prevent a callous obliviousness to the clients' pain. The judge in Joe's case, about whom we are necessarily speculating, may have been struggling with this dilemma, and may have been doing so without an adequately supportive framework. His response in the apparent absence of avenues for getting proper help and advice seemed to be to rely on the defensive maneuvers of imposing ever greater secrecy on proceedings that were spinning ever more out of control.

☐ A Parallel Case

Had we been naive enough to believe that Joe's case was unique, we would have been disabused by other stories of sane children being hospitalized in mental institutions at the insistence of welfare departments. One example was an account of a case of a "Kafkaesque Nightmare," that appeared in the *Ha'aretz* newspaper of 5/1/2000 (Rotem,

2000). The unusual press coverage, which is normally very hard to stimulate in cases involving juveniles and the caregiving system, apparently came about because, as members of the recently arrived Ethiopian community, this child's family was able to enlist the help of influentials who lobby for the rights of this immigrant group.

R. was a nine-year-old who, unlike Joe, but apparently like a significant number of fellow immigrant youths, had major adjustment problems that, apparently, had not been effectively addressed by the educational and welfare system. He truanted frequently, was unable to read or write, and hung out with a gang who sometimes vandalized school facilities. He thereby came to the attention of the local welfare department, which removed him from home to an emergency shelter in another city. A few days later, when the boy reacted violently to the move, he was allowed to go home. The newspaper account (Rotem, 2000) continues as follows.

> At the start of November, social welfare case workers turned up again in juvenile court; and Judge Dalia Keren sent R. for a week-long period of psychiatric observation. A social welfare officer, accompanied by policemen, arrived late one night to forcibly bring the boy for this diagnosis at the Eitanim institution. Contrary to the original order, R.'s stay at this psychological facility lasted longer than a month. Two weeks of this extension were approved by another court order, and then R. remained for yet two more weeks because the social worker went on maternity leave, and the boy was simply forgotten in the institution.

According to the newspaper,

> When the child's mother got help from the Ethiopian community worker from a local help association, the director-general of this local agency, Tikva Levi, was quoted as follows, "I visited the boy at Eitanim (a mental hospital), and he was in a desperate state. Who would place a normal boy amongst ill children? That wasn't the place for him."

Paradoxically R. was luckier than native-born Joe because his mother could get help from those assisting the integration of her community into Israeli life. Their intercession led to R.'s release both from hospital, and from the boarding school to which he, like a disproportionate number of other allegedly troubled Ethiopian children were being routinely sent. The judge permitted R. to return home for a trial period. However, people trying to help the boy were concerned that influentially placed agencies, including the Welfare department, might not abandon their preconceived plans.

> Tikva Levi believes that the "success of the boy's recovery depends, among other things, on the good will of the municipality, particularly

that of the social welfare department officials who originally wanted to forgo giving care, and sought to remove him." Levi is worried that these officials are not committed to giving R. a second chance. She fears that they are waiting to seize a pretext to fulfill their original plan of sending the boy to an institution away from his home in Ramle. (Rotem, 2000)

Ms. Levi's fears are well placed, not only because of the histories of other children caught in what the reporter calls R.'s "Kafkaesque Nightmare" where caregivers seem determined to carry out preexisting stereotyped plans, but also because such plans reflect a value system apparently shared by a variety of caregivers from different fields, so that children who try to improve their behavior begin with two strikes against them. As the article continues, the guidance counselor at the Ben-Gurion school from which R. had truanted, and where he had failed to learn to read and write,

> makes the boarding school sound like utopia. [Sounding] sceptical of the likelihood that R.'s current provisional arrangement will succeed, Sofer [the counselor] says that "In R.'s case, it is imperative to separate him from his home. You separate him for a year, you sever him from the local surroundings that have influenced him, and then later he can begin anew."

The myth of rebirth in new surroundings that we encountered in the case of closed adoption and that characterized the "philanthropic abductions" of the nineteenth-century poor reemerges to justify the removal of disadvantaged and troubled immigrant children to boarding schools. In the case of Ethiopian children (who represent a third of the pupils in such institutions), there is a dropout rate of 20% in ninth grade (Rotem, 2000). According to Uri Temiat, the director-general of the Israel Association for Ethiopian Jews, R.'s troubles are a symptom of the general neglect of these children.

> He (Temiat) thinks that the indiscriminate policy of sending troubled youngsters from this community to boarding schools is an attempt to sweep a social issue under the rug. In the past, he explains, there was a policy of automatically sending Ethiopian children to boarding schools. Today, with dropout rates from such institutions no secret . . . and with many of their students embroiled in substance abuse . . . it's clear that this policy was misguided. (Rotem, 2000)

Tikva Levi added: "Sending the child away to a boarding school is a lot simpler than dealing with him in his own community" (Rotem, 2000).

☐ Institutional Cocooning of Damaging Behavior

Among the cases we have cited, there is a progression not only in the severity of outcome and the amount of damage generated, but also in the degree of culpability of the damaging caregivers. That progression ranges from those who are doing their job badly because of poor understanding, skill, or objectivity, to those who are being forced into malfunction by unconscious drives, to those who are acting with conscious intent, using their position to distort the principles of humane, professional functioning. The latter category of damaging caregivers is in many ways the most troublesome, since they are often determined and skilled in achieving the goals of their hidden agenda whether because of ideology or because of narcissistic needs. Moreover, we must not assume that such damaging workers are always examples of eccentric individual behavior. On the contrary, they may be following normative standards and guidelines. When the judge in the case of R., for example,

> criticized social welfare authorities for the way they handled the boy's case, Galit Hevan, the director of the Ramle social services, denies that R.'s treatment was flawed. She claims that the utmost was done for the boy, and the policy derived from purely professional calculations; and she refused to elaborate in detail on this case, on privacy and professional grounds. (Rotem, 2000)

The Difficulties of Preventing Iatrogenic Damage

Our commitment to primary preventive community psychiatry has led us to identify iatrogenic damage as a significant hazard that increases the risk of ongoing psychosocial distress in the population, especially among those families that are already vulnerable because they are disrupted and may be socially marginal. For these clients especially the added stress of being victimized, unconsciously or not, by caregivers who ostensibly exist to help them can be disproportionately devastating. It is therefore within our legitimate role to attempt to derive some orderly and feasible methods to understand and reduce the incidence of this phenomenon and to support both clients and caregivers who are enmeshed in its processes.

☐ How Prevalent and Salient Is Iatrogenic Damage?

It may be asked, however, whether iatrogenic damage is common enough to warrant so much attention, or whether it should be regarded as the inevitable by-product of dealing with large numbers of extremely difficult cases, a percentage of which are liable to fail in some way. In our own practice, 8–10% of the cases sent to us fall into the category of victims of iatrogenic damage, and these absorb a disproportionate amount of staff time and effort. But since we are seeing a skewed sample of particularly difficult cases in general, our impressions of prevalence may not mirror the true, overall picture. Colleagues in a number of countries have said that there are "a lot" of such cases, but again, this is only an impression, and hardly a statistic.

☐ Defining the Category

One of the curious features of this issue, and one that apparently precluded its being addressed in an organized manner, is how rarely professionals have identified this as a distinct category with consistent patterns. While many colleagues say they have encountered examples of iatrogenic harmful behavior, apparently they have tended to view these as isolated or unique phenomena. There have been periodic discussions of organized instances of large-scale damaging behavior, usually brought to light long after the events involved, like the Swedish program of forced sterilizations of "defective" children, or the exporting of children from post–World War II English slums to Australia; or the suspicions about the fate of vanished Yemenite babies in Israel in the 1950s, believed by their community to have been spirited away for adoption. Yet to our knowledge, nobody has linked such episodes by identifying common ideological and methodological issues, or has suggested that similarities of mind set and organization may exist between these events and individual cases of harmful professional intervention that, on a smaller scale, appear to be driven by a similar dynamic.

Concerned professionals who encounter instances of iatrogenic damage apparently have been reluctant to talk about them, perhaps because they doubt their own perceptions, or feel that nobody would believe that such "absurd" situations could exist. Perhaps they are reluctant because they are wary of appearing disloyal and of threatening the reputation of individual colleagues, perhaps because they fear antagonizing powerful, well-organized groups of professionals, or perhaps because they feel that the system is indifferent to, and powerless against the Kafkaesque situations that legal and caregiving bureaucracies erect to enforce their preplanned disposition of certain cases. For whatever reason, we have noticed that caregivers who have noted and been disturbed by cases of system-induced damage are relieved to learn that they are not alone in their sightings, and that their world of practice is not more irrational and unjust than what is to be found in other places. We have noticed also that once these apparently absurd phenomena are given a name and a pattern is extrapolated by which they can be identified and categorized, concerned professionals feel more confidant about what they themselves are seeing. They may then be better able to discover ways to prevent the damage that such cases generate, and perhaps to find internal mechanisms within professional groups and agencies to lower the incidence of damaging behavior.

☐ A Problem Worth Solving

Whatever the actual rate of iatrogenic damage may be, we may accept that a percentage of failures in case management is statistically inevitable, (for despite our belief in practicing primary prevention, we know perfectly well that we cannot eliminate all psychosocial stressors, but can only try to reduce their incidence). On the other hand, we may feel that even if the rate of casualties is statistically insignificant, it would still be unacceptable not to try and lower it.

The issue of preventing iatrogenic damage is not only a matter of a particular professional commitment, nor is it only a matter of preventing suffering in a larger or smaller number of individual clients, it is also a matter of pragmatism. When the British General Medical Council put so major an effort into attempting to redirect the attitudes of thousands of licensees in order to forestall damage and insult to patients, they were responding not only to isolated, though alarming, incidents in which doctors caused harm. Serious as these incidents were and great as was the threat to future patients if malfunctioning practitioners (including alcoholic surgeons, laboratory workers and pathologists who misinterpreted data, and even a mass murderer), had remained unchecked, the British General Medical Council was also attempting to restore wavering public and government confidence in an entire profession and its regulatory institutions. The policy issues involved in controlling iatrogenic damage, therefore, go beyond reducing the actual number of unfortunate victims, present and potential. Since the subject affects public trust and support of caregiving frameworks, it is worth investing considerable effort to control malfunctioning individuals and systems, even if it should turn out that a relatively small number of cases are actually harmed.

☐ Complications in Identifying Iatrogenic Damage

If preventing iatrogenic damage in nontechnological caregiving systems had been easy, the many frameworks established to control malpractice and ethical lapses would have succeeded in curbing most instances long ago. The problem is that there are major obstacles in the way of forestalling damage that, initially at least, may not be obvious.

The first of these obstacles involves the fact that the source of psychological damage is often difficult to prove and to ascribe to a particular intervention. Especially in cases where caregivers enter a case in response to a real or supposed trauma which itself may be expected to produce psychic and social disturbance, it may be difficult to prove that a particular aspect of professional malfeasance accounts for the client's deterioration. Moreover, unlike the field of physical medicine, where particular mistakes are known to produce not only measurable, but also often inevitable damage, psychosocial interventions give variable results over a variable time span. What works well in one case may be catastrophic in another. For example, certain children who have been alienated from one parent may ultimately be immeasurably relieved when the breach is healed, despite initial reluctance and fears about restoring contact. In other cases, as we have seen, the same situation handled initially at least in an apparently similar way, can lead to considerably less encouraging results. Whether a technique should be tried or persisted in every outwardly similar situation may be a matter of experience and sophistication beyond the capacities of the relatively poorly trained workers on the front line of caregiving.

Another problem in identifying iatrogenic damage comes from the fact that obtrusive cases tend to occur in problematic populations that attract the attention of child protection services and the courts in disproportionate numbers, populations such as socially deviant and disrupted families. These cases are not only emotionally burdensome and liable to stir up unconscious antipathies and conflicted feelings in caregivers, but they may also involve the type of clients who are duplicitous, quarrelsome trouble makers, and who, whatever may be the objective quality of the care given by professionals, will complain and portray themselves as injured innocents. But they may also rouse such anger and confusion in caregivers that the latter may be moved against all judgment and training to take improper actions that in calmer moments they themselves may deplore.

Drawing on ambiguous events in his own relations with patients, a Canadian psychoanalyst, John A. Sloane, in an article on "Offenses and Defenses Against Patients: A Psychoanalyst's View of the Borderline Between Empathic Failure and Malpractice" (1993), points out that caregivers are being faced by impossible demands, attacks, and seductions to abuse from severely disturbed clients whom therapists are obliged to help despite the subjective and objective dangers of so doing. In the client's desperate need, the inability of a caregiver to give enough empathy, support, and love becomes inevitably but inescapably damaging.

Because of the increasing use of litigation, clients may sue for what they see irrationally as unsatisfactory service by a caregiver. The latter may then find himself or herself unbearably beleaguered, humiliated, and punished as a result of complaints filed by grossly disordered clients. In this regard we must realize that we too are in danger of losing our own objectivity when we are told an "impossible" and harrowing tale of abuse at the hands of the caregiving system. Indeed, a case may be just that—impossible—the product of the diseased imagination of a seemingly plausible client. In our eagerness to help a distressed member of the community, we must beware of engaging in the same style of stereotyped thinking and the tendency to demonize that characterizes damaging professionals, and in our credulity, thereby become damaging in our turn.

If it cannot be agreed who is doing the damage, and what, if any, damage is being done, it is clearly difficult to create unified programs to deal with nontechnical iatrogenic harm. This is made even more difficult by the fact that any mention of the issue tends to raise hackles, as the professionals involved may feel that their "sacred mission" is being jeopardized by ill-informed and ill-natured outsiders. Thus the very broaching of the problem is apt to precipitate a battle with those entrenched in power positions. They may view the prospect of intervention meant to prevent iatrogenic damage with the same irrational expectation of doom that characterizes a theme interference. When we told one professional in a policy-making position about our interest in studying and preventing iatrogenic damage, she said, in horror, "Do you want to tear the whole country apart?"

☐ Falsification

As we have already noted, whatever its cause, the presence of potentially damaging professional behavior may be identified by evidence that the perception of a client's situation is being falsified. This falsification may be due to deliberate development of an error-filled, stereotyped file that fits the criteria for intrusive action by the caregiving system in accordance with its own prejudices or needs, or it may be due to an unconsciously triggered blindness to, and inability to examine reality, leading to a consequent false, but good-faith perception of the client. Falsification is also achieved by the deliberate selection of experts and witnesses to support a preexisting view of the outcome in which the caregiver has invested intense personal emotion, interest, and prestige and where judicious professional distance has broken down.

We saw an example of the latter when a highly placed worker in an adoption agency ran out of our office literally in tears at the suggestion that we might interview a child, because, she sobbed, the child would be "destroyed" if we were to mention her mother from whom she had been removed and whom, we had been told by the potential adoptive parents, the child longed to contact. The adoption worker had apparently crafted a false front of appropriateness on a fragile match between the child and a new family, and she did not want her work spoiled by meddlers who might discover, before the legal system could cement the deal, that the whole scheme was unsound. The child's feelings, the adoptive parents' actual compatibility and depth of commitment, and, indeed, the mother's real parenting capacity could not be looked at impartially because scrutiny might lead to disrupting the lovingly constructed edifice in which the worker was invested, irrespective of the well-being of those involved.

In our experience, falsification, deliberate or inadvertent, is a key contributor to the typical Kafkaesque, lost-in-a-labyrinth atmosphere in which victims of iatrogenic damage are enmeshed. Falsification by caregiving professionals in general, and deliberate falsification in particular, is seldom, if ever, written about. It is a particularly sensitive and unpleasant topic to research, not because the data are necessarily hard to find, but because one does not like to impugn the veracity of one's colleagues. Yet we must remember that the high value most of us place on truth, be it for ethical, legal, or scientific reasons, is not universal, but is culturally based, and in certain groups, the opprobrium attached to falsehood lies not so much in its perpetration as in its being discovered and publicly revealed. Moreover, there is a range of gray areas in which many otherwise principled people are apt to sacrifice the truth in order to achieve a goal that they consider paramount.

In the examples of professional malfunctioning that we have described hitherto, the falsification of a client's situation in order to achieve the prefigured end designated by caregivers from their earliest contacts with the case has been central to the damaging process. Most interestingly, in our experience, it has generally proved impossible to correct the ensuing damage caused by these inaccuracies. How harm caused by falsification becomes indelible can be seen in the following example, one of our earliest and most disturbing and disillusioning encounters with this phenomenon, unusually disturbing, perhaps, because our inexperience at that time with cases of iatrogenic damage made us emotionally vulnerable.

According to the official record composed of file entries and the court testimony of various welfare and adoption workers and their experts, Shoshana, a cleaner of North African ancestry, was unfit to care for or associate with her five children, whose safety, it was said, required that all contact with their mother be severed. Shoshana was said to be significantly retarded, filthy and immoral in her habits, with a home infested by roaches, unable to "set limits" for the children, unable to stimulate their intellectual development, and so impulsive and verbally and physically abusive that her children were all terrified of her. Therefore, it was proposed that the children, all of whom had been recently removed to institutional and foster care, be declared available for adoption.

Our psychological testing of Shoshana showed that she had a number of problems. She had low average intelligence, but was not retarded. She had low impulse control, and a hitherto undiagnosed learning disorder that had probably contributed to her failure to complete her education. Thus, she had remained a cleaning woman while her siblings had successfully risen out of the deprivation into which they had been born to become teachers and small businessmen. Shoshana had attracted, or had been attracted to a series of shiftless men, each of whom had fathered one of her children and had then decamped, leaving her dejected and bitter. Nevertheless, Shoshana had significant positive features. She had never used drugs or alcohol or been accused of any acts of dishonesty. She had been in stable employment by the same people for years; and she was courteous and formal in her manners. One felt that she had been "well brought up." On inspection, her modest apartment turned out to be spotless; and her appearance was tidy. She professed to be deeply attached to her children and was devastated by their loss. She had, therefore, engaged her own lawyer, not one appointed by Legal Aid, and had paid his fee in full out of her wages.

The lawyer made a video of Shoshana interacting with two of her children, a boy of three and a girl of four, during a regularly scheduled visit to their foster family. This film, which lasted for over half an hour, showed the mother unselfconsciously playing with the children, helping them to assemble jigsaw puzzles, and getting them to sing counting rhymes with her. When the children showed signs of being about to squabble, Shoshana intervened firmly but quietly, and explained that siblings must be patient with each other. Throughout, she acted with appropriate physical and emotional warmth, but never smothered the children. Most significant, however, was the way the children related to her, with great affection and physical closeness, and with no hint of the terror that the official file claimed that they manifested in her presence.

The video was shown to two senior pediatricians, both of whom felt that they were watching a normal and healthy mother–child interaction. The foster parents attested to the fact that what was seen was characteristic of their observations of Shoshana's relationship with the children. As a couple who had served as foster parents for years, they had noted that Shoshana never missed a visit, that she always arrived punctually and brought suitable toys and clothes as presents, and that she devoted the whole session to the children rather than to talking to the foster family as, according to their experience, is usual with disturbed parents. "We were surprised," they said, "by how quiet and polite she always is. The welfare workers had told us to be very careful because she is so violent. But in fact, she seems quite normal and always thanks us for taking care of her children." The foster parents also noted that the children looked forward to their mother's visits and were sad when she left.

The lawyer took his video to court. The judge, however, ruled against its being accepted in evidence. The adoption worker had claimed that it had been staged. Had this been true, it would have required no mean acting ability over a sustained period from the supposedly retarded and unaffectionate Shoshana. More significantly, no staged performance could have elicited such authentic, loving behavior from the little children, and it is unlikely that deep-rooted fear could have been so entirely repressed before the camera.

While the video revealed that many of the allegations against Shoshana were doubtful, nevertheless the five children were subsequently divided between three adoptive families, and Shoshana's contact with them was legally terminated. Naive as we were in those days about the processes of iatrogenic damage, we were incredulous at this outcome. For while Shoshana certainly had problems that might have benefited from support, parent education, and some counseling to minimize her impulsiveness, she was not the monster she had been painted, nor did she represent any catastrophic threat to the children with whom she was mutually bonded. But in order to effect the certain removal of the children and their subsequent adoption, those producing the official file had created an unambiguous and compelling case against a supposedly pathological mother that in its many repellant details could admit of no outcome other than her total separation from the children. Significantly, though the main features of this horrific characterization were disputed by a number of qualified observers, the caregivers' version was so constructed and defended that the court accepted the false picture, stereotyped, as we were later to realize it was after we saw many other instances, so that all independent evidence was effectively silenced.

Falsification, however, is a more complex matter than perjured testimony, the biased opinions of chosen experts, or the entry of prejudicial inaccuracies into case records. In iatrogenic damage cases, falsified material can be buried in, and used to support the foundations of an edifice of consequent court judgments and officially sanctioned actions. The ensuing events, generated by, and derived from these false first premises, become embedded in an ever-burgeoning case record. This takes on an independent legitimacy based on the sheer number of entries, many of which may be made by caregivers and their experts in good faith. Those experts, after reading, assumed the accuracy of what earlier contributors had written, and their own judgments about the case were thereby shaped by preexisting documentation the validity of which apparently is often taken for granted. This case record can become virtually unassailable, even with the help of unimpeachable witnesses, and can remain a determining factor in every encounter between the client and the system. We once attended a superior court hearing in which a lawyer was severely reprimanded because he had appealed for an emergency ruling to stop a highly damaging disposition of a child. The justices, who had scheduled the hearing at short notice in order to hear his plea, had been outraged to find that aspects of the fight between the parents and the welfare department had been meandering through the courts for years, thereby generating a gargantuan file. Although this chronicle had little bearing on the present emergency in which the child had been swept up, the justices would not consider this crisis without reviewing the history; and as they had not been forewarned, and had had no time to react to this convoluted chronicle before the emergency hearing, they refused to interrupt the recently created pathological situation without a careful, time-consuming review of the entire official record.

The way in which a false element can mold and determine the subsequent course of events, so that even its exposure may become irrelevant to repairing the ensuing damage, can be seen in the following example. During a postdivorce struggle, a father managed to prevent a child visiting from abroad with his mother who was the custodial parent, from returning to her. He informed the welfare authorities that the child detested the mother and was refusing to leave him. After an unfriendly interchange with the indignant mother, who thereby alienated the caseworker, a welfare officer took charge of the child, placing it "temporarily" in a foster home in the father's community, while the mother successfully petitioned the local court for the child's return. Instead of transferring the child back to the mother as ordered, however, the welfare worker claimed that the child had threatened suicide if forced to rejoin the custodial parent. Later, questions arose about whether the child had actually made such a threat, and if so, whether it was made directly to the social worker or whether the father had reported it to her. Based on whatever evidence, the welfare officer contacted the local mental hospital and arranged, via a young staff member, that a senior psychiatrist see the child and mother. After observing the child, the latter phoned the welfare officer to report that there was no cause for concern. The child was neither suicidal nor depressed, the psychiatrist said, and the mother–child relationship appeared normal, with no sign of any alleged antipathy. According to the mother's lawyer, the welfare officer then communicated with the young staff member who had been her initial contact in the mental hospital, apparently asking for a written account of the phone conversation with the senior psychiatrist. The young staff member then sent her an unsigned memo, incorporating the name of the senior psychiatrist who had seen the child, and saying that it would be detrimental for the child to be returned to the mother and to travel abroad with her. Although the senior psychiatrist later repudiated the memo, it remained in play long enough to energize the subsequent course of the case. It was cited repeatedly in reports by various welfare and child protection workers who periodically reviewed the situation in order to support arguments to the courts to delay or reverse earlier decisions to return the child to the mother and to her country of residence. Questions about the authenticity of the memo soon became irrelevant from the point-of-view of the damage being engendered, not only as decisions based on what it purported to prove multiplied, but as time was thereby gained for the father and his supporters to successfully prejudice the child against the mother. Disproving the original falsehood that had formed the rationale for an ongoing and damaging intervention—for the child's mental health was deteriorating in consequence—became irrelevant, because facts had been established on the foundation of the dubious memo which had decisively altered the initial legal and psychological configurations of the case.

After several weeks' delay in transferring the child, the latter had internalized the antipathies that had been alleged prematurely in the memo. Ensuing recommendations by caregivers assigned to review the situation now echoed what had once been, allegedly, a falsehood, but had now developed into a new reality. Thus, false imputations about a client's situation can engender subsequent damaging events that may not be reversed by correcting the record because falsehoods can shape the dynamics of the handling of a case so profoundly that repudiating them may not materially change the trajectory of the client's fate.

This last example may suggest a further point to the attentive reader, for there would seem to be a parallel between the allegedly doubtful memo and the revised opinion elicited by the Welfare Worker from another young psychiatrist in the early days of Joe's case. This may lead us to suspect that what we are seeing may not be coincidental. Certain falsifying tactics, like elements in the negative stereotyped characterization of clients in official files, would appear to be tactics shared by certain caregivers who need a fall-back policy if an expert's opinion disappoints expectations. Experience may have shown that expert witnesses do not always double check that what they intended to say is what is indeed recorded, and the legal process may not catch such questionable revisions, or if it does, the time gained in the interim has already fixed the course towards the outcome desired by the damaging caregiver. If complaints about unprofessional or unethical behavior are made, as was done by the mother's lawyer in the example just cited, the review process tends to be internal and protracted, so that even if the complaint is eventually found to be justified, it may yield only a symbolic victory, coming too late to materially change crucial events.

☐ Secrecy

If falsification is the marker of iatrogenic damage, secrecy is its bulwark. The edicts of subjudice and the confidentiality governing all cases involving children, for example, should logically be invoked at the discretion of the client, but in many damaging cases like Joe's, laws enforcing secrecy actually serve the best interests of those who are thereby rendered immune to exposure. In the interest of preventing iatrogenic damage it might be expedient to limit secrecy and the penalties that are now imposed against disclosure in the press and elsewhere, for professionals might be more scrupulous if they knew that details of their handling of a case could be open to question.

Secrets, it should be remembered, give power and a sense of importance to those who control them, so there is little motivation on the part of professionals to relinquish such valuable assets. It is no accident that, historically, many religious and social groups have distinguished their elect by endowing them with secret knowledge that is forbidden to the uninitiated. Among caregivers, jealously guarded compartments of secrecy can effectively subvert the treatment of clients by other professionals. A foreign colleague, for example, told of the following incident: As a mental health consultant to a school district, she had received an emergency summons from a principal. A child, newly assigned to the school by the local welfare office, had been found crouching under her desk, in apparent terror. She was complaining of chest pains and shortness of breath, and the school nurse suspected a recurrent panic attack. The consultant called the Welfare Officer for information about the background of the case and was told that the child's history was confidential and no business of either the school or its consultant. The latter vainly tried to explain that the ability of the school staff to help the child was being hindered by enforced ignorance. The welfare personnel, however, remained adamant that their knowledge was privileged and could not be shared.

The defensiveness of various professional groups in the face of any hint of outside scrutiny that might breach the walls of secrecy needs to be reconsidered in their own best interests. Only if the management of clients' files can be audited impartially would it be possible to differentiate between tough cases that have been handled in a necessarily tough manner and those that have been manipulated by caregivers in order to achieve their own goals, which do not necessarily correlate with the well-being of clients. The superficial appearance of a case may deceive not only caregivers with blind spots and a hidden agenda, it may also afflict the judgment of critical outsiders whose own sensitivities are triggered by a suspicion that clients are being victimized. Therefore, allowing the auditing of hitherto secret information by impartial outsiders would benefit professionals as well as their allegedly victimized clients. Such auditing would not only oblige caregivers to become more scrupulous and therefore more effective in their helping role, but it would also prove that their hands are clean when angry clients, against whom reasonable judgment has been given, bring accusations of damage against the professionals they blame because, in fact, they were doing their job correctly.

☐ External Regulatory Mechanisms

In the allocation of public money, it is understood that strict, independent auditing procedures are required alongside the internal bookkeeping of the body receiving the funds. In the same way, it may be necessary to recognize that agencies that are given the power to intervene in the lives of others, in addition to their internal supervisory procedures, should have independent oversight. Consequently, we might consider the expediency of forming a voluntary and administratively independent body of experts composed of civil liberties lawyers, mental health specialists, retired judges of stature, and other relevant professionals, who would examine official files when clients allege gross falsification, and where laws of secrecy preclude a public airing of the issues involved. Such a unit would have the specific job of dispassionately sifting the material on which charges are brought in cases that carry the signs of the Kafkaesque, and of reporting its findings to an appeals court, even while a case is being continued in a lower jurisdiction. The group, ideally, should have sufficient status to be immune from the fears for their own careers that keep other professionals silent when they know that lies have been told, and the experts who compose it should do so on a rotating basis in order to avoid developing the sort of corporate biases that would nullify their usefulness, and in order to avoid the inevitable burnout and routinization that would come from too much exposure to emotionally burdensome and time-consuming cases. Such testing of file material would be expensive, but it would not be impossible, especially given the stereotyped nature of many falsified records. Of course such a task force would not be omniscient or universally successful, but it might cut down the prevalence of the hitherto remarkably safe practice of professionals manipulating the facts of a case despite all the legal safeguards that now exist to punish perjury and to censure unethical professional behavior.

☐ Limited Effectiveness of External Regulatory Mechanisms

Nevertheless, we must realize that even if such bodies could be established, we would have to be modest in our expectations of their ultimate efficacy. Since in iatrogenic damage cases cited earlier a host of legislative and administrative safeguards designed to prevent harm to clients failed, we must accept the fact that passing yet more laws or establishing more systems to oversee and control practice in the field are methods that can always be circumvented or suborned. Externally imposed programs like statutory regulations that define and punish harmful behavior, over-sight boards, ombudsmen, and professional ethics committees are clearly necessary, but their complete efficacy should not be assumed because they tend to be porous. Outside auditors can be hoodwinked or they can come to identify with the professionals involved and thereby lose impartiality. Politically, regulators may be weak and ineffectual, especially if they belong to the profession under question and are required to stand up to powerful colleagues who are found to share the biases, failings, and hidden agendas of malfunctioning subordinates. Most adept at evasion are agencies that have carved out a semiautonomous niche, creating a small bounded area within which damaging individuals can wield disproportionate power and whistle blowers can be effectively silenced. By preempting a field, they absorb the resources that would have enabled alternative service providers to evolve. These ever more specialized agencies and law courts may become virtual monopolies, routinizing functioning and dulling the human sympathy of practitioners. For, despite the advantages of specialization, a general caseload may dilute the damage caused by a caregiver's blind spot or a theme interference, since professionals are less likely to harm a significant number of clients in a general practice compared to those who deal with hundreds of potentially similar cases. It may be helpful, therefore, if caregivers working in specific and specialized areas rotate periodically to refresh their sense of the general client population.

☐ Coercive Power Versus Damaging Caregivers

If one is acting from a position of strength, as is the British General Medical Council whose edicts are binding on licensees and which has the power to bar delinquent colleagues from practicing, one may attempt to control damaging behavior by fiat. Such power, however, can be more apparent than real. For example, some years ago, a local mental hospital became the "cause" of an energetic and charitable community leader who set out to modernize its fabric and treatment methods. An eminent foreign psychiatrist was invited to become the new clinical director, answerable only to his philanthropic patron. When the doctor first visited the institution, he was shocked to find many patients tied to their beds in a manner long outmoded elsewhere, and he ordered the inmates released. The staff promptly rebelled, and their machinations eventually forced his resignation. When his successor made the same demands, the staff learned to substitute drugs for straight jackets.

The staff had been functioning according to the way they had been trained and may have known no ways to treat "lunatics," other than by restraining them. Nevertheless, limited knowledge and skills may not have been the only bar to introducing progressive treatment modes. The type of candidates for staff positions in a mental hospital that routinely restrains patients may be expected to differ from the type of people who apply for work in an institution where control of inmates and their long-term custodial care are not seen as primary professional goals. To require the former type of staff to behave towards patients in a more "modern" therapeutic and liberal manner might run not only against their training, but also against the bent of their personalities. In the same way, the suggestion that the general adherence to complete separation and secrecy in adoptions give way to the possibility of some degree of contact between adoptees and their blood relatives may rouse resistance among workers who have always functioned within the traditional mode, and have chosen to work within precisely such a framework. A change of policy might well reduce iatrogenic damage among adoptees and their families, but it might also threaten workers who would have to reorient more than their professional functioning. It might require them to develop a different psychological and characterological orientation, which may be harder to bring about than raising and renewing their professional skills.

☐ Limitations of Planning and Reform

Given the difficulties of reforming malfunctioning systems, there may be a temptation to side-step the vested interests and the limitations in abilities and philosophies of existing institutions and their staff by creating new frameworks that will give superior results. Unfortunately, the history of reform shows that the practical obstacles are such that while the new system may be established in the face of opposition, may look good, and for a time may perform well, eventually it will run down. It may then sink not only to the level of the status quo ante, but may ultimately produce a worse situation, because its label and outer appearance make it sound progressive and benign, thereby disarming critics and lulling potential reform. We are then left with an unwittingly created falsehood—something that is "as if" caring, "as if" modern, "as if" just, and "as if" efficient and effective. If one scratches off the label and peers at what remains of that new organization, it may, in reality, be none of these.

One reason for the deterioration of new programs and for their tendency to revert to iatrogenically damaging results is a glaring planning failure that we alluded to earlier. When new theories are conceived and programs based on them are implemented, the innovators, in their own minds and in their promotional campaigns tend to emphasize the benefits that will accrue to sufferers and to the community at large from the new system. Bureaucratic and financial obstacles to implementation are commonly factored into planning; but there is less thought, if there is any at all, about what negative consequences might arise as a result of the components of a new venture. Consequently, there is less thought about what could be built into the structure of the program from the beginning in order to lower the risk of its precipitating such ripple effects as iatrogenic damage which may be caused, for example, by poor understanding by staff of basic psychosocial principles, or by lack of control over selection and supervision of workers from other fields who are given a double mission by their inclusion within the new program. No responsible military planner and no experienced chess player would make an apparently promising move without first calculating what even far-fetched negative reverberations might occur as a result, and without assessing the relative risks and options to countering them. But historically, in proposing new social programs, emphasis has been placed on optimistic and sometimes Utopian predictions. Negative consequences that might have been foreseen then come as a nasty surprise. In the planning of community mental health programs, for example, it might have been possible to predict early on that the benefits of involving many other caregivers in a supportive and preventive mission might have some drawbacks as well as positive features. Not only was this element of caution absent from planning, a paucity of authentic feedback from the community, and particularly a failure to amplify the voices of dissent, meant that, once programs were launched, problems were not identified soon enough for solutions and safeguards to be implemented early in the process, before damaged cases proliferated.

☐ The Backsliding of Reformed Institutions

Not only do reforms cause unforeseen reverberations that many rank and file professionals are ill-equipped to handle, but there is a tendency for reformed institutions to be taken over by those very workers from traditional settings whose practice was once deemed so unsatisfactory, because of their professional philosophy and personality types, that reforms were originally instituted to exclude them. For example, as a result of clinical findings in Israel in the late 1940s, Gerald Caplan realized that children who had been sexually abused by strangers were often less traumatized by the event itself than by the ensuing investigative and judicial processes. It was the questioning by police about intimate and embarrassing details, and the need to testify and be challenged in court in the presence of the accused that proved most damaging to many abused children. Consequently, with the help of the then Attorney General and later Chief Justice of the Supreme Court, Haim Cohen, a law was enacted that established a new role called Youth Investigators.

Youth investigators were envisaged as intermediaries and proxies, technicians trained to conduct all questioning of the victims in a stress-free atmosphere, and then to act as the child's mouthpiece in court where the youth investigator was to testify and be cross-examined as the child's representative. The new system worked well enough to overcome the initial suspicions of judges and lawyers. But gradually, the nature of youth investigators began to change, not quite out of all recognition, because it was gradually reverting to an older and potentially damaging guise. Those who were increasingly recruited into the new field were those workers who were already experts in techniques of investigating witnesses and in managing reluctant children, such as police detectives and probation officers. Gradually, the youth investigators began to interrogate in the style of an earlier mode, with long sessions including hectoring and leading questions, and in certain cases they began to produce the very damage to the children that the law that created their role had sought to prevent.

The reversion, however, was not to the preexisting state; it was, if anything, to something worse. Judges now treated youth investigators as *the* experts on children, accepting their word on what had happened to the child above the opinion of other experts whose depth of knowledge in fields of child psychology and development was far greater than that of the often scantily qualified youth investigator. Moreover, the law forbade anyone other than the youth investigator to question the child, and forbade the child appearing in court, so that the youth investigator's account of what the child's evidence was worth could not be corroborated, and the child would no longer express himself or herself except through a filter which might not, in fact, represent what the child actually wanted to say. This was despite the fact that the interviews were tape-recorded and the tactics used to gain evidence in certain cases were manifestly not the type that would ensure a credible answer.

In a number of cases we have seen, information had been elicited from very young children that was of questionable worth in the eyes of child psychiatrists or clinical psychologists, but which proved conclusive in convicting a defendant. The process of extracting it had reinforced the children's impression that something awful had happened to them and had left them guiltily aware that it was their own sometimes grudging words that had made somebody disappear into prison, even though they may have said what they did only in order to placate an insistent stranger and to give him or her the answers that the powerful adult clearly wanted to hear. In his article on the various ways that the investigation by professionals might disturb allegedly sexually abused children, David Jones (1991) cites studies that demonstrate that an interrogator's preconception of what the "correct" answer should be can alter the nature of a child's response.

Most dangerous of all, the regressed system of youth investigators was now operating under the tranquilizing and disarming label of reform that could justify those who served in it and could distract their critics. Labels of this type provide camouflage since many observers tend to accept the outer appearance as substance. For example, the name of the Israeli governmental adoption service is "The Service for the Sake of the Child." At an international conference some years ago, one of the pioneers of this agency dwelt at length on the fact that the name chosen for the service exemplified and proved its high and single-minded purpose. It is often hard to remember that names have no substance of their own. The ideals and high purpose expressed by a name may indeed exist, but that does not mean that debatable motives and practices cannot coexist with noble labels.

Since there is a tendency for complex ideas to be simplified during assimilation, and for outer trappings of institutions to be confused with underlying principles, the actual original rationale of having a youth investigator was obscured. Instead of this technician acting as the child's mouthpiece in order to spare a victim the trauma of police interrogation, court appearances, and confronting the accused, the youth investigator could become an instigator of additional stress. We saw a child who had been questioned about possible sexual interference five years earlier, and who had since developed a compulsive need to masturbate which both parents ascribed to the youth investigator's explicit and reiterated questions, over several sessions, about what had happened to his bottom. A number of children we have seen suffered from subsequent guilt because the interrogation made it inescapably clear that it was their testimony that had led to someone's imprisonment. The original rationale for a youth investigator, namely, avoiding iatrogenic damage by professional actions subsequent to the alleged abuse, was thus sometimes nullified. An even worse situation had been created because these were not average police, but interrogators accorded exaggerated respect by courts as supposed specialists in the handling of children and with expertise in sexual issues, and, like their colleagues in the police, their implicit goal was, apparently, successful prosecution, rather than being supportive in order to facilitate a healthy outcome for a vulnerable child.

☐ Limitations of Manpower Pools

Deterioration of reformed institutions can be hastened by the fact that the available pool of professionals is limited and already inadequate to cover the needs of the population. When new frameworks are created, the manpower to staff them must be drawn from somewhere. Either it comes from the ranks of existing professionals who have been imbued with old habits of thought and patterns of functioning that tend to reemerge under pressure in the new setting, or there are new caregivers who have been trained by the old guard, and therefore unwittingly perpetuate older models of practice. New institutions are like the regimes established in post-Communist Eastern Europe that were obliged to rely on the existing pool of bureaucrats, those who had been the mainstay of the Communist system that was now being replaced. The fact that those schooled in the older system are now called upon to implement a quite different one means that assumptions of the older system inevitably color the new.

One reason for the erosion of reform, as in the case of youth investigators, is that in the short run, while the originators of the plan are actively involved in its implementation, while the excitement of innovation enlivens the field, and while financial resources are pumped into the hopeful, new scheme, idealistic staff are recruited and are motivated to be creative. However, once innovators have overcome the entrenched system, their motivating drive tends to drop, and they move on to new areas of challenge. Public funds that were offered to new schemes are often curtailed in favor of supporting yet newer legislative enthusiasms, which further inhibits the commitment of the innovative staff. As the new system becomes routinized and perhaps implemented on a larger scale, thereby encountering more pressures and setbacks than were envisioned in the planning, it succumbs to the limitations of the general pool of available professionals. These may be called on to meet the needs not only of clients, but also of the other branches of the community caregiving network, such as the legal system.

Overburdened judges, for example, came to rely more and more heavily on the decisions of youth investigators about whether and by whom abuse had taken place. As a lawyer told a client trapped in accusations of having been involved in an improbable sexual encounter with a manipulative, disturbed adolescent, "The verdict of the youth investigators is the verdict of a judge!" Despite the evidence for the man's innocence, the judgment of the youth investigator that an indecency had occurred did, indeed, carry the day. The man was convicted, his own children were traumatized and pilloried by their schoolmates, and the disturbed adolescent was reinforced in her irrationality, all despite the fact that a defense lawyer established during six hours of cross-examination that the youth investigator's understanding of psychological issues in general and adolescent psychology in particular was minimal, though his skills as an interrogator were noteworthy.

While he had elicited a histrionic story, told with a relish that enlivened the tape recording of the young lady's story, he could not grasp the fact of the girl's clinical hysteria, nor her pleasure at being the center of flattering attention in a drama of her own devising.

☐ Exploiting Available Frameworks

Another factor that mitigates against the long-term efficacy of reformed institutions is a tendency to heap onto an existing, and apparently successful framework other tasks that need doing, whether or not they are suited to that framework and its resources. The havoc that can ensue when such a process outpaces the practicalities imposed by limited manpower and funding was illustrated recently when, according to an account in the *Ha'aretz* newspaper, the Israeli Parliament amended the Evidence Law (Protection of Children) that governs the role of youth investigators (Kra, 2001). In 1990, over the objections of the already overburdened workers from the Ministry of Labor and Social Affairs' Juvenile Probation Service, their client population was expanded to include not only young victims of sexual abuse, but also all children under the age of 14 "who had suffered or witnessed parental violence constituting real battery (leaving a mark on the body) or severe battery (causing permanent changes to the body), or who had been abused or neglected by their parents" (Kra, 2001).

The account in the *Ha'aretz* newspaper of the expansion of the law continued,

> The result was a staggering workload for the Juvenile Probation service. According to the police, hundreds of cases remain unattended because, while its officers are no longer legally allowed to look into them, the probation service is too understaffed to deal with them. (Kra, 2001)

Despite this added burden on the youth investigators, in 1998, according to *Ha'aretz*, a further increase in their workload was suggested, to include, "All cases in which violence against children was allegedly perpetrated by a responsible adult—a parent's partner, teacher, babysitter, or any other person entrusted with the care of a child for some period of time" (Kra, 2001).

After preliminary passage of this amendment, and the beginning of its implementation, and despite the fact that the legislative authorities knew that this would constitute a "great burden on the system," they nevertheless "were pleased with the way their planned reform was progressing," and proposed to bring it to a final reading for parliamentary passage. At this point, the newspaper article continued, a yet further expansion of its terms was proposed,

> to require that the Juvenile Probation service also be responsible for investigating all violent incidents involving children, school fights, even car accidents. "If you are going to initiate reform" (Knesset member Ophir) Pines told the officials, "you have to do it right."

Despite protests, in 1999, this new, expanded amendment was passed.

> The Ministry of Labor and Social Affairs now found itself faced with a task for which it had neither funding nor professional training. Moreover, public defenders and police officials argued that by shielding from cross-examination the alleged victims of the crimes now covered by the law, the amendment infringed on the rights of the defendant.

The result of the accumulated reforms was that "the justice system came close to the point of having no legal means of properly interrogating the children who were exposed to or implicated in violent crimes" (Kra, 2001).

Although the relevant parliamentary committee came to agree that the new provisions were now too broad and the law had become impossible to implement, nevertheless, new suggestions for its expansion were proposed, to include "children aged 14 and under who had witnessed a homicide or murder committed by their parent, their parent's partner, or their sibling." Even further suggestions were included into the law until Superintendent Suzy Ben-Baruch, head of the Youth Section of the Israel Police, commented, "Today we already have 200 cases piled up, because there are now no child interrogators to handle them." She added, "The Probation Service employees—*social workers who undergo only two weeks of special training* (our italics)—are simply not qualified for the job they now face" (Kra, 2001).

The head of the Juvenile Probation service, Dr. Dvora Horowitz commented,

> Budget issues aside, there is no reason why the Ministry of Labor and Social Affairs should become another interrogation division. . . . The Juvenile Probation service workers do a wonderful job of obtaining testimony. But now, they'll be saddled with investigating car crashes. (Kra, 2001)

Taking into account all of the above, we may become pessimistic about any chances of affecting the factors that generate iatrogenic damage. In the next chapter, however, we will begin to consider whether that pessimism, though based on undeniably realistic factors, is nevertheless entirely justified.

Some Suggested Solutions

We must now face the question of whether combating damaging behavior by caregiving professionals is at all feasible, or whether attempting to do so is like tilting at windmills—a noble ideal, but so naive as to be destined to futility.

Although it is relatively simple to list ways of remedying obvious defects in our helping programs, our past attempts to accomplish this, like the creating of the Youth Investigator Program, have sooner or later degenerated. Must we therefore conclude that our attempts to stop or to prevent iatrogenic harm are impossible? As mature planners should we realize that, because of the vagaries of human nature, and because of the inertia in the dynamics of institutional life and the social balance of forces, all attempts to limit the effects of human error and malevolence are destined to fail? Perhaps we should accept the inevitability of a certain proportion of harm in any of our welfare programs and not waste our time and energy in efforts to plan some ideal system. Before surrendering to pessimism, however, we wish to explore some ideas that may make it possible to reduce the incidence of iatrogenic harming.

There are various ways of approaching an attempt to prevent and attenuate iatrogenic damage, all of which require a hardheaded recognition of the complexity of the professional and political realities involved. If we wish to influence the genesis and course of iatrogenic damage, we may confront the problem from its source—individual caregivers who occasionally lose objectivity or who are habitual victimizers, and self-validating nests of damaging professionals. We can also approach the problem by informing and influencing the judges who control the final common path through which many of these cases pass. Finally, we can intervene with the victimized clients in order to help them to master and overcome the pathogenic experience. In this and in the following chapters, we will consider each of these options.

☐ The Individual Damaging Professional

One might attempt to prevent iatrogenic harm by weeding out workers with potentially damaging personality types. Selection, however, is a blunt instrument. While it may exclude some unsuitable candidates, it may also discard potentially effective ones. Predictive testing may fail to differentiate those whose unconscious motivation to enter a field will make them particularly sensitive, insightful, and empathic to the plight of those whose fate strikes an unconscious chord in the caregiver, from those who will damage because of the punitive quality of their reaction to identification with a client's situation. A caregiver drawn to child protection work because of a personal encounter with violence or neglect, for example, may see and crusade against abuse where none exists, but a colleague who has also experienced similar trauma and deprivation may have emerged particularly perceptive and empathic, just the type of caregiver that is best suited to the job. Selection inevitably leads to waste, to discarding those who do not fit the projected and desired mold but who may function well in spite of this and may do so in unanticipated ways. Discarding workers willing to do the frequently burdensome work of community agencies, unless they are positively vicious, is uneconomical, since such workers are chronically in short supply. Instead, attempts should be made to mold their functioning so that they rise to a required standard.

☐ Handling "Wrong" Answers

A possible solution to lowering the prevalence of iatrogenic damage, therefore, may not be found in wasteful and probably ineffectual attempts to prophesy who will or will not malfunction, but rather in identifying problems as they arise in the workplace, making use of such cases as learning experiences, and focusing on encouraging growth in professional expertise and sophistication. In our own teaching, we have always felt that, while right answers from students are gratifying, analyzing "wrong" answers makes real progress. In "wrong" answers, one comes across the unanticipated, hitherto undiagnosed misunderstandings or a student's novel and potentially valuable insights. The mishandling of cases may be presented negatively, or it can be treated as an opportunity to widen professional perspectives, to understand unforeseen complexities of human nature, subtle or ambiguous interpersonal cues, or unfamiliar aspects of culture. In doing so, of course, the real suffering of clients must be assuaged as quickly as possible. While this may sound perverse, elements of this method have proved to be a viable option in dealing with damaging behavior in some fields of human services.

☐ Psychoanalysts and Boundary Issues

Psychoanalysts have shown that the irrational trigger to damage clients can be treated openly and in an educational way. After a number of scandals in which some leading colleagues had been exposed as sexually involved with patients, the profession brought the issue into the open. The temptation to have an inappropriate relationship with patients was given the value-free term, "boundary issues." Certain colleagues became experts in how to handle and avoid boundary issues, and were available to discuss the topic with tempted peers, and the subject of ethics in relation to boundary issues was incorporated into the core training program of the profession.

Boundary issues happened to dovetail with the central psychoanalytic concept of countertransference, the irrational reaction aroused in a therapist by a patient because some aspect of the latter resonated with a significant aspect of the therapist's own history or relationships. For this reason it may have been easier for this profession to confront this type of iatrogenic damage among its members than it would be for other groups of caregivers for whom transference and countertransference are alien concepts. It might be well to widen awareness of this concept and introduce it into the curricula of such specialties as school teaching, where there have also been scandals involving boundary issues.

☐ Controlling Damaging Caregivers

Some individuals, however, will be impervious to attempts to mold their negative attitudes and practice. There are traditional and established ways of dealing with those who damage clients—closer supervision, further education, mental health consultation, and, if all else fails, dismissal. However, we must beware of oversimplifying. As practitioners of primary preventive psychiatry, we must differentiate between condemning the harmful actions and condemning the iatrogenic harming person, otherwise we may fall into the trap of losing our own professional objectivity and stereotyping and dehumanizing the victimizers, whom we will begin to perceive as monsters, just as they view clients whom they have victimized. That we, too, may behave in this way should give us pause when we find ourselves dehumanizing them. This is not just an ethical issue linked with the human propensity to become judgmental, dogmatic, punitive, and closed-minded when we are upset over our own inability to prevent the suffering of an innocent victim for whom we feel responsible. But such behavior, which is so similar to what we are trying to combat in the malfunctioning caregivers, is likely to interfere with the clear thinking that is essential if we are to succeed in solving the complicated problems involved. Moreover, if one of our underlying assumptions is correct, that certain types of damaging behavior are basically defensive on the part of the victimizers (defensive against psychologically threatening issues or against a lack of knowledge or techniques to handle the human complexities involved, or defensive against what is felt to be unfair hostility from problem clients or from what is perceived as unfair political or public pressures), our punitive attitudes are likely to be sensed by them and will make them even more defensive.

Instead, we must seek an approach that condemns the harming of clients and alerts people to the signs that this is occurring and to the need to stop it, while not demonizing the offenders, even though it may be necessary to intervene to stop their harmful behavior. The model that comes to mind is how we manage typhoid carriers. We do not blame them for having been infected, but at the same time, even though we feel that they may be innocent of wrongdoing, we know that they endanger others and that their movements must be controlled, so that, for instance, they must not be allowed to have significant contact with food services.

☐ Noncoercive Versus Coercive Approach to Damaging Caregivers

Consultee-centered mental health consultation techniques, developed by our team at Harvard Laboratory of Community Psychiatry to help caregivers regain a balanced professional functioning that would correct inappropriate treatment of the client and the distorted perception caused by a theme interference, were based on a nonhierarchical relationship with consultees which by careful design was noncoercive, thereby allowing mentally healthy consultees the complete freedom to accept or reject whatever the consultant said (Caplan & Caplan, 1999). But in the case of caregivers who suffered from a personality disorder, this freedom to choose enabled them to continue to impose their irrational stamp on their perceptions of the clients, so that the noncoercive, nonhierarchical stance proved ineffectual. For such people, the situation demanded the opposite approach—reality-based control underpinned by coercion. In any particular case, the decision by a consultant as to whether or not it was necessary to move from a nonhierarchical to a coercive, directive approach depended on the power of the irrational impulses in the consultee and the countervailing influences of the situation in the consultee's workplace, namely the amount of leeway afforded by the supervisors and administrators for caregivers to decide for themselves what they should do in any case. In an agency where line workers are only loosely supervised, therefore, it might be necessary for a consultant to step out of a noncoercive, nonhierarchical role in order to prevent damage to a client, whereas it would be less imperative in institutions where supervisors could be relied on to closely monitor workers and to actively protect clients.

While most caregivers may inadvertently harm clients when some unsolved emotional problem outside their conscious awareness and control is energized in them, and when they deal with it by utilizing the unconscious defense of displacing it onto the situation of their client, it should be possible to detect and to interrupt the development of such situations by supervisory and consultation techniques. Such detection may help us to learn enough about the circumstances that promote these lapses so that we may reduce their frequency by organizational and educational means. For instance, if we know that a particular member of staff has habitual difficulties with certain types of cases and cannot be taught to overcome them, then such cases should best be assigned to another colleague. But when such patterns of harmful behavior occur in caregivers who suffer from personality disorders or similar forms of mental abnormality that express themselves in the manipulation of others, and the patterns are apt to resist modification by education and persuasion, the caregiver also is likely to hang on to the cases compulsively and not allow them to be transferred to others. Then, clients may be protected only by controls imposed by coercive authority.

The biggest danger of our losing our own objectivity occurs in those extreme cases of professionals who engage in habitual and apparently compulsive victimizing behavior. They resemble mentally disturbed parents, particularly those suffering from severe personality disorders, who terrorize and exploit other family members. In our work with divorcing families, we have learned not to treat such people by mediation and reconciliation techniques because they usually manipulate discussions in order to perpetuate their exploitative hold over others. We have learned that the only way of dealing with such parents effectively in order to rescue their family members is to insist on their being removed from contact with potential victims by judicial fiat. In the same way, caregivers with analogous personality disorders are generally impervious to education programs that encourage self-assessment and foster greater sensitivity to clients' pain.

It would be helpful if we could accurately and fairly identify those who often manipulate clients in order to serve their own unconscious needs. This may refer to those who play out their own unresolved, unconscious dramas by means of their clients, those who enjoy asserting undue power over the lives of others, and those with a dualistic view of society who see themselves as representing the forces of light who must battle with forces of moral and cultural darkness to save what they perceive to be vulnerable souls. However, as we have noted earlier, it is doubtful whether we can differentiate these people from dedicated and balanced professionals whose caseload in fact consists of many realistically terrible cases, and whose zeal may only be due to the fact that they are overalert to ambiguous warning signs.

☐ Influencing the Culture of an Agency

A most potent determinant of severe iatrogenic damage, as we have seen, is not merely the malfunctioning individual caregiver, it is the receptivity of the institutional setting that embraces and perpetuates the distortions caused by the unconscious theme and stereotyped perceptions of any individual professional. Such a setting may share and foster the professional's hidden agenda. Therefore, efforts to control iatrogenic damage must aim to influence not only the immediate perpetrator of harm, but also the culture of his or her caregiving agency, which otherwise cannot be relied on to control or discipline damaging workers. It may be necessary, therefore, by means of education and supervision, to attempt to create a professional climate in which all caregivers are made aware of the ubiquity of damaging behavior. That climate would sensitize them to the value that, despite the often unconscious roots of iatrogenic damaging behavior, it is unacceptable to harm clients or to use unscrupulous means to determine the disposition of a case, however desirable that solution may appear to the caregiver. This would serve, ideally, to instill techniques of self-assess-ment and self-awareness as part of the culture of every caregiving professional group.

To change the damaging methods that are embedded in normative professional practice is difficult and may sometimes be affected only by the impetus of open scandal and consumer revolt. The progressive and unprecedented directives of the British General Medical Council mentioned in Chapter 2 appear to have been impelled by a number of high profile cases of repeated malpractice in physicians that led to the withdrawal of their licenses to practice. Protest by clients, who no longer accept an older paternalistic model for the patient–doctor rela-tionship and who see themselves rather as consumers entitled to courteous and high quality service in return for the fees they pay directly or as taxpayers, is also a sharp goad to reform.

☐ Internalizing the Value of Not Harming

Success in combating iatrogenic damage, therefore, may come less from imposing external constraints and creating temporarily more benign, reformed frameworks, than from encouraging professionals to inter-nalize as a primary value that of not causing harm to clients. Training programs that stress the need to consciously question one's own performance and cultivate sensitivity to clients' feelings may help, but only if such teaching does not become perfunctory and easily dismissed by students, the bent of whose personalities may not be receptive to such messages.

In this respect, one cannot rely on institutionalized safeguards sub-stituting for internalized values. The ancient Rabbinic courts system, for example, which has existed from before the destruction of the Second Temple, two thousand years ago, has evolved both a general sense of the dangers of iatrogenic damage and intrinsic methods for attempting to lower the risk of its occurrence. Its body of laws and customary procedures has evolved over the ages to encourage fair and independent deliberations. All important decisions are made by an odd-numbered panel of judges, usually three, each one of whom is fully autonomous. There is no hierarchy of authority, though each panel has a presiding judge; each member of the panel must indepen-dently exercise his own judgments and conscience. All deliberations must take place in the presence of both parties to a dispute; and a reduced number of judges may deliberate on an issue only with the expressed agreement of both litigants. Theoretically, these procedures mitigate against corruption, individual bias, and theme interference, since colleagues watch and contest each other's decisions. Corporate bias remains a danger, but a supreme Rabbinic court of appeal exists that can question regular court decisions.

This system, based as it is on the cumulative wisdom of centuries, can be circumvented, however, because judges, while more or less adhering to the rules, do not always recognize their implications for our present subject and may allow a certain casualness to seep into procedures. Therefore, though the Rabbinic court system has inherited tools to impede iatrogenic damage, and though the tools may work if applied properly even without the judges fully understanding their implications for avoiding harming clients, nevertheless, the fact that this dimension of their rules may not be consciously recognized for its role in this regard means that procedures may at times be carelessly followed or omitted, and damage can then ensue.

From this it follows that however well-designed institutional procedures may be for averting professionally damaging behavior, unless the professionals cultivate a conscious value system that explicitly links these procedures to their intended goal, the safeguards will often fail.

☐ Establishing Widely Acceptable Goals

We operate on the basic assumption that most caregivers *want* to engage in good practice, even though some are actually endangering or even damaging their clients at times. We prefer, wherever possible, to work collaboratively with them on problems on which we can agree in the hope that this may raise the level of practice in these areas and build relationships on which we may eventually rely in order to produce changes in areas where we do not currently see eye to eye. There is no need to obtrude this motive on our colleagues, for like some of them, we too have our hidden agenda. Were we to disclose it, it may easily be misinterpreted as provocative; but we see no need to hide our intention of reducing iatrogenic damage, and by this policy we offer them an equal chance to influence us to change in conformity with their values and attitudes.

This line of thinking leads us to identify the following significant goal which most caregivers may be prepared to accept as desirable: *We favor reality-based perceptions and oppose premature cognitive closure in situations of ambiguity that lead to oversimplified stereotyped perceptions.* We have identified this to be a crucial cognitive difficulty in many cases of iatrogenic harming. Leaving aside the underlying cause of such stereotyping, most people would agree that in its own right it is undesirable. How then can we reduce its incidence?

R. H. Ojemann (1948, 1958, 1961), one of the pioneers of preventive psychiatry in the United States, showed that teachers could be trained to instruct children in what he called "causal" thinking instead of the "manifestational" thinking usually taught in schools. Namely, children could learn to analyze unfamiliar situations by thinking about possible causal factors and then working out how these might be modified in order to alter the outcome, instead of learning by rote a list of manifestations and a matched list of appropriate reactions. He evaluated the problem-solving capacities of a population of children taught by each of these methods, and showed that among the many benefits of the causal teaching approach was an increased tolerance for ambiguity and a perseverance in grappling with complicated problems, thereby leading to more effective results.

Using Ojemann's insights, we may reduce the incidence of premature cognitive closure and of associated stereotyped perceptions among caregivers by providing them with appropriate training that focuses on the expectable complications of family conflicts and in particular teaches them that, however confusing a situation may seem at first, if they keep collecting information in an unhurried way, they may expect that they will eventually understand enough about what is happening to intervene effectively. Moreover, they can be taught that, if the situation continues to confuse them, they can ask for advice from a supervisor or a consultant, and that this will be regarded positively by their superiors as a sign of growing sophistication and will not be interpreted as failure. This implies that the administrators of their agency should also increase their own knowledge of problem solving in complicated family conflicts, which implies, in turn, that they also may need further in-service training in this area.

Training programs for management and line workers, therefore, should be designed to increase their capacity to react in a reality-based way to confusing and ambiguous human conflict situations, and they should reduce the incidence of stereotyping. We would be naive to suggest that this would prevent all or even most cases of damaging behavior by professionals. In previous chapters, we have discussed a number of commonly occurring phenomena, such as theme interference, acting out, and the presence of hidden agendas. These can lead a caregiver to stereotype a particular client despite the caregiver's having an excellent capacity to understand complexity and to tolerate ambiguity as shown by successful handling of such issues in other cases. Moreover, in dealing with these problems, we must also realize that many caregivers and their supervisors are likely to resist further collaboration with us, feeling that we may be endangering their interests by threatening to find fault with their ways of working. Most caregivers would be upset if they were forced to face clear evidence that they were damaging a client. Some would deny the possibility that this is happening, or that they could be considered culpable.

For the moment, let us set aside the important question of how we may help overcome such resistance. We will return to that question in the next chapter. Let us focus here on the crucial issue of how we may help caregivers, supervisors, and the policy makers of their agency assist the line workers to overcome stereotyping and premature cognitive closure that is unacknowledged or unconscious but may be potentially damaging to the clients.

This may entail encouraging caregivers and their superiors to build into their agency an atmosphere of intercollegial trust. Such trust will enable workers to feel secure in revealing details of their daily work with clients to fellow workers on an ongoing basis without the fear that any inadequacy in their operations will be dealt with by derogatory criticism. We are reminded here of a waggish remark by a very senior mental health administrator who had suggested that certain information about the prevalence of a particular condition might be garnered by asking therapists to recall any relevant cases in their practice. "Of course," said the administrator, "therapists are very secretive about their cases; and I know why. It's because they aren't accomplishing anything in all those sessions, and they don't want anyone to find out!" In a collegial atmosphere it is to be hoped that such defensiveness could be overcome so as to help ensure both that a therapeutic outcome is indeed taking place, and that an iatrogenically harmful outcome is avoided.

In pursuit of this goal and anticipating probable negative as well as positive results of our proposal, we must convince caregivers of the need for tact—convince them to accept that every one of us is entitled to privacy as regards the workings of our own unconscious. Most of us have sensitivities to themes that may intrude without warning into our conscious world, and many of us may act out on occasion when our rational judgment is overwhelmed and our focus is narrowed by ghostly visitations from a mercifully repressed past. Nobody can be blamed for suffering such episodes, and it must be stressed to colleagues that such eruptions of unconscious material in a coworker are in no way shameful or bad. If a supportive atmosphere could be fostered, workers may be encouraged to establish dyads or small groups in which they may share supportive surveillance over each other's daily work on a mutual basis. Each caregiver then may feel secure that he or she will be alerted by his or her supporter (who is not personally involved in this particular case and is therefore less likely to distort his or her perceptions), whenever the colleague involved with the client seems to be closing his or her thinking about a case prematurely, thereby coming to impulsive or irrational conclusions without being aware of doing so. Because the roles of giver and receiver of helpful surveillance would be rotated regularly in response to alternating needs, there should be no loss of face or feeling of undue dependency in such a mutual support system.

The weak link in this positive sounding plan is that it is completely dependent on the collaboration of the policy makers and the supervisors of the caregiving community agencies, and this may be lacking. A not uncommon reaction to our approach has been that the whole idea sounds absurd. They may claim, for example, that it takes a tough staff to stop abusers, and such a project would turn staff into soft, touchie-feelie liberals, like those who thought up such a plan and who obviously have no personal experience in the dangers and complexities of this field.

Persuasion by rational argument requires that the discussants listen to each other. Often, damaging systems react with a virulent attack on observers who point out that there may be problems in the handling of cases, and these systems seal themselves off from even sympathetic suggestions of how to alter the situation. When the capacity to listen is missing, we must utilize another approach.

☐ Agency Policies: Some Suggested Steps

Administrators who are really intent on reducing iatrogenic harm will have little difficulty in recruiting workers whose personalities and talents fit their own philosophy. We see little merit in spelling this out, except to say that it is usually better to focus on selecting out workers who repeatedly cause harm despite guidance and training by their supervisors rather than trying to select in by testing and interviewing those who are likely to be appropriate.

Second, in order to cope with the cognitive and emotional burdens of grappling with the complications of the human relations conflicts of clients without utilizing defenses that stereotype and damage, workers must be given adequate support. This is costly, and administrators must make sure that they include enough funds in their budget to pay for effective supervision and consultation and for regular peer support groups to prevent burnout. High staff morale not only makes an agency a more attractive place in which to work, it ensures that clients will be better treated.

Third, an ongoing media campaign should let potential clients know the kind of problems that are likely to be helped by that agency, and while taking care to demonstrate confidentiality, the kind of help they may expect from its staff. One important message to potential clients should be that they should be active in reporting when they feel that their problems are not being adequately handled and that such negative feedback will be welcomed by the staff as an important help in keeping their efforts on target. This should also help recruit the kind of workers who are needed and suited for this work. Information that opens up to public scrutiny what is actually going on in our community agencies is an important, if small, step in the right direction.

CHAPTER

10

Adapting Techniques of Mental Health Consultation to Influence Unwelcoming Agencies

One possible way to gain leverage on iatrogenically damaging behavior and on the agencies which may harbor it, is to confront the component of irrationality, the unconscious biases in individuals and collectives that distort the perception and treatment of clients and create unwarranted emotional involvement. This produces exaggerated repudiation of any attempts by outsiders to limit and prevent victimization by professionals. The title of this book echoes that of our earlier volume, *Helping the Helpers to Help* (Caplan & Caplan, 1972), written years ago, in which we described and analyzed theme interference and the techniques of consultee-centered mental health consultation that we developed to counteract it. In those days, we did not realize how restricted was our view of damaging professional behavior, and therefore in what way aspects of our technique were limited in their applicability to other, and possibly widely occurring types of iatrogenically harmful situations.

At that time, we felt that two prerequisites were needed to create a viable mental health consultation program for a community agency. The first was salience, which meant that the agency was strategically placed to have a high potential for influencing the mental health of its clients by supporting them in the face of stressors that our studies had led us to believe would produce a statistically significant elevation in

171

rates of psychosocial pathology in an exposed population. Second, we felt that entry to the agency must be feasible; that is, the administration of the agency would understand the need for our service and would have the capacity to make use of it effectively.

Since, like every other mental health service provider, we were limited by available time and by the number of highly trained staff able to carry out so sophisticated a technique, we did not feel it necessary to expend efforts recruiting agencies that might have had high salience, but also had low feasibility because for various reasons they did not welcome our overtures. Indeed, we could pick and choose readily among institutions that fulfilled our criteria, and occupy all our time providing a service that these welcoming agencies felt was benefiting their clients and staff alike.

Unwittingly, however, we thereby restricted ourselves to a select, and therefore unrepresentative arena of practice. For example, one of the agencies that used our consultants and provided practical experience on the basis of which we developed and refined our ideas and techniques was the Boston Visiting Nurse Association, which recruited a select staff, trained them highly, and continued to supervise and educate them throughout their employment. This agency provided us with pure laboratory conditions, as it were, to study theme interference. Lapses by nurses in expected standards of case management were quickly noted by a supervisory system that demanded a high order of effectiveness so as to safely maintain gravely ill patients out in the community. Supervisors were sensitive to changes in the functioning of their nurses. Sophisticated and self-assured, they had the confidence and pragmatism to absorb whatever help from outsiders would enable their organization to accomplish its mission more efficiently. We met a similar welcome and lack of defensiveness among the bishops and parish clergy of the Episcopalian Church of the United States, and among certain groups of school administrators in Boston.

When we encountered cases of iatrogenic damage caused by theme interference among these groups of caregivers, we assumed that we understood them and could manage them. We overlooked the fact that we were operating in privileged circumstances, among a population of agencies and professionals who had been highly selected to fit our needs as well as their own. Unwittingly, our operation had become analogous to that of private individual-oriented patient practice, or a traditional mental health clinic where, given the limitations of professional resources and the vast sea of need, it was legitimate to choose to treat only those patients with a good prognosis for benefiting from the services of that institution, patients who were interesting, who were clean and civilized, and who were prepared to follow our rules. When Gerald Caplan, for example, was on the child psychiatry staff of the prestigious Tavistock Child Guidance Clinic in London, great effort went into devising criteria for screening out cases that were "unsuitable" because they would not be expected to complete a course of therapy. Parents were identified whose values and characteristics led staff to expect that they would not break off treatment for their children for at least a year so that the clinic's students would have "good" cases to learn on. Similarly, there are other institutions that legitimately limit their services to those whom they judge will best utilize them and whose success, not coincidentally, will satisfy the needs of the service provider. Elite schools, for example, select students with the potential to best benefit from their system and who, incidentally, can be expected to achieve the high exam results that ensure the school's reputation for excellence. These high results, like the successful therapy of select clinics, or the satisfaction of the community agencies that used our Harvard mental health consultants, are not due solely to the merit of the service provider. They are the product of a not always consciously recognized interaction whose results can be disrupted if the match between professional and client is altered. In other words, our success in controlling iatrogenically damaging behavior in those early years depended not only on the efficacy of our mental health consultation techniques, but also on the sympathetic atmosphere created by the management of the agencies in which we had been invited to work and on the high caliber and motivation of their personnel.

When we moved out of Harvard Medical School into the Hadassah Hebrew University Medical School and the wards of its teaching hospitals, our view of theme interference and mental health consultation technique began to change because we were now operating in a qualitatively different sphere. Now we had to deal with an institution with high salience, but whose feasibility was not always optimal because the staff was now heterogeneous and no longer as select and sophisticated as we had been used to. The traditional mental health consultation techniques required us to work as outsiders with a recognized mantle of status due to our superior qualifications and our prestigious university affiliation, but at the same time we were to assume the role of equals, deferring to the expertise of the consultee about the issues of that particular case. Now we became insiders and fellow members of diagnostic and therapeutic teams in various hospital departments where mental health issues might be secondary to immediate questions of life and death. In this setting, we developed the techniques of mental health collaboration, in which we had to set aside certain aspects of the egalitarian, noncoercive consultant's role to assert the primacy and authority of our ideas when we saw that the management of a case was endangering a patient's mental health.

In our latest setting, where we are operating out in the community to lower the risk to children of disrupted families, we are not only seeing a much wider variety of cases and caregivers, but we are often operating among forces of very low feasibility, where entry and sanction to operate at all are major obstacles, and where, unlike the welcome offered by the Boston Visiting Nurses, the local agencies may regard us as interfering interlopers. In this more complex and inhospitable setting, our view of characteristics of, and solutions to malfunctioning by caregivers and how to gain access to them becomes much more complicated.

A traditional program of consultee-centered mental health consultation would probably be impossible to implement within the defensive and secretive organizations that may generate damaging behavior. Paradoxically, the techniques of consultee-centered case consultation are well suited to dealing with a measure of iatrogenically damaging behavior on both an individual and a collective level. However, the formal role of a mental health consultant and a formally drawn up consultation program would probably be rejected by those who deny that they need any outside help or that they are doing any harm.

☐ Working Within the Displacement

The essence of the mental health consultation technique is tact, namely the avoidance of uncovering types of interpretations by the consultant. The consultant is trained to identify the presence of irrational projection by a caregiver of his or her own unconscious problems onto a client and to spot enough of the details of that unresolved problem to understand the terms in which the misperception of the client's situation is operating. While the mental health consultant is trained to perceive the linkage, he or she is never to reveal its existence to the consultee. The consultant works within the displacement, preserving the psychic defenses of the consultee by only discussing the situation of the client. He or she is trained never to follow tempting leads into the personal life and psyche of the consultee. As far as the consultees are concerned, the process is therefore safe. Their privacy is preserved, as is their right to safeguard their biases and secrets, the tactless uncovering of which might prove embarrassing or even devastating. That element of safety for consultees and their agency may be the factor that might counteract the irrational defensiveness with which agencies deny that they may perpetrate iatrogenic damage.

The final common path of damaging professionals, as we have noted, is that they become defensive and secretive when threatened by the exposure of their prejudices and hidden agenda, since any investigation of the handling of the case might not only reveal professional incompetence but might also expose their biases, thereby destroying the defenses that are controlling the unconscious conflicts of iatrogenically harming professionals. To be confronted by the fact that one is damaging clients when one's self-image is that of a savior would not be pleasant. To see one's drive to carry out a "sacred mission" exposed as a narcissistic need to play God, would not necessarily be a welcome revelation to those who are engaged in sublimating their own need to dominate others.

Therefore, the first constructive principle that can be derived from mental health consultation technique is preserving and working inside the displacement, thereby avoiding threatening and endangering the individual consultee's privacy and the integrity of his or her defenses. In inhospitable settings, by extension, this means, being particularly tactful by avoiding as much as possible engaging in frontal attacks against the hidden agenda and what for us are questionable techniques of other professionals and their institutions. Since much professional malfunctioning is in part linked with defensive strategies, as we have already noted, frontal attacks only exacerbate the need to evade and counter outside scrutiny.

☐ A Supportive Setting

A second core element of mental health consultation is that it should provide a safe, supportive setting in which that which the consultee finds threatening or repugnant can be reflected on in a calm, orderly, and professionally dispassionate way. The consultant conveys the message that human relations are expectably complex and that it is possible and worthwhile to consider how to disentangle this complexity at length, avoiding the oversimplified and stereotyped view, the intolerance of ambiguity, and the premature cognitive closure that characterize iatrogenically damaging interventions (Caplan & Caplan, 1999).

☐ A Nonhierarchical Stance

A third core element lies behind our placing so heavy an emphasis on the consultant maintaining a nonhierarchical stance vis-à-vis the consultee. This is not based on a liberal ideology, nor is it a purely manipulative procedure, because a noncoercive approach in fact makes it emotionally easier for a consultee to choose to adopt and internalize the mental health consultant's less inhibited and more hopeful view of the client's situation. The nonhierarchical relationship also encourages free expression without fear of disparagement. In these highly defensive organizations, therefore, this is a significant advantage. The nonhierarchical, noncoercive aspects of the mental health consultation relationship encourage and enable the consultee to think freely. Within a setting that is safely insulated from the dogmas and political correctness of the consultee's normal professional framework, he or she is set free to play with ideas, to think heretically and unusually, to be inventive about solving an unusual problem about which he or she may have felt constricted not only for individual, unconscious reasons, but also because of the limitations posed by the ideological bias and covert agenda of his or her colleagues.

This is in line with our discoveries about crisis intervention, which began in Israel in the 1950s and continued at Harvard. The essence of a crisis, as we noted earlier, is that it is a novel situation that taxes an individual by demanding novel responses that are beyond his or her current capacities. The consultant is supporting the consultee during a crisis induced by a problem at work that may be reverberating with a more personal problem. The process of mental health consultation, therefore, involves supporting the consultee during the disequilibrium and confusion of the crisis created by a work situation to arrive at a novel, mentally healthy solution to the present challenge that will be incorporated into his or her ongoing professional problem-solving repertoire.

☐ Initiating Contact with Unwelcoming Agencies

One of the principles of creating a mental health consultation relationship with a salient institution is to first create proximity. When attempting to approach an agency that offers a less than cordial welcome, creating this proximity is a challenge, but not necessarily an insurmountable one. One form of proximity may be an intellectual one, namely we can try to establish a superordinate goal (Sherif et al., 1961). We operate on the assumption that although they may not welcome us, most community care systems share our desire to engage in good practice and would agree in theory that it is desirable to reduce iatrogenic damage and the misery it causes, although they may deny that they perpetrate it. Most caregivers would also agree about the importance of encouraging reality-based perceptions and opposing premature cognitive closure in situations of ambiguity that then lead to oversimplification and stereotyping that foster iatrogenic harm. Without focusing on their own possible involvement or assigning any blame, we could attempt to gain their participation in a joint community-oriented search for ways of achieving a common objective. This may be done by disseminating information about the existence of iatrogenic damage and devising ways to counter it. Such a joint educational venture would aim to foster among veteran professionals and their students the value that, despite good intentions, we are all fallible and thus liable to cause damage, even inadvertently. Consequently, we must all guard against it, and when it occurs, we should face its reality and not try to brush it aside and deny it.

As in mental health consultation, the issues involved in professional malfunctioning should be discussed tactfully and jointly within the defensive structure, otherwise agencies will increase their withdrawal and evasiveness. This echoes a well-practiced mental health consultation technique, in which we do not confront the consultee with questions about what he or she has done with the client, but we sit next to him or her, as it were, and together look at the problem from the same side of the table (Caplan & Caplan, 1999). Similarly, if we all sit on the same community committee to examine the problem of iatrogenic damage out there, we become coordinate, mutually supportive partners, where everyone's good will is taken for granted in focusing on reducing damage to clients.

☐ Peer Surveillance as Peer Support

In order to avoid damaging patients, professionals can be taught to constantly engage in self-analysis. Since even this is not an infallible solution, they should also be encouraged to use mutual surveillance by colleagues in their own agency, who by definition share a non-hierarchical relationship with each other.

Peer oversight became the key component of the mental health consultation program that we and the Episcopalian Church developed jointly, and which is described in our 1972 book (Caplan & Caplan, 1972). The program, which came to be called "Bishop to Bishop Coordinate Status Consultation" evolved after certain bishops approached us to learn our mental health consultation techniques. At first, we had assumed that they wanted to use these to help their parish clergy. In fact, they really wanted to use them to support each other in grappling with the many psychological pressures of their lonely, elevated role. The rather clumsy name they chose for the program underlined one of their major concerns, to establish a method of nonhierarchical support within a heavily hierarchical system. They worked out a program in which consultation dyads were organized. Inherent within each was a mechanism for role rotation. Thus, each member of the dyad took turns acting as consultant and consultee for the other, thereby preserving their nonhierarchical relationship.

The consulting couples met at every available opportunity, including before and after the plenary sessions of annual meetings of the House of Bishops, the supreme governing body of the American branch of their Church. When the number of bishops whom we had trained in our mental health consultation techniques exceeded a certain threshold, their informal operations during meetings of the House of Bishops suddenly changed the atmosphere and procedures of this body as a whole. Plenary session meetings that in the past had been heavily politicized and divisive, spontaneously changed to become mutually supportive for their members. This development had been consciously desired by many of the more liberal bishops whom we had trained, but nobody had been able to work out a way of achieving it against the opposition of the conservatives who exercised political control by virtue of their seniority. Change in feasibility occurred spontaneously, when a critical mass of individuals coalesced and thereby affected the culture of the body as a whole, not when any attempt was made to alter individual behavior by first changing the values of the collective. This is like the way a flock of birds changes direction in midflight, when a deviation by individual birds at the periphery is copied by more and more neighboring birds, whose growing numbers swing over the whole population. This process of course correction of the collective by an increasing number of individuals copying each other appears to be a fundamental aspect of biosocial behavior in many social animals.

If we wish to start this procedure in agencies that regard us dubiously, we will not necessarily be believed if we approach them with a direct message about our benevolent intentions and the proven safety of our methods. Instead, we should arrange that they overhear and observe what is taking place in our mental health consultation program in a feasible agency, where the doors and windows have been left open, as it were, so that staffs of neighboring systems can see and hear what we are doing. Influencing by catering to the urge to copy and to identify with the modeling behavior of others is quicker, cheaper, and more effective than directive communication and persuasion. Once again, it involves working obliquely within defenses and establishing proximity so that those who are dubious can see for themselves that we are safe and useful.

What we hope to help these unwelcoming agencies to discover is that it is possible to achieve various mission-related as well as intra-organizational goals by creating an atmosphere of mutual support for their workers. That such an atmosphere is inherently attractive was illustrated for us many years ago, when, engaged in mental health consultation in the field for the Peace Corps, we explained the purpose of our journey to the local American ambassador. We were bringing a message to the volunteers from Sargeant Shriver, the head of the agency and brother-in-law of President Kennedy. He wanted them to know that, when they encountered inevitable pressures in the field because of differences of culture, he understood that they might become personally upset. This, he wanted them to remember, was expected, and he would arrange to help them master the discomforts and the resulting inefficiencies in their operations. "I wish we could have a program like that," the ambassador said wistfully. "In the Foreign Service, everyone is watching everyone else for the slightest mistake, and when they find one, they jump on you and it leaves an indelible black mark on your record." One way to control iatrogenic damage, as we mentioned in the previous chapter, is to work with caregivers and their management to build into their agency an atmosphere of intercollegial trust that will enable workers to feel secure in revealing the details of their daily work with clients to fellow workers on an ongoing basis without the fear that any inadequacy in their operations will be dealt with by derogatory criticism.

In this respect, we should remember Joe's eminently mature and perceptive analysis of the behavior of the judge in his case. He saw that the inexperienced judge had been led astray by the Welfare Officer, had subsequently realized that he had made major mistakes, but was now unable to find a way of extracting himself, and therefore, had no alternative but to make more decisions based on the expediency of covering himself for as long as possible. Had the judge belonged to a supportive peer group in which such problems could have been revealed without incurring censure, and help could have been elicited, the entire case might have had a different configuration.

☐ Alternative to the Formal Role of Mental Health Consultant

If we abstract the basic techniques of mental health consultation from the role of a mental health consultant, we may create an analogue that follows a pattern characteristic of the epidemiological, public health aspect of community mental health. That pattern extracts from an intensified and highly specialized modality that requires considerable expertise and investment of professional time those essential principles that can be imparted to and used by less highly trained caregivers under mass conditions in the field. Thus aspects of intensive psychotherapy have been extracted and used in the less intensive form of counseling which enables less narrowly specialized professionals to treat a greater number of cases. We may dispense with the formal role of the specialist mental health consultant who operates according to formal contractual arrangements, periodically revised to fit the explicitly stated mutual needs and expectations of the host agency and the home institution of the consultant, because this formal framework requires feasibility, namely the explicit acceptance by the consultee agency of the fact that it needs help in limiting the damaging of cases.

While these formal roles could not be maintained in agencies of high salience but low feasibility, we may consider abstracting the essential features of the mental health consultation method and instilling them in nonspecialists, like the supervisors of any salient caregiving institution. The first essential feature to be imparted is how to spot whether or not an unconscious problem is interfering with a colleague's professional functioning. This is done by identifying the presence of constricted vision and inhibited data gathering, the stereotyping, dogmatic, and punitive misperceptions, and the resistance to any suggestion that the case is not as bad as it seems to the caregivers. Second, if such interference is found to be taking place, the nonspecialist consultant would be taught how to remedy it while never making the unconscious conscious and never attacking psychic defenses. Nonspecialist consultants must be taught always to work inside the displacement by talking about the case, never about the colleague's feelings or the history of the latter's private life, and by avoiding unlinking the case from the unconsciously held prognosis of inevitable danger. The main issues in training our colleagues in these principles is inculcating tact, a categorical prohibition against blurting out the obvious, and against any urge to intrude in someone's private world by direct questioning. Such a nonspecialist consultant process could be formally built into the routine of an agency's supervisory or peer interaction, or it could be informally triggered when any colleague noticed signs of loss of objectivity in a fellow worker. This also implies that the consultant must control any urge to derive narcissistic satisfaction by demonstrating his or her cleverness in solving the case through explicitly and openly identifying the unconscious sources of the consultee's difficulties.

Involvement of Judges

In order to select a professional group to be a model of openness to concepts of preventing iatrogenic damage, and whose attitude in this respect may be seen and copied by low-feasibility caregivers and their leaders, we need people who are secure enough to be relatively nondefensive. In addition, their role should constitute a leverage point, controlling the path along which many iatrogenic damage cases are carried, and they should be strategically placed to alter the functioning of other agencies. The profession that would appear to fulfill our criteria of status, location, and power is that of judges.

Within the overall system of community caregiving, judges are most prominently placed not only to affect the fate of individual children and their families, but also to discourage the perpetration of iatrogenic damage. Although the courts themselves are not immune from generating iatrogenic damage of their own, if judges are motivated to act and are fully aware of likely patterns of injurious behavior against clients, they are potentially among those wielding the most influence and power to change the situation. In order to identify the course of conscious and unconscious falsification of the reality of clients and of chronic harassment, judges may be most effectively placed. They cannot only interrupt damaging activities against an individual who appears before them, but also force changes in long-entrenched practices within institutions that, by their punitive behavior, premature closure, and imposition of a preplanned outcome, endanger the interests of children and families, culminating in the distorting of the court process itself. In theory, judges weigh all evidence impartially and provide a defense against the falsification that causes a caregiver's preconceived and predetermined outcome to actually take place and paralyzes the client's ability to counteract and appeal against it. In practice, however, often because of habit, cognitive overload, or personal views, judges may take the well-fortified word of a so-called responsible professional against the more weakly supported word of the client. In theory, defense attorneys should contest false accusations. In practice, many of the clients caught in such cases are disadvantaged and must use public defenders who have less time, inclination, or motivation to go to the lengths required to disprove an elaborately and expertly scripted official story. In Joe's case, we saw an additional factor, where falsehoods are carefully contrived with the often unwitting corroboration of other professionals and with the supposed consent of the child as proved by doubtful documentation. Thus, experienced, seasoned lawyers, asked to examine the material and appear for the defense, threw up their hands before so massive a task. In practice, rules are bent or ignored, whether by custom, by a lack of aggressive countermoves by opposing lawyers, or by the accommodation of a judge sympathetic to the caregiving system. Motivated judges who are on the alert to identify such sources of damage can stop all these practices.

☐ Proposals for Collaboration with Judges

We have been exploring ways to build a joint program with judges of the Rabbinic Courts and the secular Family Courts. Potentially, if we could offer them mental health consultation to increase their range of understanding of psychological issues, and their capacity to deal with complex and disturbing cases, these judges are the key individuals through whom the findings of our researches on preventive mental health might be implemented as part of a program to lower avoidable, institution-generated stress on divorcing families in general. They might also recognize the signs of strain and disorder in individual cases so as to help relieve pressures that may start a pathological process because of the family's basic problems, or because of the additional burden of iatrogenic harm.

Accordingly, we made a number of efforts over the first 10 years of our studies of the mental health problems of children of divorced parents in Jerusalem to develop an organizational framework for mental health consultation with the judges of the Rabbinic courts and the secular courts. We found, however, that this approach was not feasible because it runs counter to prevailing legal traditions in Israel, where it is forbidden in both court systems for judges to discuss current cases with outsiders except in open court hearings, where experts may be invited to give occasional evidence in accordance with a formal procedure. However, we did learn from a Family Court judge that we might maneuver around this obstacle and achieve analogous results by communicating our preventive formulations in an educational format. We therefore developed a proposal to establish joint study groups for mental health specialists, Rabbinic judges, and secular court judges, who would meet regularly once or twice a month to discuss commonly occurring problems that confront courts in cases of parental divorce. Our plan called for each meeting of the study group to focus on a fictitious case presented by one of the judges, which would be based on one or more real cases that he or she has recently handled with the help of a member of our team of mental health specialists.

We hoped that this format would be conducive to the development of collaborative activity between our team and judges of the two court systems. The proposal neatly overcame the obstacles posed by the requirements of the local legal system which precluded a consultation technique. Among its many other advantages, it was hoped that it would lead to the formation of joint religious and secular reference groups for judges who were basically working in the same field, and would provide sanction for new techniques of preventive intervention guided by the combined knowledge and experience of the three professional groups involved. The plan was sufficiently attractive to secure the agreement of both the authorities of the Rabbinic and secular court systems to the joint program. This was in a sense historic, marking the first time that the two frameworks had united in this way, for despite what outsiders might see as common ground logically entailing joint efforts, in fact, the two systems are so separated that their judges never formally mingle in their professional capacities.

☐ Unexpected Shortcomings in Planning

Once again, what seemed a promising step forward soon ran into unexpected obstacles, as is not unusual when one ventures out of one's office or clinic into the complexities of other community institutions. By hindsight, these pitfalls should have been predicted and should have modified the proposal before it was made public. As soon as we began to implement the plan that all the leaders had accepted, we discovered that the line workers had serious reservations that led them to resist doing what was expected of them. At the first scheduled meeting of the study group, all the Family Court judges and all the mental health specialists came, but only three of the invited Rabbinic judges turned up, even though 10 had accepted our invitation and we had carefully arranged the day and hour of the meeting to suit them. A judge of the Family Court presented a case marked by cultural and class conflicts, acute personality disorders in both parents, questions of possible violence and intimidations, ambivalent feelings in its principals, and the need to establish the least detrimental alternative for the conflicted, manipulated, and frightened children. The case, which bristled with difficulties in analyzing and balancing the various issues it presented, sparked an active discussion of important technical problems, both legal and psychological. This was exactly what we had planned. The presenter of the case was very satisfied with the session, for although several colleagues had argued with him about some of his decisions, he had been able to explain and expand on the dilemmas that had faced him. He seemed to feel that he had acquitted himself well in the eyes of the group, while increasing his own understanding of possible options and dangers that were implicit in the case.

We noticed, however, that the Rabbinic judges took little part in the discussion, and when we later asked for their reactions to the meeting, we were surprised to learn that the two most senior rabbis had been bored. Other Rabbinic judges whom we contacted did not want to meet with secular judges at all, because, they argued, the two court systems differed so much in philosophy and interests that it would be unlikely that we would be able to find topics in which both sides would share an interest. "In our daily work, we deal with resolving complicated issues of Rabbinic law. The secular judges would not be interested in this, nor do they have our background knowledge of religious writings to engage in such discussions." Other Rabbinic judges pointed to the difference in professional seniority of the two groups that we were trying to merge. With the exception of a senior justice of the Magistrates Court who was appointed to organize the newly established Family Court, the other secular judges were relative novices, the most senior of whom had had only three years experience on the bench. "You should not be surprised," the Rabbinic judges said, "that discussion of elementary issues of courtroom practice that was so interesting for the junior judges of the Family Court was not of equal interest to senior judges of the Rabbinic Court, who have had 15 to 20 years experience handling routine problems of judging conjugal conflicts."

Differences in professional culture and philosophy between caregiving frameworks with overlapping interests could be just as divisive in less exotic settings. What may seem like a logical step in bringing professionals together to discuss what outsiders perceive to be common interests may expose more differences than common ground, and this possibility must be factored into the planning of such joint meetings.

☐ A Case in the Rabbinic Court: A Psychiatric and Hallachic Solution

At the first meeting of our study group, we announced that in the second session, a senior Rabbinic judge would present a case in which we had made a psychiatric diagnosis that gave rise to an unexpected and unusual interpretation according to Rabbinic law. The case involved a man who had abandoned his pregnant wife shortly after their wedding, and had since been living as a homeless tramp. Although he now showed clear signs of mental illness, he was able to discuss his situation logically with the Rabbinic judges, rejecting their arguments that he should divorce his abandoned wife, and insisting that he loved his family. By the time the Rabbinic judges asked for Professor Caplan's advice, they had held innumerable hearings to which the police usually brought the husband, and during which interminable and repetitive arguments had led nowhere.

Professor Caplan, discovering that the man hardly spoke any Hebrew, offered to act as an interpreter for the court. He then spent several hours not only translating, but also using the opportunity to build a relationship with the man and to conduct a diagnostic interview in the presence of the judges. Caplan concluded that the man was suffering from paranoid schizophrenia and was actively deluded and hallucinated. Believing that he was in close contact with God, the man claimed that he had married his wife by order of the Almighty. The Deity had then told him to leave home and come to Jerusalem to the site of the Holy Temple. As is not unusual in such cases, despite his psychosis, he was able to discuss his case with apparent rationality, so that the fact that he was irrational most of the time had escaped the Rabbinic judges. Caplan then examined the reports of the psychiatrists and psychologists who had treated the man in his country of origin. The psychologists who had tested him at that time had felt that he was suffering from a personality disorder. Caplan phoned two psychiatrists who had treated the man. They said that, although they had not recorded their own diagnostic beliefs in the documents which had accompanied their patient to Israel, they agreed with our conclusion that the psychological testing had erred, and they too felt that the patient was suffering from a paranoid psychosis, not a personality disorder.

Professor Caplan then reported his opinion to the court. He found that the man had been suffering from paranoid schizophrenia before, during, and after the wedding, and consequently was at no time responsible for actions which had been driven by his delusional system. Therefore, from a psychiatric point of view, the wedding was invalid because, at the time, the bridegroom was unfit to make the necessary rational judgments. Professor Caplan also testified that the man was currently mentally unfit to take part in any court procedure and was unfit to grant a divorce. He validated his opinion about the duration of the man's psychosis by obtaining a signed statement from the psychiatrists who had treated the patient just before, and immediately following his wedding.

The court, and particularly its President, who had already decided that the only solution to the judicial impasse was to annul the marriage, received this psychiatric opinion with great interest. That judge had buttressed his own opinion by discovering that one of the official witnesses to the wedding ceremony had been a relative of the bridegroom's, which, because the latter could be classed as an interested party rather than an impartial witness as required by religious law, invalidated the wedding ceremony. However, the President of the court had felt that this was not a completely convincing ground for an annulment, because it could not negate the fact that the couple had cohabited for several months after the wedding, which of itself created a potentially legal marriage. Thus, even if the judge had established that the actual ceremony had not been conducted in accordance with religious rules, the couple would still need an official divorce to part them, and for this to take place, both parties had to consent freely and rationally to giving and receiving the Bill of Divorce which the husband was unwilling and mentally unable to do.

Our psychiatric evidence therefore broke the impasse by strengthening a case for the retroactive annulment of the marriage because according to religious law, legal marriages have to be both entered into and terminated only by free and rational choice. Since the husband's choice had not been rational, the wedding could be shown unambiguously to have been equally invalid. Retroactive annulment of marriage was a most unusual ruling by a Rabbinic court, but it obviated the need for fruitless arguments with the psychotic husband to free his wife. The wife and child would thereby be spared prolongation of an uncertain legal status that would itself generate iatrogenic damage since the system's inability to act would have impeded their chances to rebuild their lives.

Even though the Rabbinic judge was willing to present this case at the second meeting of our study group, he had doubts as to whether the Family Court judges would be as interested in discussing what was for him and his Rabbinic colleagues the most salient issue, the fine points of religious law. In any event, he was forced to postpone the meeting because of urgent business that took him abroad for several weeks, and by the time he returned, we had decided to delay further meetings until we had clarified and worked through the complications of implementing our original plan for joint sessions with both groups of judges. By then, it had become clear that we had too hastily over-looked the major differences of interest and approach of the two groups of judges. The mental health specialists and the leaders of both court systems had been attracted by the political and public relations advan-tages of the joint program, and only when we began to implement it at the line workers level had the impression emerged that we had too easily dismissed the difficulties. We realized that, if our primary objec-tive was to provide a learning opportunity for the judges about mental health aspects of their work, this might be better achieved by having separate sessions for Rabbinic and secular judges with mental health workers.

☐ Obstacles to Changing our Plans

It became clear to us that our original conception of joint groups con-tained basic flaws, but we encountered a most instructive obstacle when we tried to alter our own further activities. We found that our funding agency had been impressed by the attractive political and public relations issues of joint secular–religious meetings, rather than by what, for us, were more basic issues of improving professional functioning. When we proposed separating the groups in order to cater to the different needs of each, the employees of the funding agency would not accept the change. This highlights a significant ad-ministrative issue in research planning. Action research, if it is to have any value, requires built-in flexibility so that emerging findings can alter the structure of the program as it unfolds. This, in turn, may generate new findings and new research processes. If funding and administrative sanction requires, and is tied to a preconceived, fixed plan from the outset, and if that plan includes values in which these interested parties are heavily invested (which is their prerogative), the research findings and the emerging programs may not reflect or meet the needs of the real world. Since the middle level administrator of the particular private funding agency supporting this facet of our program could not grasp this, we had to terminate a relationship that was hampering our ability to mold our program to fit the emerging picture of actual needs. From this we may conclude that when arranging for such funding, from the outset both parties should understand the need for flexibility and for anticipating the unexpected. What may seem logical and attractive in theory, may turn out to be less so in practice, and midcourse corrections may well become imperative if money and effort are not to be foolishly wasted.

☐ The Reactive Versus the Proactive Role of Judges

This set-back in our original plans for the joint judges and mental health workers groups has led us to think through some of the complications of trying to involve divorce court judges in collaborating with us in preventing mental disorders and iatrogenic damage in the children of divorcing parents. In the field of family conflicts and divorce these judges usually conceptualize their basic role as mediators and arbiters in resolving conflicts between contending adult family members, but they are also supposed to supervise parental planning for the future care of the children after the divorce. In Israel, as in other countries such as the United Kingdom, there is increasing dissatisfaction with the routine arrangements for fulfilling the latter role (Murch, 1998). Perhaps one of the reasons for this is that it requires proactive behavior by the judges, which is a departure from their customary role of reacting to the evidence presented and to the demands for judgment by contending parties in a court suit. This complicated issue is also linked with the caution felt by judges in intervening in the lives of people beyond the immediate demands to establish the rights and wrongs of a current case. It may be that when a couple sues for divorce, the spouses thereby invite judicial intervention in all the consequences of the dissolution of their marriage, including how their children should be cared for, particularly in light of the increased risks to the mental health of these children, but it is not clear to what extent the judges feel it is appropriate for them to intervene.

Rabbinic judges may be more comfortable adopting the role of mentor and accepting responsibility for guarding the interests of the children of divorcing parents than would secular judges because of the pastoral aspects of their primary role as rabbis. There is a Hallachic tradition that a Rabbinic court has the duty to act as "the parent of parentless children." But it is not clear how far individual Rabbinic judges are actually prepared to go in initiating intervention that is not demanded by one of the parties to a dispute, particularly in view of the pressure on them to adjudicate among the rising numbers of divorcing parents.

Judges often rationalize their reluctance to extend their interventions beyond the fulfillment of their basic role as arbiters in marital disputes by emphasizing the fact that judicial action is likely to be a one-time affair whose continuing effect on the life of the family depends on the acceptance of its details by both plaintiffs in the future. Implementation will depend on the motivation and capacity of family members to act in the court-prescribed way in their daily life. When a dominant parent refuses to accept the opinions of the court, and when judges exert little force because they are not sure that they are justified in intervening, little will be gained. Moreover, we have seen a number of cases where one of the parents has been able to determine the boundaries of court intervention through manipulating the judges. Whether the latter realize what is happening or not, they go along with it because they apparently feel that to oppose this limitation of their role would not be worth the effort.

While the professional posture of judges may tend to be reactive rather than proactive, responding to evidence and situations submitted rather than initiating interventions in policy, precedents exist for their stimulating developments that mold the behavior of other caregivers. For example, divorce court judges in Toronto decided that divorce litigation should proceed by mediation in order to help the contending parties work together to find the best alternatives for the children. It did not take them long to influence the lawyers to alter their traditional confrontational tactics, even though this involved a loss of income for the advocates and required them to learn a new set of professional techniques. Judges in Georgia and in neighboring states in the U.S.A. have initiated a most interesting program of primary prevention that requires every divorcing parental couple to participate in a standard seminar that focuses on the reactions of children to the divorce of their parents and on the methods that many parents have developed to support their children's efforts to cope. In both these instances, there was considerable opposition to the changes proposed by the judges, partly by conservative colleagues on the bench, and partly by lawyers. In all cases, the innovative judges have overcome this resistance.

As far as we know, in these campaigns to force radical changes, it appears that the idea and the initiative started among the judges. Mental health workers, educators, and child welfare workers were brought in by the judges to help them in their efforts. In Jerusalem, our Rabbinic Court judges are known to be conservative and independently minded, therefore we can only succeed in our campaign to involve them as active collaborators in a joint preventive mental health program for the children of divorcing parents, if we can persuade each

Rabbinic judge as an individual to interest himself in this field. Perhaps if a sufficient number of Rabbinic judges become convinced of the importance of the topic, and interested enough in this addition to their role, there might be a change in the atmosphere of the Rabbinic Courts as a whole. But, we should not expect this to happen quickly.

☐ Proposed Approaches to Reach Our Preventive Goals

Our present plan is to try to achieve our objective of changing the consciousness of individual judges about iatrogenic damage as well as about issues involved in children's vulnerability in divorcing families by a number of different approaches.

We would like to organize seminars for interested Rabbinic judges that will be open also to Family Court judges, and that will present systematic courses of lectures and discussions about our theories of preventive psychiatry and the techniques that we use. These seminars will be an addition to our program of separate joint study groups for mental health specialists and Rabbinic and Family Court judges.

We hope to raise funds to pay for us to investigate and offer counsel to poverty-stricken conflicted parents who are considering divorce. When a Family Court or a Rabbinic Court with which we are affiliated accepts these cases, it will provide an opportunity for us and the judges to work together in achieving a superordinate goal (Sherif et al., 1961). In this way, we will ensure a flow of cases to be judged by those Rabbinic judges and Family Court judges who have appointed us to be their expert witnesses and with whom we seek to develop relationships.

We also hope to focus our attention on a series of populations that will become target groups as described in the introduction to this book. These target groups, it will be remembered, include children of mentally healthy but ineffectual parents, children of a parent who covertly manipulates family members in order to solve his or her intrapsychic problems, and children of families who are victims of iatrogenic harm. We would explain the common characteristics of certain high-risk groups so as to alert judges to the need for taking special care of particular types of cases. One such population on which we are currently working is child survivors of the Holocaust. We expect this population to be our fourth target group, and after working this through we will search for other similar populations.

Based on our early, disappointing experience with the joint meeting of judges, we will advance our plans slowly in a series of successive steps with the expectation that we are likely to make more mistakes in our planning. Our continually evaluating and hunting for missteps that will be exposed by unexpected reactions of the field of forces will slow our progress. It is important to identify such errors as quickly as possible so as to choose a different route to achieve our goal. Flexibility on this point is essential, and we must beware of any interference with this flexibility by, for instance, a grant-giving agency that quite naturally wishes us to abide by the plan for which they have donated their money, or by a representative of an organization with which we have developed a partnership to implement our preventive program.

☐ Influencing Individuals Rather than Reforming the System

We are also developing a new conceptual model for planning and programmatic operations that will guide us in deciding on priorities that determine our choice of one path over another in dilemmas such as the above. In our campaign to prevent and control iatrogenic harming, we have decided not to seek new laws and reform programs because experience shows that these will all eventually be sidestepped or taken over by the harming caregivers or by those professionals with hidden agendas. New laws and reformed institutions can be likened to the static defense lines in military situations such as the Maginot Line in the Second World War or the Bar-Lev Line in the south of Israel before the Yom Kippur War, both of which were considered impregnable, but were overrun or circumvented without much trouble. Instead, we are opting for mobile tactics, by identifying key workers who may exert power and influence over discreet areas in the field, such as divorce court judges, and then finding ways of motivating them and equipping them with ideas and techniques with the expectation that either they themselves will develop ways of dealing with the problems, or that we will be able to work together with them in achieving joint aims. As we have stressed earlier, the defenses against damaging behavior that are likely to be most effective are not those imposed by outside agencies or laws, but rather by the internalization of values by individual professionals, in this case, judges. It is to be hoped that, when a sufficient number of such individuals have absorbed the message that it is necessary to prevent damage to clients, then the general climate of opinion may be altered, as was the case in our example of the changed atmosphere in the meeting in the House of Bishops.

However, even proposals that sound logical and simple are very complex. In countering damaging behavior, it may be futile to attack the power bases of the iatrogenic caregivers by frontal means, but it may eventually be possible to erode their capacity for harm by placing obstacles in their path. Those professionals who are driven by corporately shared themes and hidden agendas will probably find new ways to get their way, but an informed and motivated judiciary will make it harder for them to do so. Stimulated by the influence of judges who are won over to taking active initiatives in the field, agencies may organize their personnel policies so as to provide a supportive system for their workers and will thereby attract the brighter caregivers and eventually probably higher levels of compensation and status rewards. Such measures may eventually erode the present power balance in certain areas of caregiving, thereby lowering the incidence of damaging behavior.

☐ Peer Support for Judges

One further advantage of instituting study groups for judges and mental health workers would be the peer support that such a forum could provide. Like the Episcopalian bishops, whose consultation dyads were described in the last chapter, secular judges would seem to share an elevated and highly responsible role that may be lonely and necessarily isolated. In a typical iatrogenic case, for example, a welfare officer, having removed a child from its family, showed open bias against the mother. The mother's lawyer appealed to the judge, who had already acknowledged that the social worker was prejudiced, to order her removed from the case. The judge is said to have answered, "If she is removed, they will only replace her with a similar worker, and if I don't accept her demands, she will repeat them every thirty days until I give in." This plaintive remark may be due to burnout after dealing with many similar cases in a specialized court and having been worn down by the personnel of caregiving agencies who appeared before him daily. Yet this note of weary impotence may also have been due to a lack of peer support that could have sustained and strengthened him in his role, so that he could have continued to assert proper judicial authority in the face of openly damaging behavior, and in the face of powerful, central agencies whose importuning workers sometimes appear to be competing with the court for primary decision-making power.

☐ A Recent Example of a Judge Interrupting the Development of Iatrogenic Damage

In contrast is the example of another judge who was not only able to withstand pressure from a number of powerful sources, but also acted with independence and insight to stop a typical iatrogenic damage situation marked by misrepresentations by caregivers and attempts by them to outmaneuver earlier court decisions. According to a newspaper account, this judge of the Jerusalem Family Court "severely criticized, government welfare officials for their handling of an adoption case" (Reinfeld, 2000), having concluded that "welfare officials had turned the child over to adoptive parents without examining their compatibility or openness, and had used 'deceptions' in curbing the mother's court-approved contacts with the child, thus 'harming the child's welfare, for which the [officials] were responsible.'" The behavior of these officials had forced the judge to return the child to its biological mother without "appropriate preparation." "The court further criticized the welfare sources for effectively dropping the child's case once it was clear that she would not be transferred to the adoptive parents."

Two years earlier, when the child was four, a judge had ruled that the girl should be sent to live with potential adoptive parents because of the opinion of the Attorney-General's office, which was in turn "based on recommendations of a welfare officer and [a] psychologist . . . appointed by the court as an expert in the field. The recommendations said in unequivocal terms that the child's biological parents were incapable of functioning as parents."

Despite this latter conclusion, the judge's original ruling had "stressed that the tie between the girl and her biological mother could be preserved in the interim." It later became clear to the court, however, "that the welfare officer had concealed this possibility from the adoptive parents. The officer told the adoptive parents that after a few visits the child was to be entirely cut off from her biological mother. The officer asked the court to order an immediate halt to visits by the mother, citing 'a most serious deterioration in the girl's mental state and level of functioning.'"

The judge, however, had noted "a growing improvement in the mother's condition," and concluded that the welfare officers "had failed to provide adequate backing for the claims of supposed harm caused by the visitations." In consequence, "Over the objections of the Attorney-General's office," the judge had asked another expert to conduct an up-to-date assessment. This second expert, analyzing the current findings about the status of the various people involved, had advised returning the child to her biological mother.

"When the adoptive parents threatened to return the child to welfare authorities if the maternal visits were resumed, the judge ordered the girl transferred to her mother without further preparation." The judge noted, "The child has since acclimatized well."

The account of this case demonstrates a judge's capacity to avoid stereotyping and cognitive closure. The mother's earlier dire incapacity apparently did not lead the judge to conclude that this was a necessarily immutable feature of her personality, and the bench was able to continue to monitor and assess new data elicited from a variety of sources over time and to adjust rulings accordingly. It is also to be noted that this judge had the apparent capacity to act decisively and unflinchingly when credible information indicated that this was appropriate. He or she then gave clear cut orders for moving the child that left no room for evasive and delaying tactics by welfare officers who might manipulate towards a different outcome, in the style of practice we saw in cases cited in earlier chapters. In this respect, we should note the recurrence of the theme of cooperation between the Attorney-General's office and the welfare officers, who in this as in our earlier cited cases made common cause, thereby implicating in damaging behavior not only the caregiving system, but also the central administration of the legal system.

The press account makes clear that this judge was maintaining open channels of information and was continuing to receive updated information about the child's development. Consequently, should future difficulties occur, it would seem likely that such an open-minded judge would have no hesitation in making course corrections in order to ensure the child's continued physical and emotional well-being.

Different legal systems in different countries will all affect the rate of both iatrogenic damage to clients and the degree of stress to which children of divorcing parents are subjected. The role of the judge is a universally influential one, though his or her position may grant greater or lesser latitude to be proactive and to determine the further disposition of those who appear before the bench. From our primary preventive mental health perspective, however, the need to inform judges about our findings, and the desirability of motivating them to forestall possibly avoidable risks to the emotional well-being of children and their families cuts across the differences in procedures and cultures. Judges have the potential to affect the proceedings of other community caregiving systems, either by colluding with damaging procedures, or interrupting them so that the imbalance of power between damaging professionals and their vulnerable clients becomes less inevitable.

Our Response to Some Critics

Throughout the writing of this book, we have consulted colleagues in various countries about their experiences of iatrogenic damage and their impressions about how we are handling the material we have gathered. On the whole, fellow professionals readily identified with our observations and felt it important and courageous (or did they mean foolhardy?) to break the silence surrounding this virtually taboo subject. There were, however, recurring criticisms that we felt required consideration both in our revisions of the manuscript and in explicit elucidation here before we conclude our observations in the next chapter. Such critical and opposing views served to correct our own perceptions, to complicate our own thinking, and to tease out, both for ourselves and for our audience, the hitherto unspoken, perhaps only half-realized bases on which our assumptions have been built.

☐ Anger

A number of those whose opinions we solicited were disturbed by what they felt was our tone of anger. This should be considered openly since if it disturbed these colleagues, it might also alienate other portions of our audience, leading to their dismissing our arguments as hysterical, paranoid, or so lacking in balance as to preclude serious consideration of the issues raised.

Individual cases did make us angry, even very angry, especially in our early exposure to this material. In time, perhaps inevitably, we became accustomed to the stereotyped pattern of events and therefore tended to view cases in a more detached and even fatalistic manner, though the remnants of our anger may not be in strict keeping with the dispassionate and nonjudgmental stance expected from seasoned professionals and researchers, nevertheless, we admit that as human beings we have been upset by the unnecessary suffering inflicted on vulnerable clients and by the virtual failure of the judicial and legislative authorities to reign in those responsible for repeated cases of this type. Even professionals can and should feel angry in the face of the abuses against human dignity and right reason that characterize many of these instances. Such anger is a negative emotion only if it narrows one's focus and preoccupies in a sterile or destructive manner. If it leads only to name-calling and to impotently shouting, "Something should be done! Why don't those in authority deal with it?", anger serves no useful purpose. However, it can be a positive force if it focuses our attention and energizes our commitment, so that we are driven to explore in an analytical, open-minded way why such things happen, and then forces us to ponder how we can interrupt a realistically bad situation. Anger is positive when it jolts us out of our comfortable, conventional mind-set, and gives us the energy and courage to look at what we would rather not see. It is positive when it overcomes our mental lethargy—what Jonathan Swift, the eighteenth century satirist, attacked as man's lazy mental tendency to engage in "mechanical thinking"—and instead obliges us to think unconventionally and creatively in order to find new ways to change damaging practices.

☐ Are We Prejudiced Against Social Workers?

Some readers felt that we were not only angry, but also prejudiced against certain categories of caregivers, and, in particular, that we were unfairly stereotyping and even demonizing social workers. In part, our apparent singling out for criticism of *some* social workers employed by the child protection, Welfare, and adoption agencies was an artifact of our caseload. We were dealing primarily with family disintegration that involved the courts, and the courts tended to involve, or be involved by the child protection agencies. Therefore, social workers were the most frequently encountered professionals in the iatrogenic cases with which we dealt. Had we been engaged in different types of cases, as we were, for example, when we worked in the Hadassah Hebrew University teaching hospitals, we might have seen more physicians and nurses in damaging roles. Had we been working in the school system, we might have seen teachers and guidance counselors engaged in iatrogenic harm.

This, however, begs the main question of whether we are prejudiced against the profession of social work. That this question should even arise is ironic and betrays on the part of those who suggest it an ignorance of the history of the social work profession and its literature, to both of which Gerald Caplan has made crucial and well-documented contributions (G. Caplan, 1955, 1956, 1959).

A brief history of that involvement is worth noting here. During the 1950s, while working at Harvard School of Public Health on the development of the United States' Federally supported Community Mental Health Program, Gerald Caplan was asked by the Children's Bureau, and later by the National Institute of Mental Health to take part in their campaign to involve the leaders of the professions of psychiatry, psychology, and social work in the newly developing field. His operations in social work centered mainly in Berkley, California, at the State Department of Public Health and at the School of Social Welfare. He worked closely with Virginia Insley, Esther Spencer, and Rhona Rapaport. He visited on an annual basis for 15 years, and taught seminar groups of leading professors of social work drawn from the whole country, who then transmitted the content to their own students. At Harvard, we taught similar material in an extension program that recruited students for week-long seminars, attended by practitioners from social work, psychology, psychiatry, general medical practice, pediatrics, nursing, and the clergy. And when G. Caplan moved to Harvard Medical School and organized our Laboratory of Community Psychiatry to train leading specialists in Community Mental Health, social workers were freely admitted and formed about a quarter of our multidisciplinary student body.

During that period, G. Caplan was an active member of the Executive Committee of the International Association of Child Psychiatry, which began as an association of national member societies that excluded nonmedical members. He led an active fight to open membership to social workers and other nonmedical professions, and eventually that fight was won, and the name of the organization was changed to include "And Allied Professions."

And so, we have now reached a stage when social workers are accepted in the field of community mental health as professionals of equal status to nurses, psychologists, educators, and psychiatrists in training programs; and after appropriate advanced specialist training and experience, they are eligible for any clinical or administrative role in our field. For example, they may appear as expert witnesses in court. But they should warn judges that no experts, including social workers, should be expected to give authoritative answers to questions about subjects in which they have had inadequate specialized training and experience.

Let us consider the question of our possible prejudices from another angle. Instead of asking, "Are we against social workers?" let us ask, "Does what we have been describing in the cases cited earlier constitute the normative practice of social work?" That the cases we have seen are handled by people with a degree in social work, who identify themselves as social workers, and who label what they do as "child protection," a traditional and necessary function of social workers, should not sway us. In various totalitarian settings, psychiatrists have engaged in the confinement and "treatment" of political dissidents. These are activities that many of us would hesitate to identify as falling within the legitimate boundaries of the psychiatric profession, even though accredited members of its professional guilds may carry them out. Few would say that to oppose such activities constitutes an attack on the discipline of psychiatry.

Comparing some damaging social workers to some psychiatrists who serve totalitarian regimes is meant to evoke the tendency of some caregivers, under the compulsion of greater or lesser personal necessity, to carry out functions that may superficially resemble a legitimate professional role, but whose underlying reality is quite otherwise. We may clarify this point by the following example, an account in the press about the childhood suffering of an Australian aborigine, Terry Olson, at the hands of white adoptive parents and schoolmates. His ordeal began as follows.

> While his aunt and grandmother sat in the waiting room (of a clinic) assuming the 18-month-old Aborigine with a milk-chocolate complexion and wavy brown hair was getting an immunization, a social worker spirited the toddler out of the back door. Unbeknown to his parents, he was eventually deposited with a white family more than 1000 miles away under a government program aimed at forcibly assimilating lighter-skinned indigenous people. He was later told that his parents had died.

Mr. Olson was reunited as an adult with his parents and now wants an apology from the Australian government (Chandrasekaran, 2000) for the policies that led to his unhappy childhood.

If we wonder how a social worker could justify such activity as described above, and view it as falling within his or her professional role, we must remember that, in an earlier chapter of this book, we remarked on a tendency for issues that are superficially similar to slide together, and consequently for boundaries between the permitted and the forbidden to become blurred. This is true not only of clients whose version of disciplining or of showing affection to children has come to be seen as verging on the suspect, but also of professional functioning. Thus the role of social workers in welfare, child protection, and adoption can be mutated into a damaging one when it blends into the superficially similar guise of philanthropic abduction if it is possible for the abduction to be suitably dressed up so as to seem indeed philanthropic, desirable, and as contributing to the welfare of all those "worth" saving, because of their physical appearance or intellectual assets. Under such circumstances, unwary professionals, or those with particular bents of personality, may be lured and lulled into believing that they are engaging in beneficent and legitimate professional functioning. Many of their colleagues as well as members of the lay public may be equally seduced by the veneer that makes such behavior look like acceptable and even necessary practice. More discerning observers, however, may realize that the boundaries of correct functioning have been shifted and that corrective adjustments in border markings are called for. While we may all condemn the injustice and prejudice that produced the situation in Australia, analogous, though far smaller scale examples of generically similar damaging practice may be happening around us.

A recent investigative article in an Israeli Russian language newspaper (Filarstova, 2000), describes a case that conforms to all the typical criteria of iatrogenic damage that we have been describing. The impressions of the journalist about the role of the social workers is sobering. Two children were removed from a mother in the process of a messy divorce, and were placed in a residential institution. The intervention of social workers, the reporter discovered, can be activated by the slightest rumor, and not necessarily by one based on facts. The article pointed out that social workers were equipped to produce mountains of convincing documentation condemning the parents which grew into a detailed, impregnable, and not necessarily accurate case against which the mother could offer only her bare word in her own defense. When asked by the newspaper to explain their removal of the children, the social welfare agency sent back a proforma, stereotyped letter stating that the mother is "a terrible woman," a conclusion doubted by the reporter who had noted "the look in the children's eyes" when they were with her. The mother, this article continues, has been rendered helpless, first by the volume of documentation arrayed against her mere word, and also by her humiliation and fear that if she were to raise a public outcry, the community at large would suspect that "so much smoke implies a fire." Like us, this reporter realized that no politician would touch such cases because there is no political capital to be made in battling the powerful and well-entrenched welfare system; and the reporter adds that such cases are hopeless and lost from their onset because a practiced system has sealed every chink that would offer any avenue of escape. The reporter concludes with an indictment of a profession that turns the misfortunes of others into a "feeding trough," and she demands that recently elected Russian-speaking city counselors investigate the social services agency.

We would submit that the stereotyping of parents, the falsifying of records, and the force and lack of scruples used to effect the removal of children from their families does not represent the role of a caregiving profession that is popularly expected to ameliorate mental and physical suffering in the community. We are certainly not against the legitimate practice of social workers, but we are against those who, using the label of social work and claiming its benevolent goals, engage in activities that are pathogenic.

The field of social work, like other caregiving professions, is defined not only by its practitioners, but also by the community at large that expects it to do a certain job in a certain way. When those expectations are not met, the public is apt to condemn this frustration of expectations. Trying to dismiss the observations of a growing number of witnesses to incidents of iatrogenic harm as prejudice against social workers will hardly improve the standing of the profession as a whole, let alone stem these practices.

☐ We Failed to Foresee Pitfalls in our Early Ideas

When, 40 years ago, some social work leaders, seduced by the lure of psychoanalysis, advocated replacing its traditional function of community outreach by mimicking and adopting the supposedly higher status role of psychoanalysts, we were among those responsible for influencing social workers to return to community work, to engage precisely in such fields as child welfare and child protection. Therefore, we pioneers in community mental health share the guilt for what went wrong. We did not anticipate the reverberations that our hopeful plans would produce, because we never imagined the complexities of actual field conditions. We had developed our ideas, as we said earlier, in what we now realize were almost sanitized laboratory surroundings, among caregivers whose culture we understood, whose motivation was assured, and whose level of intelligence and excitement at sharing in a pioneering and innovative experiment enhanced their response to unanticipated difficulties. When such endeavors became the routinized daily work of ordinary, minimally trained line workers, who had to function in situations and cultural milieux that we could not have envisioned, the glamour and hope of early ideas was apt to prove overblown. Innovations were harder to sustain in the colder atmosphere of real communities. The judge in Joe's case, for example, began to do something daring that we have long been urging a whole range of caregivers to do. He left his courtroom in order to go into the community to look at the boy's real situation. Unfortunately, as far as we can tell, he had neither the training nor the support to handle the next step, to use what he may have seen to correct the course of events and to refresh his outlook. Like this judge, we have to face the mess that some of our ideas have created, but we cannot then retreat, as he appears to have done, into a defensive posture. We must rebuild our plans based on even the disillusioning things we have learned. We are better off now than we were decades ago when we formulated our early ideas. Now we have seen firsthand the pitfalls and complexities of real professionals working in real communities, so we have the materials to revise and plan a range of new techniques. But this time, we know that we must plan for flexibility, remembering that, when things inevitably go wrong, we will have to make running repairs. Therefore, we had better have our tools and alternate strategies for doing so prepared and close at hand.

We must also remember that one of these pitfalls is that ideas take on a life of their own, and are apt to become so distorted in practice as to become virtually unrecognizable. It is imperative, therefore, that senior theoreticians and educators retain direct contact with their field in order to monitor, and if possible compensate for this inevitable process of mutation, and not advance so far into an insulated academic and administrative framework as to lose touch with "out there," as some of our senior social work colleagues appear to have done. What we did in Jerusalem, by going back into direct contact (and confrontation) with the actual grass roots of the current community mental health field, without the buffering of a research staff and of a prestigious university affiliation, would have been unthinkable at our level of seniority had we stayed at Harvard. The university setting would have been a great deal more comfortable, and probably we would have been treated with a great deal more deference, but we would not have seen the gritty reality that demands and inspires new ideas. We might have grown even less cognizant of how far the implementation of our ideas in the community was veering away from their source. We would not have seen that there is a pattern imposed on the drift, a pattern towards oversimplification that can reduce necessarily complex ideas to nonsense, and towards turning humane theories into screens behind which to engage in quite alien and possibly damaging practices.

Our early readers are correct in perceiving that we are upset. Indeed, this whole book is a testimony to our emotional arousal as we view a damaging situation. However, they have not accurately pinpointed the reason for this upset. It is not that we are opposed to social workers. It is, on the contrary, that we are identified with these fellow professionals and know that the lapses in professional behavior that can occur among them are common to all of us. All of us, whether psychiatrists, psychologists, teachers, guidance counselors, judges, or others are guilty at times of closed-mindedness, of stereotyping, of losing objectivity for conscious or unconscious reasons, and of using our clients for our own conscious or unconscious benefit, rather than catering to their needs. This sense of "There but for the grace of God go I" is one of the engines that has driven this research, since we are just as capable of being closed-minded as any other service provider. We will return to this in the next chapter. Here, however, we should note that we are aware of this danger, and we actively guard against it. Gerald Caplan, because of his psychoanalytic training has been drilled to include self-scrutiny in every clinical interaction. As members of a multidisciplinary team that includes nonprofessionals, we all watch and challenge each other. Even when we come to a conclusion about a case, we never close it. Though we must act on these conclusions and cannot remain in Hamlet-like indecision, we remain open to revising our ideas and recommendations as new information comes in. We remind each other to keep every option open, admitting to ourselves that like the colleagues described in earlier chapters, we can and do make mistakes. We are sensitive on this subject, as our readers have noted, and we try to stay as emotionally raw as the young pathologists who watched Robinson's film, *A Three-Year-Old Goes to Hospital*, mentioned in an earlier chapter, and to fight the defensive strategy of losing empathy not only when dealing with burdensome situations in clients, but also in reacting in an anaesthetized way to the damaging behavior of colleagues. One does not have to man the barricades, but one should openly acknowledge that a problem is present for every practicing professional, and one should apply the lesson to oneself. That it is possible to avoid stereotyping may be seen from the example of Joe, who did not demonize the judge, but instead considered the latter's dilemma, a good person vainly trying to extricate himself from a quagmire of mistakes. If a young boy in the midst of such experiences can be so open-minded, so can the rest of us.

Finally, we should note that dismissing the observations of a growing number of witnesses to incidents of corporately supported iatrogenic harm as prejudice against social workers will hardly improve the standing of the profession as a whole, let alone stem the practices of these well-entrenched and self-justifying groups. If certain groups of professionals, who happen to be social workers, driven by a need to gratify their own psychological needs and ideological agendas, have set up a damaging and secretive system under the legitimating aegis of social work, it is up to the profession itself to decide whether such people can be allowed to represent them, or whether the safe-guarding of their own good name requires some determined housecleaning.

☐ The Criticism of an Anonymous Colleague

Among our critics was an anonymous reviewer, one of a group whose opinions were solicited by the publisher as a step towards deciding whether or not to accept this book. When excerpts from this person's assessment were shown to us, we felt that it would be worth quoting this professional at some length and then considering his or her points in detail, because they are cogent and may anticipate the impressions and doubts of other readers. The reviewer is first concerned by

> the theme of the authors' criticism of professionals, particularly those in the child welfare field, whose combination of ignorance and bias lead them to intervene in ways that are insensitive and destructive. As a child psychiatrist who has done research in and consulted to the child welfare field for 37 years, I had more trouble with this section. It is not that the iatrogenic abuses that the authors describe do not occur in the child welfare field; of course they do, *sometimes*. But I found the authors so critical of child welfare practices that it seemed to me that they had little understanding of the dilemma of the child worker. While working under intense pressure, workers are forced to choose between two potentially life-saving but also potentially destructive alternatives. They can remove children from their families when, if support for the family would have helped improve the parenting to an adequate level, the act of apprehension will prove damaging to both child and family. Or they can decide not to apprehend, when failure to do so or returning children again and again to families that are unable, even with the most supportive interventions available, to meet their most basic physical and emotional needs can be a threat to the children's cognitive, emotions and social development and, possibly, to their lives. I would add that the threat is not just that of physical or sexual abuse, but also of chronic and severe emotional abuse and severe and chronic neglect which, over time, can be as damaging as all but the most life-threatening physical

abuse. I got no sense in this section that the authors appreciated the danger involved in failing to apprehend a child from a neglectful or abusive family—especially during the first few years when so much brain development is occurring that is so strongly influenced by the quality of care the child receives and by the level of conflict and violence in the family to which the child is exposed. That risk is no less than the risk of apprehending inappropriately, although I did not get the impression that the authors were aware of that. I was not clear as to why what I considered a lack of balance was present in so many examples. Are there problems unique to the exclusively orthodox and ultraorthodox Jewish community with whom the Caplans work? Is the child welfare system in Jerusalem that much more inadequate than it was in 1982–83, when I had some exposure to it as a consultant, and so much more inadequate than those in Canada to whom I have consulted? Is it that the Caplans, who work primarily with parents, are over-identified with them and, therefore, are biased against apprehension even when nothing less can protect the children's safety and potential for development? (Objectivity, in this situation, consists of being prepared to do everything possible to support the parents but, at the same time, open to seeing when the "help" is not helping and when apprehension is indicated.) Could the authors be demonstrating some of the same bias and demonization of others (i.e., a service system from which they have been polarized) that they describe in some of the examples in the book? Or am I misreading and misinterpreting this part of the book? For whatever reason, the tone of many of the examples will, unfortunately, offend, and therefore alienate many of those in the child welfare community who, if it were more balanced, would greatly benefit from the discussion of the potential hazards of allowing less well trained professionals to work beyond their capacity and without a proper commitment to adequate supervision, consultation and in-service training.

☐ Is Damaging Behavior the Inevitable Outcome of the Need to Make Critical Decisions?

The reviewer's first point, based, as he or she says, on 37 years of experience in the child welfare field, that the abuses we described occur "sometimes" and occur, he or she implies, as an almost inescapable concomitant of the dilemma faced by pressured workers caught between doing too much or too little in potentially life-threatening situations, would have been shared by us before we were drawn into this study by the cases that arrived in our office. In fact, the iatrogenic damage cases we have encountered have seldom involved the dilemma posited by the reviewer. Though the justification for intervention was often stated as the need to protect a child, an analysis of the facts showed that no real danger existed, but that did not prevent intervention. In such instances, one is forced to conclude that the rallying cry of protecting a child from abuse was a red herring. Had an adequate, open-minded evaluation of the circumstances of these clients been conducted by caregivers who initiated intervention, it would have been clear that any early suspicions about danger were exaggerated or even chimeral. But one of the hallmarks of damaging systems is their lack of flexibility because of investment in a preplanned outcome, and their consequent inability or unwillingness to admit mistakes and the need to change course.

The instances that we have been, and continue to be exposed to are not the product of what we might term "honest" mistakes of the type suggested by this reviewer, in which, after careful gathering and weighing of compelling evidence professionals draw an ultimately wrong and possibly pathogenic conclusion, such as returning a child to a family that is abusive because the degree of danger had not been recognized. Nor, for example, are these the type of cases, unfortunately not unknown, in which an unscrupulous or overburdened caregiver acts in contravention of accepted norms with sometimes terrible consequences, claiming, for example, to have maintained oversight while never actually doing so. If such behavior is brought to public attention and to the notice of superiors, presumably it would lead to repudiation, disciplinary action, and some measure of compensation for the damage caused to clients. In many of the more disturbing cases we have encountered, on the contrary, the damaging professionals were well-disciplined workers acting in accordance with the apparent standards of their agencies and enjoying the support of superiors. Though an outsider might view their actions with dismay, by their own lights they were apparently proceeding correctly. This may have been because they were self-selected, sharing a corporately held irrational theme, or were the bearers of personality types that gave them affinity for authoritarian or Utopian philosophies of professional functioning. For whatever reason, activities which to us were patently damaging appeared to be regarded as correct within their groups. What forced itself onto our notice, and perhaps accounts for both a measure of our anger and for the skepticism of our reviewer, is the chasm we found between publicly-stated theories expressed by academics in the field on the one side, and the actual realities of practice on the other. It is here that the hidden agendas and the secrecy that masquerades as confidentiality do such a disservice. Those of us, like the reviewer, who have long worked in this field, would once have taken an oath that such things are the rare and isolated outcome of chance mistakes or of incompetent, badly trained, and inadequately supervised rogue workers. Actual exposure to dozens of such cases, however, has left us sadder but perhaps wiser.

Those of us who worked in academic surroundings or model programs, and whose knowledge of colleagues' professional behavior comes from their own reports about their activities or our impressions of them seen under sanitized circumstances of conferences, seminars, and other venues, may not be able to conceive of how these same caregivers behave when they are not "on show," and may not realize what is happening out in the world of real practice. Victims of iatrogenic damage and their friends, however, view the matter from another perspective, and are apt to complain about their experiences, so that eventually a wider public will hear and draw conclusions that may be uncomfortable for all of us, inevitably eroding the financial basis and legislative sanction that underpins our work.

☐ Are Our Perceptions Distorted?

While it may be conceded that participant observers like us may legitimately experience anger in the face of damaging behavior by colleagues, to what extent does that distort the accuracy of our observations and of our analysis of events? Clearly, subjective elements affect judgment. Nevertheless, such cases are a matter of public record, and we were hardly their only observers. Lawyers, educators, physicians, and mental health workers, as well as an increasing number of people in the media, agreed on what had happened and corroborated the facts and the outcome of damaging professional behavior.

☐ Are We Prejudiced Because of Being Excluded?

The anonymous reviewer asks pertinently whether our view has been jaundiced by our being marginalized by the system. We would agree that this has been narcissistically wounding, especially in our early experience of rebuffs, and that it is frustrating to know that over 50 years of research, consultation, teaching, and clinical experience are curtly dismissed by workers with barely adequate academic preparation in fields like child development and psychopathology and with apparently disturbingly shallow perceptions of the consequences of their interventions. Nevertheless, one gradually comes to accept even such mortifications, and their emotional impact dulls over years and becomes an expectable part of the job, especially when one realizes that one shares the experience with other reputable clinicians who have been similarly blacklisted.

☐ Is There a Lack of Balance?

The reviewer's impression that there is a lack of balance in our analysis of cases, so that, like those whose activities we criticize, we are stereotyping and even demonizing caregivers, has validity. It is caused in part by the fact that a critical dimension is missing from this study, namely, those caregivers' own versions, or, if one likes, "defenses" of their actions. Presumably, they all had a consciously held rationale about the correctness of their behavior. In the course of analyzing the dozens of cases that lie behind this book, we attempted to create a research design to examine the other side of the story, to interview the workers whom we had identified as destructive, and to get them to explain and reflect on their view of the cases and on why they chose the course of action they did. We were not able to do so. Those involved would have nothing to do with us, for while we may be suspected of stereotyping them, there was no doubt that they had demonized us. To digress for a moment, it may be instructive to consider a recent and illustrative incident.

Our secretary was conducting office business in the small bank branch that handles the account of our Center. The clerk with whom she was dealing, noticing our name on a form, said loudly enough to attract the attention of other staff and customers, "You work for Caplan? He is the most evil person! He does the most terrible damage!" She then proceeded to recount to a rapt audience details of a case in which we had "interfered" with the efforts of the child protection workers to "rescue" a child. Our embarrassed secretary, now scrutinized by hostile bystanders, asked the clerk how she knew the details of a confidential case that was currently sub judice. "My sister told me. She is a social worker." It later transpired that the sister was the senior Welfare Officer in the case. Setting aside the ethical impropriety of the social worker disclosing details of a case to family members, and the defamatory outburst in a public place, it is clear that the social worker believed passionately that she was on the side of the angels in a case that many others judged to be damaging the clients. We would have liked to have known why this caregiver and others like her believe as they do. We sought out senior academics in the caregiving fields and tried to work out a viable research design. We tried to interest graduate students in interviewing such caseworkers. We could neither find anyone prepared to risk the link with us being discovered, nor any ploy that would gain information about the sensitive material we wanted without raising defenses and thereby distorting the authenticity of the material. Clearly, the publicly-stated goals and motives of the leaders of such professionals provided little guidance in understanding what was happening in certain parts of the field. An explanation of actual field conditions and any gap between the jointly-held biases of the workers and the publicly expressed position of their superiors, which often seemed mutually contradictory, would be fascinating, important, and, for us, unattainable. It would be well worth the while of other researchers to delve into this area.

☐ Is the Local Child Welfare System More Inadequate Than Elsewhere?

Our anonymous reviewer asks whether iatrogenic damage cases occur more frequently in Jerusalem than in other places. As we mentioned in our first chapter, we saw cases of iatrogenic damage from all over the country, not exclusively from Jerusalem. In fact, the Jerusalem child welfare department has had a history of good service and of a high level of staff education and supervision, and some of its earlier directors, to our certain knowledge, recognized and attempted to prevent certain types of system-generated damage.

That practices we have described are far from idiosyncratic to Israel becomes even clearer as we talk to colleagues in other countries, and we get an ever sharper picture both of the ubiquity of iatrogenic damage and of the factors that render such situations semi-invisible, thereby enabling caregivers to get away with, and even routinize damaging practices. At a recent international conference, for example, a young psychologist from the American West Coast told us of a "unique situation" in his region. Child welfare workers had asked him to prepare a negative report to the court on a family. When he pointed out that he had not yet seen the family, and might not come to a negative assessment when he did so, the child protection worker said, "Then we'll go to someone else." "Suppose," said our young colleague, "I go ahead and put in a report that disagrees with what you want?" "Then," he told us the worker had said, "We'll destroy your career." The young psychologist told us that he then found out that this situation was widespread and an open secret in the region. Dissenting practitioners had had their careers spoiled locally, and had had to find work elsewhere. Being young and idealistic, however, he had determined to beat the system by faxing dissenting reports to judges at the last minute and only then sending copies to the social workers, thereby allowing the latter no time to replace his report with a new, compliant opinion. He agreed with us, however, that this would only work once or twice before the wrath of the system caught up with him. Until our discussion, he had assumed that this situation was a local aberration, and he was amazed to hear that it existed elsewhere. A professor of psychology from southern Europe, overhearing our conversation, chuckled. "Do such things happen in your country too?" we asked. "Of course," she said. "They happen everywhere."

Since Israel is a tiny country, geographically and socially, where everyone tends to be known, once a group dominates a field and imposes itself in the way described by our colleague from the West Coast, it is difficult for any dissenting group to operate. Presumably, the blacklisted professionals in our American colleague's area can get clients referred from many sources within a population and an area so large that the territory cannot be fully controlled by any vengeful caregiving system; and *in extremis*, noncompliant professionals can move to another state. In a country as small as Israel, it is far more difficult to escape the implications of a negative reputation and a blacklist. Control of the field by any determined system, therefore, is much tighter and more effective.

☐ How do we Judge Colleagues?

The larger issue suggested by our critic is how visible to even sophisticated observers are practices that induce iatrogenic damage? When the reviewer asks whether conditions in Israel have deteriorated since he or she observed them some years ago, and presumably at that time detected little or no evidence of iatrogenic damage, we must conclude that damaging practices existed at that time too, but our reviewer, presumably a high status visitor, would not have been aware of them any more than we were aware of them for years while we were well-placed insiders.

Unless we actually watch colleagues dealing with clients, and unless we see the larger picture of the circumstances of those clients, what do we actually know about the real activities of fellow professionals? We may hear them giving a good lecture, or read a persuasive article they have written. We may be impressed by the nice way they talk about their work, and we may be pleased by their manner, especially if we are foreign guests being welcomed in for a short visit and accorded flattering attention and hospitality that would naturally dull vigilance. But the reality may be quite otherwise than what we are led to expect, and it may be well-hidden. After all, until it was proven in a court of law, we could never have imagined that certain of our highly respected and eminent colleagues in the Boston Psychoanalytic Society were engaged in sexual misconduct with patients. How many of us have referred a case for further treatment to a seemingly competent professional, only to learn later that the case has been mismanaged? Often, when one hears complaints from those dissatisfied clients, one's first impulse is to side with the colleague and to dismiss the criticism as a symptom of the client's pathology.

This tendency to side with, and exonerate colleagues is exacerbated by a sense of solidarity and identification with one's own peer group. It may be worth observing that the very category of iatrogenic damage cases was noted by the coauthor of this book who is not an accredited mental health specialist, but is, instead, an intellectual historian, and who therefore felt no collegial loyalty to any caregiving profession, who had not introjected their world view, and who observed their actions as a dispassionate outsider with none of the unconscious assumptions that legitimized their actions. Professor Caplan, on the other hand, at first had more difficulty accepting evidence that his colleagues could be acting in consistently damaging ways.

☐ Secrecy: Uncharacteristic of Israeli Culture?

We must also remember the role of secrecy in covering up iatrogenic damage. It has been acknowledged by people in Israel in a position to know such things that the adoption and child protection services operate with a higher level of effective secrecy than do the National Security secret services. In fact, secrecy is alien to Israeli society in general, where everyone seems to know things that would not circulate so freely in larger, less tightly interlinked societies. It was Ben Sirah, in the Appocrypha to the Bible, who said that if one whispers at one gate of Jerusalem, it emerges as a trumpet blast at another gate; and it is still true that official attempts to keep scandals and even security issues secret generally fail. A cherished memory is of a fellow customer in a supermarket, who spotting a friend in another aisle, shouted across the store, "Miriam! Guess what! My Yossi has a top secret job in Military Intelligence!" In a similar vein, a lady we know was a friend of a family member of a judge who was presiding over a state inquiry commission on a question of iatrogenic damage of considerable social sensitivity. We remarked to this lady that the commission had not yet produced a report after months of deliberation, and we wondered whether, given the potentially explosive nature of the material, they ever would. "Yes," said our friend, "They have concluded that public suspicions were correct," and she proceeded to tell us the details of an as yet unreleased judicial document.

The contrast between this transparency and the stringently enforced secrecy of certain agencies that deal with children is striking, and not reassuring. This degree of secrecy, in which even the press will seldom publish details of iatrogenic damage cases, however dramatic, may not be characteristic of Israeli society. It resembles, however, clandestine episodes in other countries in which caregivers have engaged in damaging behavior that they were apparently convinced would improve their society or even mankind in general. Those other episodes include those who engaged in sterilizing the "unfit" in Sweden, those who detribalized indigenous populations in Australia and North America, or those who dispatched children from British slums to a "new life" in the Antipodes. All of these perpetrators of iatrogenic damage no doubt believed that they were working towards a goal that could ultimately improve the life of the community and would contribute to the welfare of the individuals involved. Apparently they expected that the benefits of their project would not be readily understood by the lay public. Therefore, the public was not told openly what was happening. It is this belief in serving a higher goal that may make it so difficult for certain categories of caregivers to accept that they may be causing harm. Therefore, when we describe system-supported iatrogenic damage perpetrated by disciplined workers, as opposed to idiosyncratic aberrant behavior of individual workers, we are describing a phenomenon that is often hard to detect unless we are sensitized to the possibility of its existence. Such behavior appears to be less a product of a particular place, as much as a set of customary views and practices that is shared by certain types of people in a variety of professions and countries who, like cultists, cooperate with each other to serve what they identify as a paramount good, and in that service appear to feel that they are entitled to circumvent the inconveniently created checks and balances that were erected precisely to safeguard the public against being damaged. While this analogy to cults may seem unduly fanciful, we have encountered damaging caregivers who behave remarkably like cultists, and who show personality traits that are similar to those found among the religious fringe. We leave it to readers to consider whether this rings any bells in their own observations of damaging professionals.

☐ Are We Proparents, or Prochildren?

The reviewer asks,

> Is it that the Caplans, who work primarily with parents, are biased against apprehension [removing children] even when nothing less can protect the children's safety and potential for development?

If we have given the impression that we work primarily with parents, that is due to a lack of clarity in our writing. We work with both parents and children and, indeed, with any members of the extended social and familial networks whose role may be significant as a source of support and information about the circumstances of the children. Although this reader got the impression that we are "proparents," we are aggressively "prochildren," a fact that we stress to all our clients. After more than 50 years as a practicing child psychiatrist, Professor Caplan indeed

> appreciates the danger involved in failing to apprehend a child from a neglectful or abusive family—especially during the first few years when so much brain development is occurring that is so strongly influenced by the quality of care the child receives and by the level of conflict and violence in the family to which the child is exposed. That risk is no less than the risk of apprehending inappropriately, although I did not get the impression that the authors were aware of that.

The authors are fully aware of this point. However, they are also aware that, while we set the highest priority on the welfare of our child clients, we recognize the concept that is currently less fashionable, that parents also have needs and rights, something that is often overlooked nowadays when it is apparently accepted as axiomatic that children's wants take precedence over those of adult family members, and that children's innocence and truthfulness can be readily assumed. In certain cases, children create misery for their family and for themselves by engaging in manipulations whose implications they themselves may not comprehend, but which when taken at face value by naive or opportunistic caregivers opens the door to iatrogenic damage.

In fact, in many of our cases, we have found ourselves at odds with those ostensibly concerned about child welfare, precisely because we were trying to help frightened children. We believe that whenever possible, most children feel safer and are better off either staying within their own families or remaining in contact with them. But there have been cases when we have recommended removing children from home, and there have been other cases where we have recommended adoption and even closed adoption. We have always tried to assess the needs of children according to their individual situations, not by imposing stereotyped solutions which may well fit many cases, but not a particular case.

It should be added, however, that although our primary focus is on children and on promoting their healthy development despite the difficult circumstances in which they find themselves, we are in favor of treating unfit parents with courtesy and sympathy, and by fair and transparent means. Whatever may be their shortcomings (and they may be perfectly horrible people), we feel that there is no justification for using degrading and unscrupulous means and actual falsification of records in order to rescue their children. We are as able as the child protection workers of taking a hardheaded view of a case, but, we hope, not a hardhearted one that degrades parents.

☐ Do We Deal Only with Orthodox Clients?

If we have given the impression to others besides our reviewer that we deal exclusively with orthodox or ultraorthodox clients, this is an inadvertent distortion. In fact, we deal with all segments of the population. Among the cases cited, we may have disguised several secular families as orthodox, but, of course, we cannot disclose which these are. Other cases indeed involved actually orthodox clients who were stigmatized by caregivers prejudiced against this group.

☐ We Offend and Alienate Certain Professionals

Our anonymous reviewer makes another point with which many will concur:

> For whatever reason, the tone of many of the examples will unfortunately offend, and therefore alienate many of those in the child welfare community who, if it were more balanced, would greatly benefit from the discussion of the potential hazards of allowing less well-trained professionals to work beyond their capacity and without a proper commitment to adequate supervision, consultation and in-service training.

While we did not deliberately set out to offend any individual professionals or professional group, it is not the function of a study such as this to hide what we have seen, however distressing it may be, in order to avoid giving offense. It seems to us to be more important to open up issues whose existence, if acknowledged at all, have been taboo precisely for fear of incurring the resentment of certain fellow professionals. Within such silence, however, damaging behavior festers, confident in its invisibility and in the silent collusion of colleagues. As we have stated often, the fact is that many caregiving professionals, including child welfare workers, are not deliberately damaging. Their jobs are difficult, sometimes dangerous, and constitute a vital contribution to any civilized community. But such workers must accept the need for self-scrutiny and always remind themselves that they must guard against wittingly or unwittingly doing harm. Some readers will be repelled and insulted by what we have shown and may consequently refuse to consider the issues, but others will realize that they and we have the common goal of improving practice by minimizing the issues described in these case studies.

☐ The Ambiguous Role of Professional Loyalties

The reviewer raises an issue that we have touched on before, the fact that loyalty to the professional collective may not only support and validate damaging behavior, but may also suppress the critical faculties of individual members. This may be explicit. We have spoken to professionals, some of whom occupied supervisory positions, for example, who have been disciplined by their groups for openly challenging harmful policies. It may also be implicit and self-imposed. Our reviewer appears to assume that identification with the professional group would make certain individual caregivers so affronted by criticism of their colleagues as to render them unable to consider the points raised here. Along with all the benefits of identification with a profession, and the supportive atmosphere that such identification fosters, there should presumably be a limit to the introjection of that identity. Affiliation with a party or a professional group may indeed carry the danger that our reviewer implies, of allowing one's ethical objectivity to be submerged in loyalty to that collective, so that one's primary professional identification becomes implicitly linked to the honor of one's group rather than to serving clients. Most of the time, these loyalties over-lap, but when they do not, mature and reasonable caregivers ought to be able to detach themselves sufficiently from their immediate allegiances in order to consider whether they are serving a hidden agenda rather than the human service mission that presumably led them to join that caregiving profession in the first place. At the very least, one may hope that they should be able to suspend any sense of affront to a collective identity in order to privately consider the issues related to damaging behavior.

The foregoing, however, casts into question the efficacy of mutual surveillance by colleagues as a method of controlling iatrogenic damage. On the one hand, people don't like to inform on their friends. On the other, people under surveillance will disguise their activities unless they are genuinely committed to the goal of acknowledging and correcting such behavior. Even in the area of physical medicine, where the British General Medical Council advocates peer surveillance, it has been possible for errant doctors to cover their steps. How much more so would that be true in caregiving fields where no physical evidence of erroneous procedures may be detected?

☐ Will Better Training and Supervision Help?

While the reviewer is undoubtedly correct in mentioning the "potential hazards of allowing less well-trained professionals to work beyond their capacity and without proper commitment to adequate training," this begs the question of institution-embedded iatrogenic damage. The workers we have encountered are not considered poorly trained by their system, and they are provided, apparently, with all the outer appurtenances of professional support, supervision, in-service training, and more. The problem lies, at least in part, in the context of these supports, the inner reality beneath the cosmetic exterior. We have reason to suspect that despite all of these aids to professional competence, the really persuasive and imperative directives that determine actual functioning do not encourage self-scrutiny, avoidance and management of stereotyping and bias, and monitoring for premature cognitive closure.

On the other hand, we are left with the issue of helpers from other fields who may over-value their own mental health expertise, and who are largely unsupervised. This was illustrated for us in a custody case in which a child was placed in a foster home for a "transition period," supposedly to ease his passage from one parent to the other. The foster father, a teacher, at first appeared neutral, but was rapidly drawn into the camp of the manipulative parent with whom the Welfare Officer had also allied herself. The teacher developed a deep and publicly expressed admiration for the Welfare Officer because, in his view, she was so "professional." When queried about what that meant, he said that she was able to remain calm when the mother berated her for "stealing" her child. The fact that she was able to remain silent under such an attack, the teacher felt, constituted her professionalism. "Would you not wish," he asked a coworker, "that your wife was like her?"

Professor Caplan had contacted this teacher in order to discuss the child's increasingly alarming, though as yet transient symptoms whenever the child had to relate to any person or object associated with his mother, and to point out that this was being exacerbated by the way the teacher was managing the confused, conflicted child. For example, the teacher had arranged a ceremony in which the child was to give the social worker a present to show his "gratitude" for her having "rescued" him from his mother. The teacher hotly defended what he termed his "treatment" of the child, and there ensued a discussion between him and Professor Caplan about their relative standing as "psychologists." "I have not asked you to show me your credentials," the teacher said, "but I understand that you are a psychiatrist with many years' experience. You don't realize that I am also not only a teacher, but that I have taken many courses in psychology. Also, you do not know that I am being advised by Rabbi G., who is older than you, and who has a great knowledge of human nature, and who gives lectures to teachers every week."

In his memorandum of this conversation Professor Caplan noted,

> I told him that I oppose his philosophy on this case, and that I thought that he was endangering the mental health of the child. . . . It is of interest to me that he has no idea of my standing in my profession, and feels that my expertise is on a par with his, or is even inferior, apart from my age and length of experience.

☐ The Existence of a False Sense of Mental Health Expertise

Those of us in community mental health share a degree of guilt in encouraging this fuzzying of professional identity by our dissemination of information about mental health among many categories of community professionals without ensuring that the latter understand the limits of this relatively superficial knowledge. When one of our children/grandchildren became a field medic in the Israeli army, it was stressed by his mentors that while he and his colleagues may have been taught a great deal of medicine, they were not qualified doctors, and were to carry out their duties only in a limited and supervised area which, for example, did not flow over into civilian life. The young medics were warned, "You are *not* an expert. Despite all that you have learned, you may not consider yourself more than front-line technicians who must follow the orders and accept the authority of real doctors on any medical question." The instilling of a knowledge of one's proper rank and station in the order of things is obviously easier in a military than in a civilian setting, yet it represents a corrective standard which should be borne in mind when designing any mental health courses for nonspecialists. We hope that they will act as our front-line scouts to alert us when an individual is displaying disquieting symptoms, but we may not have instilled in them the prohibition against meddling in what we know is probably beyond their capacities, though they, in their relative unsophistication, may mistake what they know as true expertise.

In our next, and concluding chapter, we will consider our role in helping the victims of iatrogenic damage, as well as some of our own reactions as clinicians to the danger that we too can cause harm.

CHAPTER

Helping the Victims
of Iatrogenic Damage

So many cases of iatrogenic damage are intractable, and obviously it will take a long time for any significant changes in professional and institutional procedures to occur that might reduce their prevalence. Therefore, we must realize that perhaps among our most feasible and highest priorities for dealing with this issue, certainly in the short term, is to intervene with its victims. This may involve explaining to them as early in the process as possible what is actually happening to them. It would involve helping them to look behind the rhetorical and legal facade at what their actual situation may be, based on the stereotypical patterns of other iatrogenic cases. Most clients, and many lawyers too, unless they have been exposed to other similar instances, will have difficulty believing that the "misunderstandings" of professionals and the legal complications that ensue cannot be cleared up relatively quickly. At first they may not believe that their experiences fit into a well-established mold that will wear them down with false hopes and mirages of solutions in a few weeks or months or in the next court hearing, which inevitably leads to another hearing and more after that. They may be puzzled and demoralized by the apparently unaccountable animosity of the caregivers. As one client kept asking us, "Why is the welfare officer being so mean to me? Why does she hate me so much? Why does she yell at me? She barely knows me. I haven't done anything to her." The answer was that the reality of the mother and her actual interactions with the welfare officer had little to do with the latter's attitudes, which were stereotypes that were impervious to the mother's arguments and to her actual personality. Clients, brought to gradually realize the futility of struggling against the Kafkaesque outer appearance of the case, and helped instead to see its inner rationality may be less liable to waste energy and resources fighting straw men. Focusing on the logic behind the apparently illogical and absurd is itself empowering, since it enables those buffeted by apparently unpredictable and random blows to orient themselves and to begin to plan realistically.

It may also be possible to reduce the irrational shame and consequent social isolation of victims of iatrogenic damage by creating support systems composed, amongst others, of past and present fellow sufferers. Filling the void in their psychosocial support system can be critical to their capacity to withstand stress. Because of the protracted nature of many such cases, they tend to exhaust and even alienate the natural support group composed of those in immediate contact with the sufferers. For, while an acute crisis state appears to stimulate an infusion of help from the social surround, as though there is a biopsychosocial urge to match the neediness and temporary emotional malleability of the sufferers, the impulse to help, like the crisis state itself, seems to be of corresponding short duration. In other words, just as the biopsychological attributes of an acute crisis state are time-limited, lasting only up to about four to six weeks, there seems to be a matched time limitation in the arousal of the social surround. Once that critical period passes, it would seem that protracted misery tends to wear down the energy and goodwill of average supporters, the focus of whose efforts and emotions must necessarily return to their own day-to-day affairs, and whose inability to assuage the victim's long-term suffering becomes, for many, a burden that may breed indifference and even irritation and a measure of contempt, leaving the still vulnerable sufferer to his or her own devices. As the elderly widow of a Chief Rabbi told us, explaining her exhausting round of charitable activities, "Nobody can stand a weeping woman. I had to find a distraction from my grief because it came to the point that I was becoming a burden to others."

Lawyers and others associated with iatrogenic damage cases that last for months and years have complained to us of the toll such situations exact and of their urge to turn and run. They may be worn out by endless phone calls at all hours from distraught clients, and by witnessing the clients' despair in the aftermath of fruitless court hearings, for the failure of which the lawyers and others involved may feel an often irrational sense of guilt and impotence. Unlike community mental health workers, those professionals and lay supporters are not necessarily trained to maintain a measure of emotional distance from clients while retaining empathy, so that they may become as exhausted and haunted by the proceedings as are the principals themselves. However good their intentions, many people are ill-equipped to sustain their involvement in chronic and essentially hopeless situations, and may themselves come to need support in order to stay the course. Thus, the ripple effects of iatrogenic damage cases may come to affect the lives of a widening circle, and consequently, may require organized efforts to inform and maintain the capacities of all involved to help each other continue to function effectively in both their professional and their informal caring roles.

Supporting the victims can help these sufferers maintain their self-image and mobilize ego strength to focus on the true essence of their situation. This may involve a realization that their goal must be to escape from the system rather than confronting its impregnable facade on the system's own terms, or it may involve helping them to come to terms with inevitable defeat. Even in the latter situation, we have a preventive mission—that of enabling clients to survive the successive crises that mark incidents of iatrogenic harm. We can help them in coping with the reality even of probable loss, and we can provide support against being submerged by the alternation of ephemeral hopes and despair, confusion, and exhaustion that characterize these cases.

One avenue for preventive intervention, therefore, may not be to confront harming colleagues who have their own well-entrenched reasons for acting as they do, but to enable clients to cope in a mentally healthy way with the intensely pathogenic stressors that these situations create, so that the clients do not become helpless and hopeless casualties, whatever may be the eventual outcome of their case.

This may be a difficult task, because clients can become so invested in the battle that the focus of their emotions becomes not only, for example, the retrieval of a child, but also the defeat of the various tormenting systems—the courts, the welfare department, the experts with opposing views, and others. The toll these cases exact includes for many clients the gnawing need for revenge, which mitigates against coming to terms with an outcome they oppose. Especially if it involves a custody battle, as many of our cases have done, the accumulated animosities of the failed marriage and all the bitterness of the divorce process are raised anew by the iatrogenically damaging situation. Working through such issues is intensely complex, since accepting an unmerited defeat is often much harder than accepting loss.

☐ The Interdependence of Professionals and Clients

One of the recurring findings in this present study is the emotional interdependence of professionals and clients and the matching or mismatching of their professional goals and practices. This can be seen, for example, in our earlier discussion of how agencies that welcomed our mental health consultation program fitted our needs as much as we fitted theirs, and how the success of programs may be due to fortuitous matches under sanitized research conditions, rather than being the exclusive outcome of the superior performance of a service provider under random circumstances. With respect to this theme of professional–client interdependence, and even symbiosis, we must be very careful to examine our own motives when we counsel clients about whether to continue or to abandon an apparently hopeless fight. We must beware of being swayed by our own often unacknowledged vested interest in perpetuating the struggle, either because we have become overly identified with the plight of the client and want to see that client vindicated and satisfied at last, or because we are exasperated by the machinations of the system and want to see its power for harming curbed, or because, as researchers, we want to study the twists and turns of the process for as long as possible in order to learn as much as we can about ways of curtailing the damaging process. This continuation of our hopeful endeavors, however, might imply sacrificing the needs and rights of our client to the needs of our research. It also hides from us the great difficulty of determining whether or not the individual problem is actually impossible to solve. If we are to separate our own needs and motives from the issues that directly affect the welfare of the clients, we must learn to identify the signs of a lost case. This involves the technical problem of differentiating impossible situations from similar cases where, if we maintain our struggle, we might eventually rescue this particular client from otherwise inevitable damage.

☐ Identifying a Hopeless Case

The first sign of a hopeless case is that the legal system is effectively frozen by the fixed negative reaction of a judge, though the case may continue to be referred for further reviews and hearings that in fact lead nowhere. A case may also be hopeless when appeals are blocked because a lower court appears satisfied with the status quo and refuses to deliver a verdict that will enable a higher court to review it, and when the administrative arm of the judicial system will not intervene to force a judge to rule within a reasonable time, or to question alleged procedural lapses, like barring the testimony of certain defense witnesses or even altering the court protocol.

The second element, which is in a way analogous to the dilemma faced by the welfare officer and the judge in Joe's case, is assessing when the means justify possible attainable and often theoretically desirable ends, or rather, assessing the chances that any victory can only be a Pyrrhic one. This can be the saddest and most reluctantly arrived at conclusion, but it may be the most realistic if one factors into the situation the wider view of the clients' circumstances and the rights of other family members. The following case, alluded to earlier, illustrates this dilemma.

A child, one of a number of siblings, visiting the divorced father in Israel, was not returned to the mother who had recently moved back to her own parental home in Belgium. The father had a severe personality disorder and was an accomplished manipulator whose domination of the child's will had always been apparent. Despite protracted court battles in a number of jurisdictions, all of which led to orders to return the child to the mother even if only with conditions attached, the father, his social circle, and the welfare officers prevented the repatriation of the child. The latter, meanwhile, had not only been indoctrinated against the mother, but had begun to develop worrisome psychological behavior. The mother had spent months at a time away from home enduring court delays, attempting to bypass the various obstacles erected against her meeting the child, and being a witness to the child's increasingly bizarre symptoms. Whenever she returned home, she was summoned back for more court hearings that she did not dare to miss. She and her family were spending their combined resources on legal and other fees, and her other children were being deprived of their mother for long and uncertain periods. They were being caught up in the emotional tug-of-war over their sibling, were growing ever more suspicious of their father, whose future access to them was now questionable given his record of capturing the other child, and were themselves developing clinical symptoms of insecurity, depression, and maternal deprivation. After more than a year of battling, an observer had to wonder at what stage some very painful calculations had to be faced. The mother, with whose desperation one could only sympathize in her determination to rescue her child from a disturbed father and from a most dubious social environment, apparently could not bring herself to accept that a time was coming when it might be wiser to cut her losses and recognize defeat.

In the best of circumstances, if she were to get unambiguous official approval to take the child home, which was doubtful, but not totally beyond the realm of possibility, she would have to contend with a host of new difficulties. Among these were the brainwashed child's probable opposition to leaving, the possibility that the rebellious child would engage in destructive and even self-destructive behavior, and the certainty that the child would need protracted psychiatric treatment. Moreover, the mother and her family had to face the possibility that the child could disrupt the sibling group, creating dissension as the agent of the manipulative father by spreading the latter's destructive and even scandalous allegations against the mother's character, and propagandizing in favor of the father's supposedly greater rectitude. As the scion of the father's prominent family, the clever and attractive child had been flattered and emotionally captured, being hailed by the father's circle as an exemplar and moral teacher of other children, a role which was appropriate neither by age, attainments, nor emotional stability. The child's incentive to return to the relative anonymity of an ordinary childhood in an ordinary school in the mother's native country, and to blend into an ordinary sibling group was consequently not high. Once the child was returned, therefore, the mother and her family could hardly anticipate a peaceful future to compensate for their emotional and financial sacrifices.

What "victory" could be anticipated in such a case, and how much longer was it feasible or rational to continue the struggle were questions that the father had doubtless anticipated in his own strategic planning. At what point would it be more expedient for the mother to return to her other children, to a more equable life, and even to remarry, accepting that this child, though beloved by her, had been placed beyond her reach for the foreseeable future? She could maintain a measure of contact by phone and by periodic visits. However, she might have to accept that the child's mental health might continue to deteriorate under the influence of the father and his supporters.

We feel that in a case of this type, unless the mother were to succeed in unlinking herself and her other children from their intensive involvement with the pathogenic situation, they will all continue to suffer despite any preventative intervention efforts. In this kind of situation, inculcating hope of a successful outcome is likely to be counter productive

☐ Do We Cause Iatrogenic Damage?

A reader may suspect that we consider ourselves immune from committing the damaging behavior that we ascribe to others. Unhappily, however, we can look back over a long career in which we too have caused our share of harm. There was, for example, a highly disturbed literary figure who told us that a respected psychiatric colleague had seduced her. We dismissed the accusations of this patient as a paranoid fantasy, instead of exploring the possible reality of the accusations further. It was inconceivable to us in our naivete, and coming from the type of religious background in which we were brought up, that such a charge had any objective validity. We failed that patient because we were closed-minded. After she had committed suicide, it became clear that her charges had been no fantasy.

Similarly, we have been taken in by our own dogmatism and by superficial appearances. In a case of a mother, whose custody of her children was being challenged by their father who claimed that she was engaging in promiscuous sex in their presence, we were swayed by our observations during a home visit. The children were clean and relaxed and the house was tidy and tastefully arranged. All the children, who had earlier testified tonelessly before the police, the social services, and us about witnessing their mother's affairs and about her neglect of them (which was corroborated by their then bedraggled and undernourished appearance), collectively and individually now said that they were happy living with their mother and that their previous accounts of life with her had been lies that their father had required them to tell. They now denied that their mother ever consorted with strange men. The male visitors whom neighbors alleged to have seen were "uncles" and "husbands of mommy's girlfriends." We were swayed by the appearances of the home, by the "obvious" sincerity of the woman's protestations of having been abused and slandered by her husband, and by the children's corroboration of her story. Our suspicions were somewhat raised by the fact that she refused psychological testing, while her former husband accepted it, and tested normal. That defensiveness in itself did not necessarily indicate that she had things to hide, but it left enough of a doubt so that we waited before coming to any final conclusions, and in that space of time, her actions and those of the children contradicted the pretty, stage-managed picture we had been shown. For, after some weeks of apparent reform, the mother reverted to her earlier neglect of the children and to behaving in an openly promiscuous way. Moreover, the children were becoming a cause for worry. One was caught shoplifting, and another, when found in what used to be called a compromising position with a boyfriend, was reported to have said, "Why shouldn't I? My mother does it." Unfortunately, caregivers cannot delay decisions indefinitely if there are questions about the safety of children. At some point, decisions have to be made and action taken. Cases cannot drag on forever, clogging the workings of agencies, so a disposition may be made in good faith that can be the product of misapprehension and manipulation. For this reason, channels for gathering additional information and for reviewing any new evidence must remain open. At least we did not close our ears and our door to the father in this case. While at one point we had concluded that the preponderance of truth lay with the wife, and that the husband was probably a manipulator and an abuser, we suspended judgement long enough to await the results of psychological testing and to look at the further evidence he brought of his wife's behavior.

We were not as flexible in a custody case some years ago, when we gave emphatic credence to a disturbed mother with unfortunate results for the child and with lasting damage to our reputation in the eyes of a key socially active lawyer. In the years since, that lawyer has asked us repeatedly "How could you have been so completely taken in?" The lady was persuasive in her manipulations; the psychological testing was inconclusive; we were naive and were charmed by her; and we held the dogmatic view that small children should remain with the mother. It all added up to potential danger for the children.

We also have on our conscience the case of a group of siblings who refused to associate with their frightening father. The welfare officers had been impressed by the father's arguments that this was a "Parent Alienation Syndrome" orchestrated by his former wife, and they had stereotyped the mother, claiming that they had witnessed her exerting absolute control over her children's behavior by means of her mesmerizing, penetrating gaze, a peculiarly Middle Eastern form of demonization, where the Evil Eye is still feared. The children, under intense pressure from the father and the welfare officers, had become phobic about leaving home, afraid of being carried off to an institution as the welfare officers had threatened their mother that they would be unless she arranged for their compliance. The mother, on whom the pressure was growing intolerable, denied that she had set the children against her former husband, and claimed to be in favor of their meeting him. When the children's resistance proved stronger that any adult persuasion, the court asked us to attempt to bridge between them and the rejected parent. With the help of a senior welfare officer, and with the cooperation of the mother, we arranged a meeting in our office between the youngest child and his father, by design removing the little boy from the united strength of the sibling group. When the mother brought the boy in and he learned that his father was present, the child tried to kill himself. The Welfare Officer, who was no longer young, had sufficiently agile reflexes to catch him as he was scaling the railing of our fourth-floor balcony, preparing to jump.

Despite the general shock that this created, we were gradually able to entice the still unwilling boy into his father's lap, while the patently terrified mother tried to assure him that she wanted him to meet his father regularly. The father's tears when, after two years of separation, he was given the opportunity, at last, to hold his son in his arms moved everyone. We were even more deeply moved, this time by a sense of guilt, when we saw the child's subsequent and violent upset and even more adamant refusal to keep the next appointment with his father. We were compelled to ask ourselves whether such suffering should be inflicted on a young child in the interests of a theoretical mental health gain. The father was indeed intimidating, even to adults. It was said that he had often returned home late at night to beat his wife and smash household objects in the hearing of the suddenly awakened children, and after the divorce he and his relatives were said to have tried to intercept the children on their way home from school and carry them off. Why, therefore, were we isolating this child from his siblings and forcing him, in this unsupported state, to experience terror and later self-disgust and remorse for having given in to the united force and blandishments of a group of adults all bound to make him do what he was prepared to die rather than do voluntarily? For all the adults involved, it had appeared to be a rational attempt to see if it was possible to rectify a contentious and possibly pathogenic situation. For the child, all these considerations were irrelevant; resisting was literally a matter of life and death.

The judge later agreed that the children's wishes should be respected, and that the father would have to suspend his pressure, at least for the time being, thereby alleviating the children's panic. But we are left to ask ourselves at what point do we carry out a theoretical precept, or even a court order, when it is clear that it is causing great suffering which is unlikely to be replaced by any gain in the near future? The issues involved are not simple ones and should not be brushed aside with simplistic, generalized formulations.

☐ We Try to Reduce the Danger of Our Damaging Clients

We would like to think that we differ from some of our damaging colleagues in our sincere acceptance of the fact that we can and do make mistakes, and in our attempts to remain open to criticism and to self-scrutiny. Awareness of the characteristics of iatrogenic damage and of our own lack of immunity in this respect has led us to build certain safeguards into our own programs in Jerusalem for preventing psychosocial disorders in the children of divorcing parents.

We attempt to reduce our own bias and stereotyping by organizing our operations so that each member of our team forms an independent view of our cases. When we refer a client for investigation to our clinical psychologist, for example, we tell him absolutely nothing about the person's background or about our own impressions. We do not even specify what questions we wish him to answer. Only after the psychological investigation has been completed and a report has been written do we compare notes and discuss possible discrepancies between his impressions and our own. We also do not read the documents in a client's official file until after we have assessed the case ourselves. Clients sometimes feel that we must be lazy or derelict because we have not yet read the reports of the social workers, the school authorities, or the psychologists about them. We explain that we do not want the development of our own diagnostic assessment to be influenced, even unconsciously, by the opinions of others. Only after we have made our own observations and have arrived at a preliminary view of the case are we prepared to consider the contents of the case file and the possibly discrepant findings of each of our team members in a carefully organized staff meeting.

Such staff meetings provide us with opportunities for all members to identify and draw the attention of others to possible professional or personal bias or to signs of premature cognitive closure that may lead to stereotyping. In this, we are helped by the multidisciplinary makeup of our staff that includes clinicians and a social scientist, and professionals and nonprofessionals, all of whom share the duty to help others to become aware of inadvertent endangering of clients. We constantly challenge each others' assessments, forcing each other to examine the evidence on which our conclusions are based and also forcing each other to confront the prejudices for and against, that may attract us to one side or another of a struggle between clients. Sometimes, the more unpleasant parent is telling the truth; and the child, despite our own antipathies, has a deeper sense than we do of the dependability of one parent rather than the other. Cultural values and social graces are poor guides to human relationships. Even "primitive," delinquent, or disturbed people can fulfill the needs of their children, and should not be dismissed as parents because we don't like them.

☐ What Constitutes Help?

At the beginning of this book, we said that one of our goals was to try to construct for the average vulnerable children of divorcing parents the conditions that invincible but vulnerable high-risk children are able to arrange for themselves in order to overcome potentially crippling stress. Obviously, we cannot endow all vulnerable children with enough energy, social skills, and physical and spiritual charm to win the support that will compensate for their otherwise unmet needs. But we can identify stressors that are overwhelming in the absence of support, and we can possibly arrange that these stressors be weakened by parent education and by sensitizing judges and other caregivers to their impact. We can also encourage the artificial provision of support if it is not otherwise available. But we must be careful. Another characteristic of invincible children is that they themselves choose and then elicit the help they feel they need. Apparently, what others define as help is not thrust on them in any stereotyped and prepackaged way. In our own practice, we see too much iatrogenic harm when a system has intervened gratuitously, where people's needs have been rigidly predetermined by outsiders, and the "help" that is then thrust uninvited onto families proves not only unwanted but inappropriate and destructive.

In one of our latest ventures—mutual help groups for children of divorced parents—we try to give children who feel that they are passive victims of parental feuding an opportunity to become active on their own behalf and on behalf of others with whom they identify. This shift from passivity to productive activity is likely to contribute strongly to mental health, as it does in the case of the invincible children. The innovative aspect of our program, which we have already shown to be feasible, is that we do not teach the group's participants how to understand and solve their problems in terms based on our professional knowledge, or impose on them our own preconceptions of what troubles them and what they must do about it. Instead, our nonprofessional group facilitators build communication and relationships among the children who then develop their own ways of identifying and meeting each other's needs. We have been impressed by the effective ways that children as young as nine years old have developed to help each other, usually not in the weekly meetings, but outside of them. Once we have helped them to make friends inside the group, they operate as nonprofessional, "natural supporters" in networks they themselves build.

As practitioners of primary prevention we have had to face up to the inevitability that we must intervene initially as uninvited outsiders. However, in our program to reach out to divorcing parents by means of our printed guides in order to inform them how to handle the expectable reactions of their children, as mentioned in the introduction to this book, we have adopted the principle of allowing those in crisis to choose the form of support that fits their idiosyncratic needs. When our guides are handed out to parents in the divorce courts, people are free to read them, to learn what is useful for them, to choose which points to adapt to their own circumstances, or to toss the paper in the rubbish bin. Perhaps what we say is irrelevant in their particular subculture. Perhaps they have other effective ways of compensating for deprivation and stress, ways that we as yet know nothing about and which we should not assume to be inferior to our own formulations. We must keep in mind that at least 60% of the children of divorcing parents will grow up mentally and socially healthy without our intervention, so we may assume that most people find their own satisfactory solutions from which we can learn, but which we should not distort by turning the presence of identifiable stressors into a green light for overhasty, rigid, heavy-handed meddling by mental health, welfare, or legal professionals.

This should not lead us to adopt a policy of laissez-faire, but rather to be extremely circumspect and tactful in our proactive intervening. We must always build into our program effective feedback mechanisms that will reveal possible discontent and will amplify voices of dissent of powerless clients who may be poor communicators. Negative feedback should cause us to interrupt our intervention immediately, before it damages the clients and should then force us to search for alternative ways of remedial action.

BIBLIOGRAPHY

Antonovsky, A. (1974). Conceptual and methodological problems in the study of resistance resources and stressful life events, In B. S. Dohrenwend & B. P. Dohrenwend (Eds.), *Stressful life events* (pp. 135–152). New York: Wiley.

American Psychiatric Association. (1994). *Diagnostic and statistical manual of mental disorders* (4th ed.). Washington, DC: Author.

Barnardo, T. J., & Marchant, W. (1903). Quoted by Wagner, G. (1982), in *Children of the Empire*. London: Weidenfeld and Nicholson.

Beck, A. T. (1970). The phenomena of depression: A synthesis. In L. Offer & D. Freeman (Eds.), *Clinical Research in Perspective* (pp. 98–128). New York: Basic Books.

Blaufarb, H., & Levine, J. (1972). Crisis intervention in an earthquake. *Social Work, 17*(4), 16–19.

Brown, G. W., Bhrolchain, M. N., & Harris, T. (1975). Social class and psychiatric disturbance among women in an urban population. *Sociology, 9*, 225–251.

Caplan, G. (1950). The treatment of emotionally disturbed children and child guidance services. *Child Care in Israel* (Jerusalem), 183.

Caplan, G. (1951). A public health approach to child psychiatry. *Mental Hygiene, 35*, 235.

Caplan, G. (1952). The disturbance of the mother-child relationship by unsuccessful attempts at abortion. *Courier of the International Children's Center, 11*, 193–201.

Caplan, G. (1954a). A public health approach to child psychiatry. *Nordisk Medicin* (Oslo), *I*, 51–78.

Caplan, G. (Sept. 1954b). Preparation for healthy parenthood. *Children, 2*, 171–175.

Caplan, G. (1954c). The disturbance of the mother-child relationship by unsuccessful attempts at abortion. *Mental Hygiene, 36*, 67–80.

Caplan, G. (1954d). The mental hygiene role of the nurse in maternal and child care. *Nursing Outlook, 2*, 14–19.

Caplan, G. (Ed.) (1955a). *Emotional problems of early childhood*. New York: Basic Books.

Caplan, G. (1955b). Recent trends in preventive psychiatry. In G. Caplan (Ed.), *Emotional Problems of Early Childhood*. New York: Basic Books.

Caplan, G. (1955c). The role of the social worker in preventive psychiatry. *Medical Social Work, 4*, 144–160.

Caplan, G. (1956a). An approach to the study of family mental health. *Public Health Reports, 71*, 1027–1030.

Caplan, G. (1956b). *Mental health aspects of social work in public health*. Berkeley: University of California Press.

Caplan, G. (1956c). Mental health consultation in schools. In *The elements of a community mental health program*. New York: Milbank Memorial Fund.

Caplan, G. (1957a). Detection in pregnancy of future disturbed mother-child relationships: Ways to forestall future emotional disturbances. Lecture reported by the *Hawaii Health Messenger, 18*(6), 2–8.

Caplan, G. (1957b). Psychological aspects of maternity care. *American Journal of Public Health, 47,* 25–31.

Caplan, G. (1958). Mental health consultation in preventive psychiatry. *A Crianca Portuguesa, 42,* 479–489.

Caplan, G. (1959a). *Concepts of mental health and consultation.* Children's Bureau Publication No. 373. Washington, DC: Department of Health, Education, and Welfare.

Caplan, G. (1959b). Practical steps for the family physician in the prevention of emotional disorder. *Journal of the American Medical Association, 170,* 1497–1506.

Caplan, G. (1960a). Emotional implications of pregnancy and influences on family relationships. In H. C. Stuart & D. G. Prugh (Eds.), *The healthy child.* Cambridge, MA: Harvard University Press.

Caplan, G. (1960b). Patterns of parental response to the crisis of premature birth. *Psychiatry, 23,* 365–374.

Caplan, G. (1961a). *An approach to community mental health.* New York: Grune & Stratton.

Caplan, G. (Ed.) (1961b). *Prevention of mental disorders in children: Initial explorations.* New York: Basic Books.

Caplan, G. (1963a). Opportunities for school psychologists in the primary prevention of mental disorders in children. *Mental Hygiene, 47,* 525–539.

Caplan, G. (1964a). *Principles of preventive psychiatry.* New York: Basic Books.

Caplan, G. (1964b). A conceptual model for primary prevention. In D. A. van Krevelen (Ed.), *Child Psychiatry and Prevention.* Bern, Switzerland: Verlag Hans Huber.

Caplan, G. (1964c). The role of pediatricians in community mental health (with particular reference to the *Primary prevention of mental disorders in children*). In L. Bellak (Ed.), *Handbook of community psychiatry and community mental health.* New York: Grune & Stratton.

Caplan, G. (1965a). Opportunities for school psychologists in the primary prevention of mental disorders in children. In N. M. Lambert (Ed.), *The protection and promotion of mental health in schools.* Public Health Service Publication No. 1226. Washington, DC: Department of Health, Education, and Welfare.

Caplan, G. (1968). Opportunities for school psychologists in the primary prevention of mental disorders in children. In E. Miller (Ed.), *The Foundation of Child Psychiatry.* Oxford, England: Pergamon Press.

Caplan, G. (1970). Schools and the challenge of change. In S. Alexander & D. Lancaster (Eds.), *Schools and the Challenge of Change.* Pittsburgh: United Mental Health Services of Allegheny County.

Caplan, G. (1970). *Theory and practice of mental health consultation.* New York: Basic Books.

Caplan, G. (1974). *Support systems and community mental health: Lectures in concept development.* New York: Behavioral Publications.

Caplan, G. (1974). When stress becomes too much. In G. Caplan, *Coping with stress.* Chicago: Blue Cross Association.

Caplan, G. (1975). A multi-model approach to primary prevention of mental disorders in children. In L. Levi (Ed.), *Society, stress, and disease. Vol. 2: Childhood and adolescence.* Oxford, England: Oxford University Press.

Caplan, G. (1976). Organization of support systems for civilian populations. In G. Caplan & M. Killilea (Eds.), *Support systems and mutual help: Multidisciplinary explorations.* New York: Grune & Stratton.

Caplan, G. (1976). The family as support system. In G. Caplan & M. Killilea (Eds.), *Support systems and mutual help: Multidisciplinary explorations.* New York: Grune & Stratton.

Caplan, G. (1980). An approach to preventive intervention in child psychiatry. *Canadian Journal of Psychiatry, 25,* 671–682.

Caplan, G. (1981a). Mastery of stress: Psychosocial aspects. *American Journal of Psychiatry, 138,* 4.

Caplan, G. (1981b). Partnerships for prevention in the human services. *Journal of Primary Prevention, 2,* 3–5.

Caplan, G., et al. (1981c). Patterns of cooperation of child psychiatry with other departments in hospital. *Journal of Primary Prevention, 2,* 40–49.

Caplan, G. (1982). Epilogue: Personal reflections. In H. C. Schulberg & M. Killilea (Eds.), *The modern practice of community mental health: A volume in honor of Gerald Caplan.* San Francisco; Jossey–Bass.

Caplan, G. (1989). *Population-oriented psychiatry.* New York: Human Sciences Press.

Caplan, G. (1993). Organization of preventive psychiatry programs. *Community Mental Health Journal, 29*(4), 367–385.

Caplan, G., & Bowlby, J. (1948). Aims and methods of child guidance. *Health Education Journal, 6.*

Caplan, G., & Cadden, V. (Jan. 1967). How to deal with a crisis. *Reader's Digest,* 80–83.

Caplan, R. B., & Caplan, G. (1972). *Helping the helpers to help: Mental health consultation to aid clergymen in pastoral work.* New York: Seabury Press.

Caplan, G., & Caplan, R. B. (1967). Development of community psychiatry concepts. In A. M. Freedman & H. I. Kaplan (Eds.), *Comprehensive Textbook of Psychiatry.* Baltimore, MD: Williams and Wilkins.

Caplan, G., & Caplan, R. B. (1980). *Arab and Jew in Jerusalem: Explorations in community mental health.* Cambridge, MA: Harvard University Press.

Caplan, G., & Caplan, R. B. (1999). *Mental health consultation and collaboration.* Prospect Heights, IL: Waveland Press, Inc.

Caplan, G., & Gruenbaum, H. (1967). Perspectives on primary prevention. *Archives of General Psychiatry, 17,* 331–346.

Caplan, G., & Killilea, M. (Eds.) (1976). *Support systems and mutual help: Multidisciplinary explorations.* New York: Grune & Stratton.

Caplan, G., & Lebovici, S. (Eds.). (1969). *Adolescence: Psychosocial perspectives.* New York: Basic Books.

Caplan, G., Mason, E. A., & Kaplan, D. M. (1965). Four studies of crisis in parents of prematures. *Community Mental Health Journal, 1,* 149–162.

Caplan, R. B., in collaboration with Caplan, G. (1969). *Psychiatry and the Community in Nineteenth-Century America.* New York: Basic Books.

Caplan, R. B. (1982). Gerald Caplan: The man and his work. In H. C. Schulberg & M. Killilea (Eds.), *The modern practice of community mental health: A volume in honor of Gerald Caplan.* San Francisco: Jossey-Bass.

Cassel, J. C. (1974). Psychiatric epidemiology. In G. Caplan (Ed.), *American Handbook of Psychiatry,* Vol. II (pp. 401–411). New York: Basic Books.

Chandrasekaran, R. (2000). Sorry for a "stolen generation?" Australia debates an apology for aboriginal policy. *International Herald Tribune,* July 8–9, no. 36, 498.

Cobb, S. (1976). Social support as a moderator of life stress. *Psychosomatic Medicine, 38*(5), 300–314.

Crawshaw, R. (1963). Reactions to disaster. *Archives of General Psychiatry, 9*(2), 157–162.

DeAraujo, G., Van Arsdel, P. P., Hughes, T. H., & Dudley, D. L. (1973). Life change coping ability and chronic intrinsic asthma. *Journal of Psychosomatic Research, 17,* 359–363.

Filarstova, O. (Jan. 27, 2000). Yanina and her children. *Novosti Nedeli.* Tel Aviv.

Fox, N. (1977). Attachment of kibbutz infants to mothers and metaplot*. *Child Development, 48.*

*Hebrew term for Child-care paraprofessionals.

Fratter, J. (1991). Parties in the triangle. *Adoption and Fostering, 15,* 91–98.

Fratter, J., Rowe, J., Sapsford, D., & Thoburn, J. (1991). *Permanent family placement: A decade of experience.* London: BAAF.

Freud, S. (1911–13). *Collected works* (vol. 11), (J. Strachey, Trans. and Ed.). London: Hogarth Press.

Garmezy, N., et al. (1978). The nature of competence in normal and deviant children. In M. W. Kent & J. E. Rolf (Eds.), *Primary prevention of psychopathology, vol. 3: Social competence in children* (pp. 23–43). Hanover, NH: University Press of New England.

General Medical Council. (1998). *Good Medical Practice.* London: Author.

Gibbons, J., Gallagher, B., & Bell, C. (1995). *Development after physical abuse in early childhood: A 9–10 year follow-up.* London: Her Majesty's Stationary Office.

Glass, A. J. (1947). Effectiveness of forward treatment. *Bulletin of the U.S. Army Medical Department, 7,* 1034–1041.

Goldstein, J., Freud, A., & Solnit, A. J. (1973). *Beyond the best interests of the child.* New York: The Free Press.

Goldstein, J., Freud, A., & Solnit, A. J. (1979). *Before the best interests of the child.* New York: The Free Press.

Halpern, E. (1978). *Effect of support on adjustment of war orphans.* Lecture at Second International Conference on Psychological Stress in War and Peace, May, Jerusalem.

Hansell, N. (1976). *The person in distress.* New York: Behavioral Publications.

Haughney, C. (2001, June 21). Weapons in U.S. schools: Do paper guns count? *International Herald Tribune.*

Hiroto, D. S. (1974). The relationship between learned helplessness and laws of control. *Journal of Experimental Psychiatry, 3,* 23–37.

Iwanek, M. A. (1987). *A study of open adoption.* Otaga, New Zealand: Petone.

Jaffe, E. D. (Ed.) (1994). *Intercountry adoptions: Laws and perspectives of "sending" countries.* Jerusalem: Gefen.

Janis, I. (1951). *Air war and emotional stress.* New York: McGraw-Hill.

Jones, D. P. (1991). Professional and clinical challenges to protection of children. *Child Abuse and Neglect, 5,* sup. I, 57–66.

Kalter, N. (1977). Children of divorce in an outpatient psychiatric population. *American Journal of Orthopsychiatry, 47,* 40–51.

Kalter, N., & Rembar, J. (1981). The significance of a child's age at the time of parental divorce. *American Journal of Orthopsychiatry, 51,* 85–100.

Kendell, R. E. (1998). What are Royal Colleges for? *Psychiatric Bulletin, 22,* 721–725.

Klein, J., & Glover, S. L. (1983). Psychiatric malpractice. *International Journal of Law and Psychiatry, 6,* 131–157.

Kluft, R. P. (June, 1993). The physician as perpetrator of abuse. *Family violence and abusive relationships, 20*(2), 459–480.

Kornberg, M. S., & Caplan, G. (1980). Risk factors and preventive intervention in child psychopathology: A review. *Journal of Prevention, 1,* 71–133.

Kra, B. (2001, Jan. 19). Spare the child, spoil the system. *Ha'aretz, 78*(24), Weekend Supplement, D5. English edition.

LeBow, H., Schiller, M., Caplan, G., & Selinger, D. (1983). The integration of the emotional and surgical treatment of children hospitalized on a pediatric-surgical ward. *Child Psychiatry & Human Development, 13*(3), 180–188.

Lindemann, E. (1944). The symptomatology and management of acute grief. *American Journal of Psychiatry, 101,* 141–148.

General Medical Council. (1998). *Maintaining good medical practice.* London: Author.

McDermott, J. F. (1970). Divorce and its psychiatric sequelae in children. *Archives of General Psychiatry, 23,* 421–427.

McRoy, R. G., Grotevant, H. D., & Ayers-Lopez, S. (1994). *Changing practices in adoption.* Austin: University of Texas.

McWhinnie, A. (1969). *Adopted children: How they grow up.* London: Routledge and Keegan Paul.

McWhinnie, A., & Smith, J. (Ed.) (1994). *Current human dilemmas in adoption: The challenge for parents, practitioners, and policy makers.* Dundee, Scotland: University of Dundee.

Murch, M. (1998). *Report by Professor Mervyn Murch of the Cardiff Law School to the Lord Chancellor, based on his recent study of "Safeguarding children's welfare in uncontentuous divorce: A study of Section 41 of the Matrimonial Causes Act, 1973."* Unpublished.

Nicholls, K. B., Cassel, J., & Kaplan, B. H. (1972). Psychosocial assets, life crisis, and the prognosis of pregnancy. *American Journal of Epidemiology, 17,* 359–363.

Ojemann, R. H. (1948). Research in planned learning programs and the science of behavior. *Journal of Educational Research, 42*(2), 296.

Ojemann, R. H. (1958). Basic approaches to mental health: The human relations program at the State University of Iowa. *Personnel and Guidance Journal, 33*(3), 198.

Ojemann, R. H. (1961). Investigations on the effects of teaching an understanding and appreciation of behavior dynamics. In G. Caplan (Ed.), *Prevention of Mental Disorders in Children* (p. 378). New York: Basic Books.

Parad, H. J., & Caplan, G. (1960). A framework for studying families in crisis. *Journal of Social Work, 5,* 3–15.

Parkes, C. M. (1970). "Seeking" and "Finding" a lost object: Evidence from recent studies of the reaction to bereavement. *Social Science and Medicine, 4,* 187–201.

Reinfeld, M. (2000, July 17). Court slams handling of adoption case. *Ha'aretz, 77*(24585), 2. English edition.

Rosenfeld, J. M., & Caplan, G. (1954). Techniques of staff consultation in an immigrant children's organization in Israel. *American Journal of Orthopsychiatry, 34,* 45–62.

Rotem, T. (1998, Dec. 16). Hillary's seal of approval. *Ha'aretz, 75*(23997), 2. English edition.

Rotem, T. (2000, Jan. 5). The history of R, the "Gangster of Ramle." *Ha'aretz, 77*(24363), 4. English edition.

Rutter, M. (1985). Resilience in the face of adversity. *British Journal of Psychiatry, 147,* 598–611.

Seligman, M. E. P. (1975). *Helplessness: On depression, development and death.* San Francisco: WH Freeman.

Seligman, M. E. P. (1976). Depression and learned helplessness. In H. M. Van Prag (Ed.), *Research in Neurosis* (pp. 72–107). Utrecht: Bohn, Scheltena & Holkema.

Shader, R. I., & Shwartz, A. J. (1966). Management of reactions to disaster. *Social Work, 11*(2), 99–104.

Shahar, I. (1999, Nov. 2). A striking example. *Ha'aretz, 76*(24299), 4. English edition.

Sheffer, H. R. (1990). *Making decisions about children.* London: Blackwell.

Sherif, M., et al. (1961). *Intergroup conflict and cooperation: The robber's cave experiment.* Norman, OK: University of Oklahoma Press.

Sloane, J. A. (1993). Offenses and defenses against patients: A psychoanalytic view of the Borderline. *Canadian Journal of Psychiatry, 38,* 265–273.

Spivack, M., Weiss, R. S., Caplan, G., Sheldon, A. P., & Schulberg, H. C. (1970). *Mental health implications of the organization of the large-scale physical environment.* Hearings Before the Select Committee on Nutrition and Human Needs of the U.S. Senate (91st Congress, 2nd session on Nutrition and Human Needs), Washington, DC: U.S. Government Printing Office.

Tayal, S. (1972). *Suggestibility in a state of crisis*. DAI, 32(12-3).

Triseliotis, J. (1993). *Open adoption: The evidence examined*. In M. Adevik, J. Kanrick, & R. White (Eds.), *Exploring Openness in Adoption*. London: Significant Publications.

Tyhurst, J. S. (1951). Individual reactions to community disaster: The natural history of psychiatric phenomena. *American Journal of Psychiatry, 115*, 107–764.

Tyhurst, J. S. (1957). *The role of transition states—including disasters—in mental illness* (pp. 148–172). Symposium on Social and Preventive Psychiatry. Washington, DC: Walter Reed Army Institute of Research.

Vobejda, B. (1998, Dec. 16). When foster kids can't beat the demon. *Jerusalem Post*, Reprinted from *The Washington Post*.

Wadsworth, M. E. J. (1979). *Roots of delinquency*. New York: Barnes & Noble.

Wadsworth, M. E. J., Pekham, C. S., & Taylor, B. (1985). The role of national longtitudinal studies in prediction of health, development, and behavior. In D. B. Walker & J. B. Richmond (Eds.), *Monitoring Child Health in the United States* (pp. 63–83). Cambridge, MA: Harvard University Press.

Wadsworth, M. E. J., & Maclean, M. (1987). Parents' divorce and children's life chances. *Children and Youth Service Review, 8*, 145–159.

Wadsworth, M. E. J., Maclean, M., Kuh, D., & Rodgers, B. (1990). Children of divorced and separated parents: Summary and review of findings from a long-term follow-up study in the UK. *Family Practice, 7*(1), 104–109.

Wallerstein, J. S., & Kelly, J. B. (1980). *Surviving the breakup*. New York: Basic Books.

Weiss, R. S. (1975). *Marital separation*. New York: Basic Books.

Werner, E. E. (1989). Vulnerability and resiliency: A longitudinal perspective. In M. Bambring, F. Losel, & H. Skowronek, *Children at risk: Assessment, longitudinal research, and intervention*. Berlin: Walter de Gruter.

Werner, E. E. (1997). Vulnerable but invincible: High risk children from birth to adulthood. *Acta Paediatr*, Suppl. 422, 103–105.

Winkler, R., & Van Keppel, M. (1984). *Relinquishing mothers in adoption: Their long-term adjustments*, Monograph #3. Melbourne: Institute of Family Studies.

INDEX